GETTING BETTER

GETTING BETTER
A Medical Student's Story

KENNETH KLEIN, M.D.

Little, Brown and Company   Boston–Toronto

First edition

LIBRARY OF CONGRESS CATALOGING IN PUBLICATION DATA

Klein, Kenneth.
  Getting Better.

  1. Klein, Kenneth. 2. Medical students — Massachusetts
—Biography. I. Title.
R154.K36A38   610'.92'4 [B]   80–27928
ISBN 0–316–49838–6

BP
*Published simultaneously in Canada
by Little, Brown & Company (Canada) Limited*

PRINTED IN THE UNITED STATES OF AMERICA

To Phyllis

Contents

GETTING BETTER

Prologue

T HE PATIENT WORE a flannel shirt, chinos, and a day-old
beard. He lay on the steel stretcher, breathing regularly;
from a distance he could have been sleeping. But when I put
my hand on his shoulder to say hello there was no response.
For a change I was spared the awkwardness of introducing
myself as a medical student to a patient who was expecting a
doctor. I picked up the emergency ward sheet that lay on his
chest. His name was Richard Hastings. He was seventy-two.
The triage nurse's note read: "Found unresponsive on
bedroom floor. Period of unconsciousness unknown.
Brought in via ambulance with diagnosis of stroke. Vital
signs stable."

I started my exam with the patient's head. While working
my way through his stringy hair I found a deep laceration on
the right temple. Had he suddenly lost consciousness, then
fallen, and hit his head? Or did he hit his head first,
becoming unconscious because of the injury? I began a
detailed neurological exam, looking for clues.

Mr. Hastings's breathing grew irregular. Also, his right
pupil seemed to be getting bigger. His lungs and his eyes
were telling me that a little lake of blood had formed

3

beneath the skull and was beginning to compress the brain — Mr. Hastings had a subdural hematoma. To help confirm my diagnosis I tested the reflexes. Sure enough, there were no reflexes on the left but they were normal on the right. So the head injury came first! He had somehow hit his head, and that caused the bleeding under the skull. This was a rather obvious conclusion, but an incredibly exciting one. It was glorious to see my studying at last beginning to pay off. Instead of merely reading a case history, I was seeing physiology in the flesh. I ran to the chief resident, Eric Costello, rejoicing over my unconscious patient.

Physiology continued to unfold before my eyes — just as we arrived back at Mr. Hastings's stretcher, he stopped breathing. Eric grabbed the laryngoscope and an endotracheal tube from the crash cart and called for help. Within seconds he had threaded the tube down the patient's windpipe. A nurse appeared and hooked up an Ambu bag; Eric began to squeeze it rhythmically, breathing for Mr. Hastings. For me this had been the transition from neuroanatomy to terror. But for Eric the intubation led as naturally from the patient's respiratory arrest as the respiratory arrest followed from the expanding clot of blood.

Doctors and nurses came running from everywhere. I was both thrilled and depressed at the incredible burst of activity. Tubes and wires were connected, drugs administered by vein, orders given and quickly carried out. How could I ever understand, much less hope to do, all that I saw going on? My pretty little piece of physiology had dissolved into a complicated mess.

A neurosurgeon appeared and even that depressed me — how did you get a neurosurgeon in an emergency?

Eric quickly told him the story. I was astounded to hear Eric say, "It was this medical student Klein here who diagnosed the subdural." There was no basking in my fragile glory though: "Excellent," the neurosurgeon said, "since my resident is sick, Dr. Klein can assist at surgery and actually see the clot he diagnosed."

I was terrified. My only real operating room experience had been removing the spleen from a black and white mongrel in dog surgery lab. I visited the dog every day in his postoperative cage and watched with awe as he recovered from my assault on his belly. Sinking the scalpel blade into the dog's flesh had been incredibly difficult; cutting into a person was unthinkable.

My most immediate concern, though, was putting on my gloves in the operating room. I had gone through three pairs that day in the dog lab before I managed to get them on with proper sterile technique. And now a real O.R. nurse would be assisting me, not just an indulgent fellow medical student. I remembered what a friend had said about operating room nurses: "You take your balls off and check them at the door when you go into the O.R. at the Boston City Hospital."

The neurosurgeon went to do another emergency consult while things were being set up for surgery. Just after he left, Eric was called away "stat" to deal with the results of a head-on car crash. "Here, Ken," he said, handing me the Ambu, "you bag him and take him up to the O.R."

"*What?*" The Ambu bag sat in my sweaty hands like a flaccid football. I squeezed and the patient's chest went up. I let go and it went down. "Hey, am I doing this right?" I asked the nurse who was arranging things for the trip to the

O.R. She looked up briefly and then went back to her patient without answering. Didn't she know herself, or was she already initiating my castration? I tried squeezing the bag in time to my own breathing, then realized it wasn't normal to breathe that fast.

"OK, doctor," the nurse said, "you're all set. Sorry the EW can't spare one of us to go with you." My eyes went from the intravenous tubing to the oxygen tank under the stretcher to the portable cardiac monitor down by the patient's feet. I forgot when I had last compressed the bag and atoned for my lapse with three quick squeezes. Then, after taking a deep breath myself, I pushed Mr. Hastings's stretcher out of the Emergency Ward.

As I passed the desk where patients checked in, I realized the tour I'd taken on my first day at the hospital hadn't sunk in — I didn't know where I was going. "Excuse me," I said to the clerk behind the desk, "can you tell me how to get to the operating room?" The patient she was checking in looked at me, at my subdural hematoma and then at the floor. For the first of many times that evening I wished that Mr. Hastings had died at home. Then I felt a flash of anger at the ambulance drivers. Why had they brought him to the short-staffed Boston City instead of the Mass. General or the University Hospital, where there would have been an abundance of skilled personnel?

The clerk gave me directions with the same flat voice she must have used to direct countless patients to the lab or the men's room.

As the elevator went up, my stomach sank. For the first time I was alone with Mr. Hastings. What if his IV stopped running? What if his endotracheal tube slipped out? And what if his heart stopped? The slowly rising coffin of an elevator resonated with rhythmic sounds. There was the low hum of the elevator machinery, the steady chirping of the cardiac monitor, and the hissing of the oxygen as it wound its way in and out of the Ambu bag. The regularity of all the sounds wasn't a bit reassuring; it almost invited disaster.

My anger at the ambulance drivers began to spread. I grew angry at Eric for handing Mr. Hastings over to me, then at the City of Boston for putting me in this situation by not hiring enough staff. Then the anger turned inward. I grew angry at myself for stupidly choosing the Boston City to do my emergency ward rotation. I grew angry at my incompetence, at my pretense at trying to play doctor, and at my decision to go to medical school in the first place. The elevator stopped at the seventh floor and I got out.

I pushed Mr. Hastings to the left, down a dark corridor. It was about eleven-thirty at night. I knew that the on-call anesthesiologist and O.R. nurses had been told to come in; I was afraid they would blame me for dragging them out of bed. Even so, I couldn't wait to find them and hand over my patient. But each of the O.R. suites I passed was dark and locked. Where were these people who knew how to care for nonbreathing subdural hematomas?

I turned the stretcher around and went down another hallway. I met a cleaning woman, humming to herself as she mopped the floor. She moved with quick, efficient strokes; she really knew her work. How lucky she is, I thought. "Excuse me," I said, "do you know where the operating room is where they do brain surgery?"

"Well, I'm not sure," she said, barely looking up. "There are some folks on the eighth floor opening up one of the rooms. Maybe that's it."

"Oh," I said weakly. "Thanks."

The elevator took forever to get back to our floor. I thought of the doctor shows on TV where they have a special key to call the elevator in emergencies. The camera always focused on the passengers' faces: expressions of annoyance quickly turned to respect as they saw the reason for the elevator's diversion. Then the passengers would solemnly file out to make room for the emergency patient.

The elevator finally came. Fortunately it was empty; I'm not sure I would have had the authority to kick anyone off for *my* emergency.

The eighth floor definitely looked more promising. For one thing, the hall lights were on. And as well, I could see several people bustling in and out of an operating suite down to the right. It was like rediscovering the trail after being lost in the woods! I hurried down the hall and swung Mr. Hastings into the brightly lit room. "Is this where they do neurosurgery?" I asked.

"Yes, of course it is," said the scrub nurse. "This must be the subdural finally." I thought again of my friend's advice about checking my balls. Looking past me and Mr. Hastings, the nurse said, "Jesus, did you bring him here by yourself?" At first I took this as a slap at my competence. But then I realized she didn't know that I was merely a medical student — she was amazed that the emergency ward had allowed just one person to transport such a sick patient. "Here, let me help you," she said, and she took over bagging Mr. Hastings. Thank God, I thought, he'll finally get some proper breaths. Then the scrub nurse and another nurse quickly transferred Mr. Hastings to the operating table and sorted out his tubes and wires while I meekly introduced myself.

They told me the neurosurgeon would arrive shortly. He wanted me to begin prepping the patient. As I reached for the iodine soap the scrub nurse suggested that I had better shave the head first. "Hair has a nasty way of sticking to the brain," she said, the bitch. I found the electric shears, which fortunately I was familiar with — they were the same model we'd used in dog surgery. I grabbed a handful of hair and applied the humming blades. Nothing happened. Surgeons, when things aren't going right, seem to deal with the situation by using more force. So I pulled the hair harder and pushed harder on the shears. Still nothing happened. The hovering nurse smiled triumphantly and took them from me. But to my glee she had no luck either.

"Here, let me do it. We've got to get this fucking case on the road!" It was the anesthesiologist. He'd recently arrived and already had the respirator smoothly breathing for Mr. Hastings. He grabbed the shears but even he couldn't make them work. After fiddling with the blades he decided that the fucking thing was broken. He told me to go change for surgery; they'd find another set of clippers and prep the subdural themselves.

I floated out of the operating room, at last without responsibility for Mr. Hastings. I trotted down the hall in search of the locker room. Without thinking I opened the first door I came to. There was a short flight of steps. At the top, instead of lockers I found myself in the little observation area above the operating room. I looked down and saw Mr.

Hastings. The nurse was just starting to shave his head with a new pair of shears. Though the idea of watching the operation as a spectator had strong appeal, I jerked my head back so no one would see me. I ran back down the stairs.

Finally I found the surgeons' dressing room. It had the look and smell of the locker room in my high school gym. High school had been so nice. I got all A's in math and science. I was going to be a chemist and do research. What had gone wrong? What was I doing in this dark smelly dressing room in the middle of the night, an incompetent medical student about to operate on someone's brain? I put on clean scrub clothes that were two sizes too big and returned to the O.R.

Dr. Rogers, the neurosurgeon, had arrived. Everything seemed to be nicely under control; it was wonderful not to be needed. The patient's head had been shaved and prepped. The scrub nurse was arranging the tray of surgical instruments, the anesthesiologist was watching the patient's heartbeat on the cardiac monitor, and Dr. Rogers was just beginning his scrub. I popped open a plastic bag containing a scrub sponge and joined him at the sink. As we brushed our nails he discussed the case. If the subdural had expanded enough to threaten vital structures, he said, he could have bored holes to decompress the brain right in the emergency ward. However, since the patient was relatively stable, he chose to evacuate the clot under more controlled conditions in the operating room. It was nice to hear that he thought Mr. Hastings was relatively stable. He outlined the expected surgery, which made little sense to me. Then he told me what he wanted me to do as his assistant, which made no sense at all. We completed the ten-minute scrub and I was sterilely gowned and gloved by the nurse, thankfully without a hitch.

I took my place next to Dr. Rogers at the end of the operating table. All I could see of the patient was a shiny bald head swathed in green drapes. There was a towel clamp pinching the drapes where I thought the nose should have been. "OK, let's go," said Rogers. The scalpel was slapped into his rubber-skinned palm, and the surgery began.

The blade arced across the smooth dome of the skull, writing a fine trail of red. I took a gauze pad and began dabbing blood. Quickly the skin flap came down and the glistening pearly skull was exposed. Mr. Hastings had made the transition from person to anatomical specimen. It was hard to remember how he had looked.

We were now ready to drill a hole in the skull to remove my theoretical blood clot and relieve the pressure on the brain. The bit was tightened in the craniotomy drill. Dr. Rogers widened his stance, took the drill in both hands, and placed the bit on the skull. There was a horrible grinding sound. Shreds of bone, like dried coconut chips, flew everywhere. Rogers cleared the debris to reveal a half-inch hole, filled with jellied blood.

"Sucker," he said. I handed him the suction device that had somehow found its way into my hand. He edged the tip of the instrument into the hole. Little bits of dark red cranberry sauce leaped up and zipped down the clear plastic tubing toward a large glass bottle clamped to the wall.

The entire clot was quickly removed. Mr. Hastings's brain peered out at us from its little hole, like delicate gray-pink sausages huddled together within the confines of the skull. I glanced up at the heart monitor and noticed frequent premature ventricular beats. The anesthesiologist didn't look worried, but then again, did he know these abnormal beats were occurring?

"Hit me," I heard Dr. Rogers say. "Hit me, damn it!" I realized he was talking to me. There were a few bleeding vessels in the dura, the covering of the brain, and he wanted to cauterize them. He had grasped a bleeder with a tiny insulated forceps. I was supposed to touch the top of the forceps with an electrocoagulation device that the scrub nurse had put into my hand. After his impatient explanation I touched the cautery blade to the forceps. Rogers stepped on the foot switch, and with a sizzle and a puff of acrid smoke the bleeding stopped. "Hit me," he said again and this time I was right there. We went on rhythmically cooking the little bleeding sites. It was a satisfying and almost relaxing rhythm — hit me, sizzle, smoke; hit me, sizzle, smoke.

"V tach!" yelled the anesthesiologist, ending my reverie. I looked up to see the regular wide spikes of ventricular tachycardia on the monitor. The anesthesiologist wound up and smashed his fist into poor Mr. Hastings's chest. The rhythm reverted to normal. Then, under our watchful eyes V tach returned and soon converted to the ugly irregular jaggedness of ventricular fibrillation, a lethal rhythm. The anesthesiologist injected some lidocaine into the patient's IV and began pumping on his chest.

Dr. Rogers grew frantic. "Jesus," he said, "I've never lost a case on the table before. Cardiac massage will never work; let's crack the chest." He tore down the fragile tent of drapes that separated Mr. Hastings's sterile brain from the nonsterile surface over his heart, ripped off the covering sheets, and shoved the anesthesiologist aside. The nurse handed him a scalpel. He slashed a deep, foot-long incision across the left chest. Then he took the rib spreaders and fixed their ends between two adjacent ribs. With an ugly series of cracks the fragile bones separated. Within seconds the heart was in Rogers's hands. He squeezed it frantically to preserve his patient and his unblemished record.

Despite Rogers's heroics, the tired heart continued its random twitching. There was no sign of return to a normal rhythm.

After several minutes even the fibrillation ceased. The glowing green dot on the heart monitor glided smoothly across the screen, a flat line. Rogers continued to pump.

"You can stop, doctor," the anesthesiologist said. "The patient is dead."

The only sound in the room after Rogers's last squeeze was the hissing of the respirator, still ventilating Mr. Hastings's lifeless lungs. Did I do this, I wondered, by improperly bagging him on my nightmare trip to the operating room? Am I the one who caused this surgeon to lose his first case?

Rogers suddenly severed the stillness. He took my hand and placed it on the warm rubbery heart. "Here, practice squeezing this," he said. "You might save someone's life someday."

1
Joining the Parochials
Getting into Medical School

I NEVER WANTED to be a doctor. There were no physicians in my family and I didn't idolize my pediatrician. Not once did I manage to sit through an entire episode of "Ben Casey." I was never attracted to a life of sore throats and heart attacks and calls in the middle of the night. But as I'll explain, during my third year of college I suddenly decided to apply to medical school.

Since then a lot has happened. I've delivered babies, put tubes into hearts, and diagnosed cancer. I've wasted countless hours holding retractors at surgery, and I've seen people kept alive far past their time. I've learned the biochemistry of some rare diseases, but I still don't know what's best for a stomachache. I've seen patients put far too much faith in medicine. But I've also witnessed miraculous cures. And more than once I've been filled with terror in the middle of the night.

I've been transformed from a layperson into a doctor. This transformation, this process of education and socialization and experiencing, is not complete when the M.D. degrees are handed out, or even after internship and residency. Nevertheless, the four years of medical school go a long way toward creating and shaping a physician. This book is about those exciting and excruciating four years. It is all true.

So how, despite my old attitude toward doctors, did I end up in medical school? I still ask myself that question sometimes. There was certainly no childhood inspiration. My earliest medical memory is being taken to the doctor for constipation. My pediatrician was a tall man named Dr. Morris. He had a sour face, thick glasses, and very shiny shoes. My mother told him my trouble and he asked me some questions about what I liked to eat. Then he did a rectal with his big fat finger and extracted a few lumps of feces. He rolled them around in his rubber-gloved palm. "Look at these," he said to my mother as I cringed in embarrassment, "like hard little marbles. Kenny needs to eat more roughage." Though I never really had anything against Dr. Morris, he hardly inspired me to become a doctor.

My mother certainly didn't push me toward medicine. She was a social worker and president of a Planned Parenthood chapter. She didn't always have good things to say about doctors. Sometimes I met her physician colleagues at parties my parents gave. I was allowed to stay up until company came. Then I said goodnight to everybody and had to troop off to bed. Instead of going to sleep, I'd spy on the party by putting my ear to the heating duct by my bed. The obstetricians always seemed to be the loudest of the guests. And they were the ones who left the sour cigar butts I found in the ashtrays the next morning.

So did I end up in medicine because of my father's

influence? Not a chance. My father's a chemist. He always seemed to think of doctors as mere technicians. These uncreative people simply fixed you when you were sick, just as a mechanic would repair a broken car. "Doctors," he once told me down in his study, "are the most parochial of professionals." I sure didn't want to be parochial. Clearly I was headed for science, like my father.

I didn't get any medical inspiration from high school, either. Some of my classmates already knew they would become doctors. They all seemed to be on the football team and had the prettiest girlfriends. In math and science courses they were different from those of us who were going to be scientists. The only thing that ever seemed to get them excited was grades.

Just as I had strong feelings about these budding Dr. Kildares, they had their own stereotypes. Scientists, they said, were unfeeling machines with no social conscience and no interests apart from their slide rules. But I didn't want to be an unfeeling machine. And I certainly had interests other than my slide rule. I was a big cheese in student council. I wrote poetry, sometimes even when it wasn't assigned in English class. I loved books too. One summer I snuck down the basement and read Freud's *Interpretation of Dreams,* which I'd lifted from my mother's bookcase. It was exciting; I wanted to learn more about psychology.

After I was accepted by Harvard College, one of the forms they sent asked for my anticipated major. I knew I'd probably stick with chemistry but I didn't want to rule out psychology. I agonized over the form for hours.

"Hell, Ken," my father said, "it doesn't matter what you say. Just put down 'chemistry.'" I wrote down "Undecided."

By sophomore year I still wasn't ready to commit myself. Psychology had deteriorated into a series of pigeon experiments. But my chemistry course, organic chemistry, was no more inspiring. To me organic chemistry was merely the memorization of hundreds of chemical reactions. That wasn't science! But the pre-meds in my class delighted in cramming all the formulas into their compulsive little heads. Organic chemistry and pre-meds became inseparably entwined in my thinking. I despised them both.

Every other day I seemed to bump into these pre-meds going to meetings of the premedical society, whatever that was. It seemed to be the doctor's equivalent of the 4-H Club. What went on there? Did they learn secret medical handshakes? How to set up a tax shelter? How to smoke cigars? I never knew, and I never cared.

By junior year I had kissed organic chemistry good-bye, and with it, most of the pre-meds. My chemistry course then was physical chemistry. It was much more beautiful than organic; what I was learning sang like poetry. I officially became a chemistry major.

But as the year went on clouds began to gather on the horizon. Now, in the midst of graduate courses, I found that things weren't coming so easily to me any more. I still loved chemistry, but doing it grew to be more and more of a struggle. Sadly I recognized the obvious: I couldn't become a good chemist if I wasn't good at the chemistry.

But if I didn't go into chemistry what else could I do? I had begun doing volunteer work in a state mental hospital. I loved this work with the mentally ill and knew I was good at it, but it wasn't very scientific. And besides, becoming a psychiatrist was out of the question. That would mean going to medical school.

A course in neurophysiology turned out to be my salvation. Martha, a classmate I had the hots for, told me about the course. I thought it might be fun to learn how nerves worked. Also, taking a class with Martha would mean I'd get to see her at least three times a week.

Things never got going between Martha and me, but neurophysiology and I really hit it off. There was both the beauty of science and the relevance to human behavior. And as time when on I even developed an intellectual crush on my professor. Neurophysiology became more and more glamorous.

I decided to apply to graduate school in neurophysiology. But one day my professor suggested that I consider medical school. With an M.D., he said, not only could I do lab work, but I'd be able to do human research too. Grant money and an academic position would be easier to come by as well. "You know, Kenneth," he told me, "believe it or not there are actually some M.D. neurophysiologists who are good scientists. If I had to do it over again I'd probably go for an M.D. instead of a Ph.D." I was startled by this heresy from my hero.

I began mulling over what he had said. Unfortunately, it made sense. For months I struggled with the shame of taking the easy way out to earn the title "doctor." For a Ph.D. you had to do research and write a thesis. To get an M.D., though, you merely needed a good memory and a strong stomach. But the more I mulled, the more sense an M.D. seemed to make. After I had agonized a lot, medical school won out.

So, as my senior year got underway, I began frantically applying to medical schools. I'd made my decision perhaps ten years later than most of the competition; I had a lot of catching up to do. The first step was meeting with Dr. Ganz, the pre-med advisor for my dorm. My classmates had been cultivating his favor for three years of premedical society meetings — how could I ever hope to wring a decent letter of recommendation out of him?

He urged me to apply to at least eight or ten schools. Some could be places where I'd really like to go, but at least a few should be "safety schools," chosen just because they would be easier to get into. He told me to sign up to take the Medical College Admission Test right away. Doing well on this medical equivalent of the SAT was apparently crucial for a good shot at medical school. Dr. Ganz also warned me I'd better get several strong letters of recommendation. And I'd better put a lot of thought into my application essays — I had to justify choosing medical school so late. I thanked him for all his advice and went home to dream up an essay.

Home, during my senior year of college, was a big house in Cambridge that I shared with six other people. I'd become friends with a classmate named Susan — we kept finding ourselves signed up for the same science and psychology courses and soon got to know each other. We'd decided to rent a house together — surely we'd be compatible housemates. We quickly found an assortment of people to fill up all the rooms but one. Then Susan got a call from her younger sister, Phyllis. Phyllis had decided to come to Boston to work for a year before going to college. Could she join us? Though it seemed rather undignified to share a house with someone just out of high school, we did need another housemate. And, Susan assured us, her sister was very mature for her age. Also she was a terrific potter; maybe she'd bring some of her mugs and bowls to fill our bare kitchen cupboards. We agreed to take her.

A few days later I answered the door. It was a woman who looked about my age. She had long fluffy light brown hair, subtle little freckles, and hazel eyes. "Hi, I'm Phyllis," she said with a shy but self-contained smile. She took the room next to mine, up on the third floor.

Sometimes Phyllis and I sat out on the third floor fire escape, overlooking the street with its row of maple trees. We'd talk and watch the leaves toast in the warm sun of early fall. "I can't understand why anybody would want to be a doctor," she said the day I came back from my meeting with Dr. Ganz. "It's not the blood and guts; that doesn't bother me. It's just the idea of spending your life worrying about people's bowel movements and headaches and arthritis."

"I feel the same way," I said. "That's why I'm not going into practice. I'm going to do research in neurophysiology. A medical degree is just a union card."

"Well you'd better watch yourself," she said. "You're going to be surrounded by medical types for four years. I bet it would be easy to get sucked into just being a regular doctor."

"Oh no, not me!"

Over the next months Phyllis and I got to know each other through our noises. Across the wall between our rooms we shared rustlings and grumblings and comings and goings. I'd hear her watering her plants; she'd hear me flipping the pages of a book. Her guitar serenaded my typewriter. She came to my room to show me a teapot that she'd just unpacked. I went next door to read her from one of my application essays, hot off the press:

> Neurophysiology is such an incredibly exciting field to me because it is where physiology, chemistry, psychology, and philosophy meet. To be creative and effective in the field one must have a good feel for all these disciplines and constantly change perspective from one to another. Being involved in this interplay of ideas and points of view would be tremendously exciting and satisfying. Ultimately I would like to do neurophysiology in connection with the study of mental illness, learning, and memory . . . .

"A little pompous, but it does sound sincere," Phyllis said.

The fall was thick with thoughts of medical school. In October I took the dreaded MCATs. I spent hours slaving over my application forms. I went to see some of my chemistry professors and sheepishly solicited letters of recommendation. I felt guilty, as if asking a rejected girlfriend to endorse me to a new woman.

In early winter, representatives of most of the medical schools to which I was applying came to Boston to hold interviews. I rehearsed answers to hundreds of theoretical questions: "I see there are no doctors in your family, Mr. Klein. How do you know what being a physician will be like?" "You've decided very late to become a doctor; can you convince me you're really interested in medicine?" "How do you feel about national health insurance?" "Do you support the AMA?"

Rumor had it that there would be trick questions, and insults designed to see how I'd react under stress. It didn't surprise me, this sadistic rush week of interviews before being considered for the medical fraternity.

"Hey, Phyllis," I said one night over the dishes, "do you think I should shave off my moustache?"

"Huh?"

"For my interviews. Doctors are a pretty conservative bunch, you know. Maybe I'll be subverting my application by looking too much like a hippie."

"No. Don't start selling out already."

"Yeah, but is a moustache worth not getting into medical school for? Remember, I'm starting in this business late. I need all the help I can get." As a compromise I got her to give it a good trimming.

Despite the rumors of gimmicks and trick questions the interviews turned out to be quite benign. I was asked why I wanted to go into medicine and what attracted me to neurophysiology and had I read any good books lately. But at the Harvard interview the issue of my moustache came up.

My interviewer was a sleek, silver-haired professor of neurology. "I see you sport a moustache, Mr. Klein," he said during a pause in the conversation.

"Yes, sir, I do."

"Have you thought about how it might affect the doctor-patient relationship?"

"No, I can't say that I have, sir. However I feel that the doctor-patient relationship is one of the most important aspects of the practice of medicine. If I were to find that patients had a harder time relating to me because of my moustache, I'd shave it off immediately. Nothing should interfere with the doctor-patient relationship."

"Yes. That's very good, Mr. Klein."

When I told Phyllis about the interview she said she was glad she hadn't been there; she would have puked.

While I was applying to medical school, Phyllis was applying to college. She wanted to study fine arts and psychology. She was accepted by Goddard, a college in Vermont that had a work-study program. By the time my interviews were finished, she had already arranged to spend two work-study terms in Boston the following year. I decided I wanted to stay in Boston too; I wanted to be near Phyllis. This would mean going to medical school at Harvard, despite its suspicion of mustachioed applicants. But the more I wanted to stay in Boston, the more impossible it seemed that I'd be accepted at Harvard, the only school in Boston to which I'd applied. As my pre-med advisor had repeatedly told me, the competition was fierce. "Harvard may be the best," he said chauvinistically, "but there are other good places too. Frankly, Ken, you should be happy to get into anyplace at all."

In late December the letters started arriving. My first, from San Diego, was an acceptance; the pressure was off. Then I was accepted at a few more schools and put on the waiting list at several others. But as January rolled into icy February I still hadn't heard from Harvard. I ran into Dr. Ganz one day. He said the final decisions would be made on Monday of the following week. He understood that those accepted would get a special delivery letter; the rejects would hear by regular mail.

Monday came. There was no letter, but I figured I wasn't out of the running yet. It might take a full day even for special delivery. But when I didn't hear on Tuesday, I figured that was that. I resigned myself to going to San Diego; at least it would be warm in the winter. "Hey, don't give up," Phyllis said. "Remember, Harvard hasn't said no, either."

By dinnertime on Wednesday I was really down. A mailman could have *walked* a special delivery letter from Boston to Cambridge in two days! "Listen, Ken, you have just as good a chance as anyone," Susan said. "Maybe you're on the waiting list."

"Remember," Phyllis said again, "they haven't said no."

By the time I came home from school on Thursday I was completely resigned to leaving Boston. Maybe Phyllis could do a work-study term in San Diego sometime.

"Ken!" Susan screamed when I walked in the door. "You got a special delivery letter from Harvard!"

"Come on, Susan, that's not funny. Let me suffer in peace."

"No, really!" She ran down the stairs with the letter. All my housemates gathered around me. "Open it already!" Susan yelled.

I retreated to the bathroom and locked the door. Then I sat on the toilet, took a deep breath, and tore open the fateful letter. "Dear Mr. Klein," it read. "On behalf of the Committee on Admission of the Harvard Medical School, I am pleased to offer you a place in the first-year class entering in September."

I walked calmly out of the bathroom and handed the letter to the waiting throng. They whooped and hollered, and Phyllis and I hugged a long, deep hug.

As spring began to green up the cold gray city I thought ahead to next fall, the start of medical school. After several years of living in a group, I decided I just couldn't face dorm life again. I began searching for a place close to the medical school. Several months later a creaky ten-bedroom house turned up in the Brighton section of Boston. It had been an old people's home; there was still a sign above the porch that said "Endale Rest Home." I recklessly put up a deposit, signed a lease, and ran an ad in the paper for housemates.

Phyllis and I had decided to go to Europe for the summer, the last fling of freedom before our respective academic incarcerations. By the time we were scheduled to leave, though, I'd found only one tenant for the Endale Rest Home. His name was Gene, a forty-one-year-old electronics firm executive. He was getting divorced from both his wife and the suburbs and moving to the city to start a new life. Gene agreed to find people to fill up the house.

When we came back from Europe in the late summer I met my housemates-to-be. At twenty-one I turned out to be the baby of the house. The next youngest were Tim, a cab driver, and Amy, a Montessori teacher who always seemed to be going out with at least three men. Besides me there was one other medical person. Her name was Bonnie, a lab technician at the Deaconess Hospital, who drank a Coke every morning for breakfast. In the room above mine lived George, an unemployed schoolteacher. He eventually stole and then married Gene's first postdivorce girlfriend.

The basement had been staked out by a thirty-five-year-old sculptress named Hannah, who lived like a hermit with her creations. A computer programmer who wanted to become a carpenter, a special-ed teacher, and a secretary rounded out the crew.

Phyllis helped me move into the Endale Rest Home and then got ready to leave for school. Just before she left, Susan threw a big farewell party. At the party I met Andy and Harvey, friends of Susan's who had just finished medical school. They were both going west for their internships.

"So you're about to start medical school, are you?" Andy said to me. "You have my sympathies."

"Yeah," said Harvey. "I tell you, it's nice to finally be a doctor, but if I could do it over I don't think I'd go to medical school. It's just not worth it."

"Come on," I said, "it can't really be that bad."

"Oh no?" said Andy. "Just wait. You've signed up for four years of incredibly long hours and incredibly intense work. You won't have time for anything else. Or any*one* else."
Phyllis later found out that Andy's long-time girlfriend had broken up with him during his third year.

"But listen, Ken," Harvey said, "don't let us scare you. Everyone's different; maybe you won't find it so bad."

With this hardly comforting reassurance I braced myself for the fall, and medical school.

2

When Will We Learn Some Medicine?

The Basic Sciences

I FOUND MY WAY to the auditorium of the Peter Bent Brigham Hospital, settled uneasily into one of the plush seats, and looked around. The walls were encrusted with paintings of famous professors, staring down with intimidating eyes. The room quickly filled with my new classmates, 140 men and women, launching into yet another four-year cycle of their education. We were all restless with anticipation; we were about to see our first patient.

Dr. Thatcher, a distinguished professor of cardiology, welcomed us to this introductory clinic. He was going to present a patient with a pacemaker to us. But first he would say a few words about abnormal heart rhythms. He drew pictures of the cardiac conduction system on the board. He described the various types of heart block. He explained how pacemakers worked and when they should be used. He spoke clearly, yet nothing made sense to me. Everyone else seemed to be nodding knowingly, though. It was the first week of medical school and already I was behind!

As my classmates continued hectically taking notes Dr. Thatcher called in the patient. She was a thin gray-haired woman who was a veteran of these presentations. She clearly knew more about heart block than I did. She told us about the symptoms that had led her to see Dr. Thatcher six years previously and how her life had changed after he put in the pacemaker. "Thanks to Dr. Thatcher," she said, "I'm a new woman. I have a hundred percent more energy now and I don't get those dizzy spells. I feel wonderful!" There were touching little intimacies between patient and doctor about experiences in the office, the hospital, and even at similar presentations in the past.

I was in awe of Dr. Thatcher. He seemed to be in total command of all cardiological knowledge, and at the same time he was so humanly warm and kind to this patient. How wonderful it must be to know so much and be able to help someone so much!

After the patient had told her story Dr. Thatcher said, "Now, Evelyn, would you mind showing these student doctors your pacemaker?"

"Of course not," she said. "I do it every year." Then she took off her blouse. On the left side of the upper chest, next to her bra strap, was a raised rectangle of flesh. It looked like a tiny pack of cigarettes, somehow growing beneath her skin. "Come on up if you want a closer look," she said.

I was astounded. This woman was perfectly willing to expose her chest in front of 140 total strangers. Somehow, because we intended to become doctors we were entitled to expect her to remove her blouse. How scandalous it would have been had she done the same thing in my chemistry class the year before!

I glumly left the auditorium. My first-day jitters, combined with all the unfamiliar words Dr. Thatcher had used, resulted in my not understanding a word of his talk. I had no more knowledge of pacemakers, or of medicine in general, than the average person on the street. Yet I had been allowed to look at this woman's chest. Would she still have let me look if she'd known I hadn't learned anything? I felt like a fraud.

After the clinic it was lunchtime. We marched back across the street to Vanderbilt Hall, the medical school dormitory. In the cafeteria I sat across a plate of fish sticks from someone I thought I'd seen in the auditorium. He was a little chubby, with light brown hair and a bushy moustache.

"Hey, how'd you like that clinic?" he asked.

"Well, Dr. Thatcher seemed very nice," I said, "and he was very articulate. But I must say, not much of it sank in."

"Boy, that's good to hear," he said. "To tell you the truth, I had no idea what the hell was going on. It seemed like everyone else understood it, though." We were both relieved. Each of us was glad to know that there was at least one other person in the class who hadn't yet mastered pacemakers.

He introduced himself. His name was David Rappaport. He was soft-spoken and friendly, not at all like the grubby pre-meds I remembered from organic chemistry.

"By the way," he asked, "what room do you live in? I haven't seen you around much." I explained that I didn't live in the dorm. I told him about my big house and invited him home to dinner.

Since each of us at the Endale Rest Home had to cook only once in ten nights, every meal was an extravaganza. When it was my turn, I liked to bring classmates home. All my grandmotherly instincts came out as I resuscitated these victims of dormitory macaroni and cheese with some good home cooking.

I was proud to show off my housemates, real working people, to my fellow students. And I was proud to show off bona fide doctors-to-be to my housemates; they seemed to be impressed with other medical students, even if not with me. The night Dave came to dinner, for example, Gene and Bonnie plied him with questions: Why had he decided to go into medicine? How did it feel to be so smart? Wasn't it tough to deal with sickness and death all the time? David squirmed and shrugged his shoulders. "I don't know," he kept saying; "I don't know."

As cook that night, I was exempt from the predessert table clearing. So I took Dave on a tour of the house. "You know, Ken," he said when we were alone on the second floor, "living in Vanderbilt Hall is making me lose touch with the outside world. People really *do* look at you differently when they know you're in medicine, don't they? It sort of gives me the creeps."

"I know what you mean," I said. "But sometimes I wonder if they're *really* treating us as something special or if it's just that we're beginning to *expect* them to." We both stewed about that until the dessert call came.

Dinner at the Endale Rest Home was filled with rituals. For example, after we reassembled for dessert someone would turn to me and ask, "Hey, Dr. Ken Klein, what's the medical fact of the day?" I always had an astounding bit of information ready from one of my classes. I'd stroke my chin pensively, brood a bit, then suddenly brighten. Then, with upraised arm and pointed finger I'd recite my fact. The night when David came to dinner, I said, "The medical fact of the day is that the surface area of the human small intestine is equal to that of two hockey rinks." Everyone gasped in astonishment, and there was applause. Unlike chemistry or even neurophysiology, medicine was interesting and accessible to almost everyone. I liked that.

Despite collecting my medical facts of the day, I rarely felt that I was learning to become a doctor. The first part of medical school is all "basic science" — you don't learn how to diagnose a stroke or deliver a baby. My housemates wouldn't accept this, though. They relentlessly bombarded me with medical questions, as if the mere fact that I was studying to be a doctor gave me instant omniscience. If Tim had a sore throat or if Amy were spotting on her birth control pills, they always asked me what to do. I never knew. "We haven't learned that yet," was my standard answer. "Go see a doctor." I felt guilty — I never seemed able to deliver the medical goods. Sometimes I wondered what it would be like after I'd finally learned some medicine. Would it be fun to be able to spew out sage answers, or just a nuisance? I looked into the future and saw myself at the archetypal cocktail party, surrounded by people looking for free medical advice. It was hard to imagine enjoying it. I wondered if my parents bugged their doctor-guests with questions at the parties I used to spy on when I was a kid. Unexpectedly I began feeling some sympathy for those obnoxious obstetricians.

If I weren't learning any medicine, my housemates asked, what *was* I being taught this first year of medical school? I sure seemed to spend a lot of time at the library. And more than once I ducked out in the middle of a household crisis to coop myself up with my books. Before we would be set loose on the wards, I explained, we had a year and a half of "preclinical" courses. The first six months was a densely packed conglomerate called "the basic sciences." These courses, which included biochemistry and statistics and histology and genetics, were designed to teach us the scientific underpinnings of medical practice. How arrogant, I thought, to call things like statistics and histology *"basic science"*! How inelegant and fumbling they seemed compared to my dear but fast-fading physical chemistry.

Some of the basic science courses lasted the entire semester. Others lasted only a matter of weeks or months. In microbiology lab, for example, we made successive generations of bacteria jump through genetic hoops, manipulating their ability to ferment sugars and do other metabolic tricks. But just as we got to be on speaking terms with our *E. coli,* microbiology was over and we raced on to embryology and physiology and immunology. Occasionally some exciting bits of science came up, but they were quickly lost in the dust of the next class. There was no time to savor any of what was being force-fed.

Most of the lectures were held in a big auditorium where all 140 of us were held captive every morning. Then in the afternoons we were dispersed to lab sessions and discussion groups and problem-set reviews. During these long days I got to know most of my classmates, some as just names and faces, others as friends. There were musicians and football players, Ph.D.'s in anthropology, former social workers and schoolteachers. I was excited by this variety — few seemed to fit my premedical stereotype. But I was also distressed. Confronted with all this diversity, it was hard to feel different or special or aloof. We were all together in this thick medical soup. We'd simmer for four intense years and then be served up to internship programs as newly done doctors.

I made some close friends. In addition to Dave Rappaport there was Karen Grieves. Like me, she had majored in chemistry. Also like me, she felt contemptuous of medicine's claim to be a hard science, and she loved working with people. "Medicine," she once said, "is intellectually the easiest but emotionally the most difficult of the graduate fields." This certainly seemed to be true. It would be good to have someone like her around to celebrate and commiserate with during the long years ahead.

Biochemistry was the most time-consuming course of the first semester. As I sat among my classmates in the big lecture hall, with polypeptides and triglycerides swirling through the air, I thought back to organic chemistry. As in organic, there was an endless assembly line of reactions to memorize. And as in organic, I was surrounded by doctors-to-be. Only now I was one of them! Again and again I wondered how I had ever ended up in medical school.

Every few weeks, to convince us that biochemistry was really relevant to medicine, we had what they called "correlation clinics." We were shown a patient, or sometimes an entire family, that illustrated biochemistry in the flesh. One clinic was on a metabolic disorder called glycogen storage disease. A roly-poly family was marched in front of the class. The professor went up behind the youngest girl and held her face in his big hands. The little girl stood stiffly at attention.

"Look at this face," he said. "Just like a china doll, hey? This is the 'china doll face' of glycogen storage disease." He pinched her china doll cheek and asked the family to sit down. They sat uncomfortably in the front row while the professor explicated their disorder, draping the blackboard with long strings of biochemistry.

Despite the presence of living patients, these clinics failed to convince me that biochemistry was really relevant to taking care of sick people. All the patients we were shown had exotic disorders we'd probably never see in practice. And even when biochemistry gave an elegant explanation of their obscure disease, there was usually nothing that could be done for them anyway. I knew all about the kinetics of glucose 6-phosphatase, but I still couldn't treat Tim's sore throat.

Though I didn't seem to be learning any medicine, I was nonetheless in medical school; there was no doubt about it. Doctors were everywhere, white-clothed medical gurus promising salvation to those who passed biochemistry. In the lobby of Vanderbilt Hall upperclass students hung out, each wearing a white coat with medical instruments bulging conspicuously from the pockets. I watched with envy as they discussed their latest cases with enthralled women from my class. A white coat with a stethoscope in the pocket was the medical equivalent of a letter sweater.

Sometimes I ate in the cafeteria of one of the nearby hospitals. There I rubbed elbows with doctors, nurses, pharmacists, and physical therapists. They all looked so comfortable in their crisp white uniforms. Clearly, they were all competent in their work — you could tell by the calm, deliberate way they ate their lunches. How I envied them!

Something called "the first-year tutorial" was designed to make us feel part of this teeming mass of medical humanity. Groups of three or four students were matched up with a professor in one of the teaching hospitals. We met once a week during the basic sciences semester to see patients or talk about medicine. Dr. Allen, my tutor, was a doctor at Children's Hospital. He was impressive, like Dr. Thatcher. Although he did sophisticated research, he was incredibly gentle and caring with patients. Belatedly I had found a pediatrician for a role model!

Once Dr. Allen took us to the neonatal intensive care unit. The five of us surrounded a tiny being encapsulated in a Plexiglas incubator box. Wires and tubes sprouted out from everywhere. I wondered how this electronic child would ever survive once he hatched from his plastic shell.

Dr. Allen wanted to teach us to increase our powers of observation. We were supposed to take turns stating ways in which the infant looked abnormal.

"But Dr. Allen," I said, "we haven't had pediatrics yet."

"That doesn't matter; just tell me what you see."

"Well, the kid's head looks big."

"No, that's normal."

It was Dan's turn: "He's almost bald. Does he have some disease that interferes with hair growth?"

"No, that's normal too. Remember, this infant is only three days old."

"But Dr. Allen, like Ken said, we haven't had pediatrics yet."

"That's OK. Just tell me what you see. For instance, Celia, what about the child's color?"

"Well, he looks sort of blue, but aren't all kids pretty blue for the first week or two?"

"No. This infant is quite blue. That's because of a cardiac abnormality. He has tetralogy of Fallot."

"What's that?" we all asked.

"Well it's a congenital malformation consisting of a ventricular septal defect, right ventricular hypertrophy, and—"

"—Wait! What's a ventricular septal defect?" I asked. "Remember, we haven't had anatomy yet."

"Well, maybe we should go over that some other time."

Amidst biochemistry and embryology and the other basic sciences was a course called "social medicine." There were lectures and seminars that dealt with the nonscientific issues of medicine. I suppose the idea was to make sure we wouldn't become parochial professionals. Social medicine wasn't exactly a top priority; most of the lectures were held Friday afternoon, and the teachers didn't even bother to grade us "pass" or "fail." One part of the course was to introduce us to different types of medical practice. The president of the Massachusetts Medical Society gave us a talk on solo private practice. "The right of free choice of the physician is paramount," he told us. "A doctor must have total control over his practice."

What? All the still-idealistic eyebrows in the room were raised. What about curing the sick? Comforting patients and their families? Working for a healthier environment? He ended his talk by denouncing socialized medicine and government bureaucracy: "Nothing must come between the doctor and his patient. There is nothing more important than the doctor-physician relationship." That slip of the tongue seemed to sum up his philosophy. I don't think he convinced many of us to go into solo private practice.

But my visit to a prepaid group practice was hardly more inspiring. I was assigned to spend the morning at the Harvard Community Health Plan in conjunction with the social medicine course. It was there that I saw my first physical exam.

My mentor was Dr. Burns, an internist who was going to do the initial history and physical on a new member of the Plan. I sat at Dr. Burns's side, behind his big desk. He wore a long white coat and gold cuff links. I wore corduroys. The nurse brought in the patient. She was a twenty-nine-year-old woman named Rita Custer who had just moved up from Virginia. Dr. Burns stood and shook her hand.

"Hello," he said, "I'm Dr. Burns. And this is Dr. Klein. He'll be watching today." I cringed as I heard myself being called "doctor."

Mrs. Custer sat down in the little chair on the other side of the desk. Her eyes kept roving the room. She was looking, it seemed, for something familiar among all the fancy furniture and light fixtures and diplomas.

Dr. Burns picked up the health questionnaire Mrs. Custer had filled out earlier. He began asking all the questions she had already answered—how old was she, how many kids did she have, had she ever had pneumonia or seizures or palpitations. Dr. Burns put down the folder, locked his hands behind his head, and swung gently from side to side in his big leather swivel chair. Mrs. Custer kept looking at him and me and tried to answer. She seemed to be shivering in the air-conditioned room.

When the questions were done, Dr. Burns asked her to go into the examining room, take off her clothes, and put on the robe he handed her.

After a few minutes we strode into the little room and Dr. Burns closed the door behind us. Mrs. Custer looked tiny sitting on the examining table in the crumpled robe. She seemed to be shivering even more. Dr. Burns took her pulse and blood pressure and looked in her mouth and felt her neck. He kept turning to me to explain what he was doing; I didn't understand much of what he said. Mrs. Custer's eyes seemed to be steadily on me.

Dr. Burns turned off the lights and looked into her pupils. Then he handed me the ophthalmoscope. I'd never seen one before. "Here, Ken," he said, "have a look." I took the thing and put it to my eye. All I saw was a very bright light. He told me I was looking in backward, and set me right. But now all I saw was a piece of a big bulging eyeball, out of focus. I couldn't seem to find the pupil.

"How you doing, Ken?" Dr. Burns asked. "You see the optic nerve and those retinal arterioles?"

"Oh yeah, I sure do, Dr. Burns. Interesting!" I hadn't seen a thing.

Dr. Burns continued the exam. After he listened to the lungs he asked Mrs. Custer to drop down the front of her robe so he could examine her breasts. Her eyes shot up to look at me. I'm not sure if the fright they flashed was hers, or if they only reflected what she saw in *my* eyes. Slowly and stiffly she reached for the bow that tied the robe behind her neck. Her eyes were fixed on me. I grew more and more uncomfortable.

"Mrs. Custer," I finally blurted out, "would you prefer it if I left the room?" It was the first time I'd spoken to her; I'm sure I didn't sound like "Dr. Klein." She immediately nodded yes. I left the room with relief and closed the door tightly behind me.

A few minutes later Dr. Burns pushed open the door and yelled "Pap smear!" A nurse appeared, and went in to help him.

After the exam was done, Dr. Burns met me in his office. "Gee, Ken," he said, "too bad you didn't stay to see how the Pap is done."

About two weeks later Hannah had a friend over to dinner. The word was out that I was a medical student; as usual we got on the subject of doctors. Hannah's friend began a little tirade about how insensitive and piggish physicians were. I agreed. Later, when I mentioned that I'd spent the morning at the Harvard Community Health Plan, she said, "Oh, I'm a member of the Plan. I found a really fine doctor there; he's different from most of them. His name is Dr. Burns; did you happen to meet him?"

I was astonished. Why had we reacted so differently to this man? I wondered if it was really I, not Mrs. Custer, who had felt uncomfortable in Dr. Burns's office.

As the basic science courses drew to a close, a housemate at last asked me a question I could answer. Amy, the Montessori teacher, had just sprouted a cold sore. "Hey, Ken," she asked, "what's this thing on my lip?"

"It's a cold sore."

"No dummy, I mean what is it *really?* You know, *medically.*"

"A cold sore," I said with authority, "is nothing more than an infection with herpes simplex." We had just gone over herpes viruses in microbiology.

Amy was thrilled with her scientific cold sore. At breakfast the next morning she sat down next to Tim. "Hey, Tim," she said pointing to her lip, "guess what I have."

Tim looked up from his Rice Krispies: "Syphilis."

"No, no, stupid. It's herpes simplex!"

Amy's cold sore was my first diagnosis. After this taste of being a doctor, my appetite was whetted for contact with patients; I couldn't wait to get on to the hospital wards. But the laying on of hands was a whole year and many courses away. The next one was pathology, which ended the basic sciences.

The start of pathology was a milestone. At last we were going to be taught about sick people! For several weeks we were tantalized with microscope slides of diseased tissue. We got to know the wavy pink lines of fibrosis, the dark leukocyte dots that meant inflammation, and the wild streamings of malignancy. This was still a long way from taking care of patients, but at least we knew we were on the right track.

The day finally came when we were ready for pathology in the flesh. Dr. Miller, our lab instructor, brought two fresh surgical specimens over from one of the nearby hospitals. They came in white cardboard boxes with little wire handles, the kind made to hold food. It was pathology, Chinese carry-out style.

Six of us gathered round the boxes and nervously flexed our rubber-gloved fingers. Dr. Miller opened the first box. He withdrew a tough hunk of pink gristle, about the size of a three-year-old's fist. There were several fleshy appendages hanging from it. "This," he said, "is a uterus."

"My God," said Gail under her breath. She was the only woman student in the group.

"Down here near the cervix is a little fibroid," Dr. Miller continued. "Here, feel it." He held out the uterus to us. After we had all delicately squeezed it through the safety of our gloves, he sliced into the fibroid with a big sharp knife. Its cut surface bulged out, as if trying to escape the uterus.

Dr. Miller passed around this pathological morsel. Everyone kept hefting it and combing it with their fingers, trying to make it real. Maybe it was the layer of rubber between our fingers and the uterus, but somehow we couldn't imagine it as part of a person. How could this thing possibly have been in someone's pelvis earlier that day? How could a baby ever grow inside something like that? Everyone kept asking Dr. Miller about the patient whose womb we held. How old was she? Did she have any children? Why did they do the hysterectomy? He seemed annoyed at all these irrelevant questions. He kept trying to draw our attention back to the pathology at hand.

Then he opened the other box. It contained an even more disturbing specimen. "This, ladies and gentlemen, represents one of the most common cancers in the United States," Miller said. "You'll all take care of patients with this disease before you've finished medical school. In fact, it's likely that each of you will discover one of these cancers in a patient sooner or later." He scooped up the specimen from the box and plopped it down on the black slate table. It was a breast.

There was a dark, stiff nipple centered on an ellipse of skin. The skin sat on a wide bed of fat, in the depths of which was an irregular grayish rock — the tumor. Gail examined the breast, then handed it to me. The slippery tissue settled into the cup of my hands.

This can't really be a breast, I thought. How could I possibly be attracted to globs of yellow fat, sealed in a bag of skin? I thought of Phyllis's breasts, I thought of the breasts of past girlfriends as I touched the nipple and lightly kneaded the underlying tissue. No, this wasn't a breast. As soon as it was removed from the body, I decided, it ceased being a breast and became merely a specimen. But I left pathology lab feeling very troubled.

3

Meeting the Dead

The Organ Blocks

"Hey, Phyllis," I said over the phone, "want to do something tomorrow afternoon?"

"Sure. What do you have in mind?"

"Oh, I don't know. How about an autopsy?"

"*What?*"

"Well, they want us to see an autopsy as part of our pathology course. I called the morgue at the Boston City and they said to come down tomorrow afternoon. They have a woman in the fridge that they're going to do then."

"What about me? Did you ask if you could bring a date?"

"Well, no. You'll be a first-year medical student too, see?"

"Sounds ridiculous. I'll do it."

It was midwinter. Phyllis had finished her first semester and was now in Boston for her work-study term. She decided to live in a halfway house for former mental patients. She was going to work in a hospital as a nurses' aide and study classical guitar. We saw each other only once or twice a week; we were both doing things that gobbled up time. But there were marathon phone conversations: I moaned about medical school. Even though I was finally learning things that seemed relevant to doctoring, I was tired of being a student. I lusted for the hospital wards, for living patients. I pumped Phyllis about her experiences: what was it like to work in a hospital? Did her patients have interesting diseases? Were the doctors good?

Her work was hard, both physically and emotionally. She loved to sit with patients and talk with them about their fears and their families, but there was little time for talk between the bedpans and sponge baths and linen changes and meal trays. She didn't have an especially high opinion of doctors. With the flick of a pen they could write orders that would generate mounds of work. One doctor, for example, insisted that a 280-pound man with bad emphysema and a leg infection be weighed daily. Maneuvering him onto the portable bed scale meant a major struggle for Phyllis, and torture for the patient, every morning. His weight had been stable for over a week — why didn't she suggest that the doctor order less frequent weighing? "What?" Phyllis said. "Me question a doctor? Do you really think an M.D. would speak to a lowly nurses' aide?" That gave me the willies. I vowed I'd be different, if I ever actually got to be a doctor.

The day after I'd made the autopsy date we drove down to the Boston City Hospital. The air was cold and gray. Greasy patches of ice lined the gutters.

"What if they discover that I'm an impostor?" Phyllis said.

"Don't worry. Just act like you know what's going on; I'll do the talking."

As we rode down Massachusetts Avenue the grimy hospital buildings rose up from their dreary surroundings. What a depressing place to come when you're *already* sick, I thought.

We parked on the street and went in through the emergency entrance. The receiving area outside the Emergency Ward was filled with official vehicles: ambulances, paddy wagons, even a fire truck. Some still had their lights flashing, and several sirens softly mooed — they were like mechanical cattle grazing on the asphalt.

I got in line at the desk where patients checked in. The waiting room was packed with people, each with a tantalizing clue to his or her diagnosis: a woozy woman in the corner held a plastic basin with one hand and her belly with the other. A man mumbled to himself as he wobbled around the room, crowned with a bloody towel. A teenaged girl with heavy makeup and chattering teeth huddled against an older man.

Finally my turn came. "Name?" asked the clerk, fingers poised on the typewriter keys.

"I don't want to check in," I said. "I just want directions to the morgue."

"I'm sorry sir, the morgue is not opened to the public."

"No, no, I'm a medical student. I'm supposed to meet Dr. Cantor to see an autopsy."

"Oh," she said, then gave me directions. I felt an unexpected thrill of specialness at the clerk's flat "oh." I wasn't the public, no indeed. I was a medical student. And she believed me!

Phyllis and I set out for the morgue. We followed the clerk's directions down dark twisty hallways, deep into the hospital. Eventually we came to a sign that said "Pathology Department," which pointed us up a short flight of stairs. The undifferentiated smells of the main corridor began to divide and sharpen. We could now smell powerful odors, sour and sweet. Was this the smell of death?

We came to a set of swinging doors. "RESTRICTED AREA. NO ADMITTANCE," warned a big red and white sign. Below it a smaller sign said, "Morgue."

"Well, toots, this is it," I said, trying to be casual. "Hold your nose." Phyllis gave me a dirty look.

I pushed open the door that barred admission to the general public and we entered the pathological world of the dead. We were in a bright empty hallway. On either side were shiny tiled rooms with stainless steel tables and counters and sinks. The walls were layered with shelves. They held neat rows of jars, each containing a hunk or two of tissue in a dark broth. I almost expected price tags.

There was no one in sight. The only sound was running water, somewhere in the distance. We walked slowly forward, deeper into this land of no return. To the right was a room with its door closed. We went up to it and looked in through the little glass window. Inside was a man wearing a white cap, rubber gloves, and a plastic apron. He whistled merrily to himself as he worked. He was deep in the belly of an old woman. "Do you think this is it?" I whispered to Phyllis.

"Well, she looks dead, doesn't she?"

I knocked lightly on the door. The man looked up. In his right hand was a knife and in his left a loop of intestine. Except for the rubber gloves he could have been a butcher at the Stop & Shop.

"Come in, come in," he said. "You must be the medical students. Welcome to the morgue."

We exchanged introductions while I looked around. Hanging from the ceiling was a scale with a big porcelain pan. On a counter were some open specimen jars filled with formaldehyde, and a collection of saws and knives. A blackboard above the counter listed all the organs of the body. There were spaces for their weights, to be filled in at each autopsy.

Lying stiffly on a long steel table with a raised rim was the corpse we had come to see. This collection of skin and bones, this former person, had wet ropy hair and a deeply wrinkled face. She looked about seventy. There were bruises all over her thin arms. On the back of her left hand was a Band-Aid. It didn't seem right — how could someone wearing a Band-Aid be dead? Her pubic hair was sparse and stringy, like an old oriental's beard. And like the hair on her head, it was gray. So pubic hair ages too, I thought. It had never occurred to me before.

A garden hose was pinned in place by her right shoulder. Water flowing slowly from the nozzle caught and twisted pink ribbons of blood and carried them toward a drain by her feet. Between her legs lay the front portion of her ribcage. The lidless chest was filled with what looked like cheap cuts of meat. The belly had been parted down the middle with an extension of the incision that allowed the removal of the rib cage. The skin, fat, and muscles that made up the abdominal wall were folded back over each flank, like the pages of an opened book. Filling the hollow of the abdominal cavity were a big chunky liver the color of cloves, a wineskin of a stomach, and glistening loops of intestines lying like a nest of enormous bloated earthworms.

"Well," said Dr. Cantor, "what can I tell you? This gal was fifty-nine. She died from cancer of the pancreas. I'm just now trying to free up the small intestine from all the metastases." He dove back into the belly and continued to skin the bowel.

"When did she die?" asked Phyllis.

"Yesterday morning, about seven-thirty. We didn't get the family's permission to do her until later in the day, so we cooled her in the fridge over night."

"What was the cause of death?" I asked.

"Oh, I don't know. She had widely metastatic adenocarcinoma of the pancreas — died of the dwindles, I guess."

The door swung open and Dr. Mertz walked in. He was head of pathology at the Boston City. He had been my favorite teacher during our pathology course.

"Hello there," he said, "come to make the acquaintance of the dead, have you? How about a little anatomy lesson while Dr. Cantor wrestles with the bowel?" Mertz put on some gloves and reached into the chest. He hefted a roundish organ with a heavy fringe of fat, slightly bigger than his fist. "What's this?" he asked.

"Is it the thymus?" I answered timidly. I remembered from embryology class that the thymus sat in the midline of the chest and had a lot of fatty tissue around it.

"Ah, no," said Dr. Mertz. "The thymus is very high up in the chest, practically in the neck, and at its biggest weighs only an ounce. Also, it involutes after adolescence; it would be tough to find this woman's thymus even if I went over her with a fine-toothed comb." He turned to Phyllis: "You try. What organ is this?"

"I don't know; it looks like the heart to me."

"Yes, of course. This is the heart." Phyllis had first crack at Dr. Mertz's questions after that.

We left the morgue and went to a nearby sub shop for lunch. As usual, we split a large meatball and a large Italian. I was surprised to see Phyllis eating so enthusiastically. "Phyllis," I said, "how can you chomp away like that? Didn't that autopsy make you feel sick?"

"Not really. I got a little queasy when he opened the intestines, but it didn't last long. What about you?"

"Of course it didn't bother me. I'm a medical student, you know."

"Listen, poops," she said, "don't pull that on me. I've seen just as many autopsies as you have."

Despite what I'd told Phyllis, I somehow didn't feel like finishing my lunch. For me that was very unusual.

By early spring the basic sciences were finally over. We then began a ten-month series of courses called "the organ blocks." In turn the cardiovascular system, the digestive system, the endocrine system, and so on would be intensively studied for several weeks. Each block would begin with a review of the system's normal anatomy and physiology. Then we'd learn the diseases that occurred when various things went wrong with normal structure and function. The days were dense with lectures, labs, and discussion sessions. New diseases flew by at an alarming rate — just as I grew comfortable in one area we moved on to the next. But for a precious few weeks the whole world revolved around the organ being studied: while doing the respiratory system, I was conscious of every breath I took; during the kidney block each urination was a special event. I was learning not to take my body for granted.

The first block was the cardiovascular system: that is, the heart and blood vessels. I rejoiced as it began — at last I'd learn the difference between an atrium and an auricle, and maybe even the significance of the heart sounds, "lub-dub." What a rich new source of medical facts of the day it would be!

We plunged right in and were soon totally immersed in the cardiovascular system. But the price we had to pay for this Berlitz approach to the heart was periods of profound incomprehension. In one of our discussion sessions we went over a case of congestive heart failure. The case description was a mixture of English and an obscure cardiovascular tongue. Amid things that made sense, such as "the patient began experiencing increasing shortness of breath and gained 10 pounds in the two weeks before hospitalization," were foreign phrases like, "he developed marked orthopnea and paroxysmal nocturnal dyspnea." The description of the physical exam was almost entirely opaque — our unfortunate patient had "pretibial edema," "rales at both lung bases," and "an S-3 gallop." The instructor tried to translate this gibberish into English, but he wasn't very successful. His message seemed to be that we should wait until we began seeing patients, then we'd understand. After all, how could he explain the sound of an S-3 gallop to people who had never even heard a *normal* heartbeat?

We read through this case and cases of other patients and saw how their doctors logically deduced the cause of the symptoms, ordered the right tests to clinch the diagnosis, and finally began treatment. A dramatic cure always seemed to follow. The congestive heart failure patient, we read, was given digoxin and a diuretic. He lost all his extra weight and the leg swelling went down and he could breathe again. Even the paroxysmal nocturnal dyspnea and S-3 gallop went away, whatever they were. I was excited by the logical inevitability of it all: diagnosis followed from symptoms, physical exam, and lab tests, and treatment from diagnosis. In its own way this was as elegant as physics or chemistry. And the result wasn't just intellectual satisfaction; it was a healthier person.

But I knew things really couldn't be as simple as they appeared in our case descriptions. I thought back to the first week of school, to Evelyn, Dr. Thatcher's patient. Could I have diagnosed her third-degree heart block from her complaints? She too was tired and short of breath and putting on water weight. Why didn't she simply have congestive heart failure, like our case history? How could I have known she needed a pacemaker, not just pills? The EKG, of course, would have made the diagnosis. But we hadn't learned how to read EKG's yet. There always seemed to be something else.

Even though the cardiovascular block exposed new vistas of personal ignorance, it wasn't entirely discouraging. Rather, it whetted my appetite to learn more and begin doctoring. I was just itching to get my hands on a real patient. I knew it would happen someday, but first there was the rest of the organ blocks. And, tucked anomalously between the cardiovascular block and the respiratory block, was gross anatomy.

Gross anatomy is the study of the structure of the body. "Gross" simply means "visible without a microscope," but took on a further meaning during the more squeamish moments of the course. The start of gross anatomy was a banner day. Studying anatomy, after all, was the very essence of being a medical student. And not only would I feel like a bona fide medical student, but as with the cardiovascular block I would at last have answers to a whole host of nagging questions: what really was the "wrong pipe" down which food sometimes went? Where did the pancreas fit into the scheme of things? Which of the arm muscles was actually the biceps? At last, my housemates would get some answers.

Gross anatomy was not taught in the traditional way. Instead of taking a year or more, as we would have done in most medical schools, we went through all of anatomy in a roaring five weeks. The philosophy was that at our stage a quick zip through the body was sufficient. Later, when we'd each settled into a medical specialty, we'd learn what we really needed to know. Finally, I thought, some curriculum committee was being sensible. At last they got the word that memorization is boring, and that facts don't stick unless they're used.

Doing all of human anatomy in five weeks, no matter how superficially, meant very long hours. The mornings began with fast-packed lectures that had us reeling for the rest of the day. They were followed by small classes where we went over slides, diagrams, and models. And finally, the essence of the essence, were the cadavers.

Unlike the old days, we didn't dissect a cadaver from start

to finish; there wasn't time. Instead, the muscles, nerves, blood vessels, and internal organs had been predissected by upper-class students who were paid for their grisly work. Near the end of the course we would have the chance to dissect an arm or a leg; otherwise all the work was already done.

The cadavers were kept in several dark high-ceilinged rooms in one of the old medical school buildings on the quadrangle. The windows were high and dusty and hard to open. This was unfortunate, since the cadavers had a terrible smell. It wasn't the smell of decay but rather, recalling our recent visit to the morgue, the sweet and acrid odor of Formalin. It was penetrating. The day after a session with the cadavers we still smelled it on our hands. Or at least thought we did.

In each of these rooms were a dozen or so medical students, an instructor, and six dead people. Each cadaver lay on its own black slate table. At night they were covered with sheets. During class sessions they were completely exposed except for the heads, which were tightly wrapped in white cloth. The heads remained mummified until the last week of the course. Then they were severed from their bodies and offered up to the dental students for dissection. I'm not sure why the heads were covered when the rest of the bodies went bare, but I don't think it was primarily out of respect for the dead. Instead, I think it was to make things easier for us students — a face is what makes a body a person.

Each of our corpses featured the dissection of a different portion of the anatomy: the heart and lungs, the digestive tract, the nerves. Everything was conveniently labeled with little white name tags. Even the blood vessels were color-coded—tinted latex had been injected into the vessels just after death, making the arteries red and the veins blue. Every day was like a scavenger hunt. We went from body to body, searching out the adrenals and the portal vein and the brachial plexus.

We were given a key to our room so we could come by in the evening to study our corpses. Once I took Phyllis. By this time I knew a heart from a thymus and could show her some anatomy on these pungent rubbery beings. It was hard to concentrate, though, with the bodies ominously covered by sheets, with the room so quiet, with no one living except the two of us. We didn't stay long.

One morning near the end of the course we came into the room to find our bodies headless. The limb dissections were about to begin. There would be an arm or a leg for every two students. We paired up and awaited our extremity. With a big butcher's knife the instructor carved away skin and fat from around the shoulders, then the hips. Next he took up the bone saw and with a terrible rasping sound the limbs came off. What was left of the body was quickly covered and removed. We were assured that the medical school provided a proper burial for the remains of the remains.

My partner, Steve, and I were handed an enormous hairy drumstick, a right leg. As we carried it back to our table I was bothered by a corn on the big toe. We set to work, starting up at the thigh. Our scalpels minced their way into the firm, greasy Formalin-flesh. Cutting through skin was the most difficult; once we were down to unrecognizable tissue it didn't hurt so much.

The dissection was slow and frustrating—there were no

labels. It was easy to get distracted. Once I caught myself carefully trimming hair from the calf, almost in a trance. When I snapped out of it I felt ridiculous — we were supposed to be dissecting out muscle and tendon and nerve, not shaving the leg.

Just after my trance broke I realized that the room had grown very quiet. I looked up and saw six carnivorous couples, each gnawing at their catch. Nervous glances shot up from around the room. It was so quiet, I realized, not because everybody was hard at work but because we were all uncomfortable. I went back to my leg.

As we puzzled over the quadriceps muscle something flew across the room and hit Steve on the left shoulder. We both jumped — it was a morsel of fat. It stuck to his sweater. He picked off the foreign body, giggled, and threw it back to where it had come from. It hit an apparently innocent bystander on the chest and bounced to the floor. This new victim sliced some skin from his cadaver's arm and threw it back. It landed in the middle of our filleted thigh, touching off a giggle-explosion.

The cadaver room became a free-fire zone. Stealthy blobs of tissue suddenly flicked into the air and sailed toward other launching sites. Everyone squirmed uncomfortably, but several people kept shooting. Eventually the tension of dissecting death subsided and the warfare ceased. We went back to our sober medical student work, feeling bad.

During this medical version of a spitball fight I kept thinking about the owner of my leg. Would he still have donated his body to medical science if he had known that his head and his arms and this leg and the other leg would be chopped off and cut up? What if he knew his skin and fat would be made into guided missiles, fired by and aimed at doctors-to-be?

We finished up the leg without absorbing enough anatomy to have justified the carnage. Steve and I put our scraps in a plastic bag, which we left for burial. I carefully washed my hands and left the cadaver room. The anatomy block was over.

On the way home, with the smell of the cadavers still on my hands, I stewed about the fat fight. I knew it was more a result of discomfort than disrespect, but the result was the same — we had done something that a short time ago would have been unthinkable. Already, less than a year into medical school, we were changing.

One night I cooked beef hearts for dinner. It was a celebration of the end of gross anatomy. Phyllis was over, as well as Dave Rappaport. "Wash it well, removing fat, arteries, veins and blood," said the baked hearts recipe from *The Joy of Cooking*. I was titillated at the idea of learning cardiac surgery from a cookbook.

As I prepared the hearts Phyllis, Dave, and half my roommates gathered round. The other half wouldn't come near the kitchen. Gradually the chef became an anatomy professor — I explained the coronary circulation, went over the cardiac chambers, and showed how the valves worked. Phyllis reminded me of my thymus-heart of just two months ago. We were both awed by how much I'd learned since then.

The anatomy lesson was delicious. I convinced everyone to try it except Bonnie, who became a vegetarian for the evening. Over dessert Dr. Ken Klein's Medical Fact of the

Day was, "In a single day the human heart beats over one hundred thousand times and pumps two thousand gallons of blood." I got a lot of huzzahs for that one.

After anatomy was over we resumed the organ blocks. The lungs, kidneys, skin, and bones each had their day in the sun. The hours were long and tiring. I hadn't read a nonmedical book in months; I rarely even went to movies anymore. Phyllis said I always seemed preoccupied. More and more of my life was being gobbled up by medicine — was I becoming one of those parochial physicians my father had warned me about?

Now that we were learning about diseases, I felt a new tension. Back in college, if I didn't understand a particular equation it just meant that I wouldn't be as good a scientist. But now, if I missed a fact about a particular disease I could blow a diagnosis someday, and maybe even kill someone! With their desperate compulsive memorization back in organic chemistry maybe those pre-meds had already sensed what was to come.

We were well aware of the stereotype: the idealistic student enters medical school only to emerge four years later as a callous, self-serving physician. It wasn't hard to see how the hours, the weight of responsibility, the constant tension could cause this grotesque transformation. We all promised each other we'd guard against changing.

One of our big worries was becoming insensitive to patients. Dave Rappaport and I had long discussions about dealing with patients, even though we had never done so. We agreed, for example, that it was important to tell cancer patients their diagnosis. But how could you be honest and still give hope and encouragement? These discussions reminded me of the highly theoretical conversations my high school buddies and I used to have about whether it was OK to sleep with a girl you didn't love, when at the time the most we'd ever done was hold hands. It was frustrating, all these months and months of studying about taking care of patients without ever having done it. We were indeed medical virgins.

One day at lunch, in the middle of the kidney block, a group of us sat at one of the big tables in the dining hall. The center of attention was Robert Siegel. He was a year ahead of me. He had actually been responsible for patients! He told us exciting and terrifying tales of life on the wards. He had started IV's, taken cardiograms, discovered pneumonias, and even helped at a cardiac arrest.

We began yet another discussion about patient care. I said I'd heard that some medical students introduced themselves to patients as "doctor." This seemed arrogant and deceptive. "Patients have a right to know who they're dealing with," I said. "A student shouldn't misrepresent himself as a doctor; little deceptions like that lead to bigger ones."

"Well you know, Ken, I used to believe that too," said Robert. "But now I think you're wrong. When you're taking care of a patient you *are* the doc. Sure you have lots of supervision, and the intern countersigns your orders, but *you* really run the show. And the patient knows it. It's nice to be honest, but hell, most patients don't understand the difference between a medical student, a resident, and a professor of medicine. And they don't care either. They just know that you're the one taking care of them — you're the doctor. When you make a big deal about being only a medical student I think you're just trying to avoid responsibility for the patient."

I was confused. Was this the sage voice of experience, or a callous, already corrupted medical student?

The first time I tried to take responsibility for a patient myself things didn't turn out very well. My brother Doug came to visit occasionally, dropping in from up north, where he pruned apple trees and cut gemstones. His current girlfriend, Madeline, was a woman who had traveled with the gypsies in Europe. I thought it was very exotic to know people like this, and they thought it was very exotic to know a medical student.

One day in the late spring, just before the start of the neurosciences block, Doug called. Madeline was in the Mt. Auburn Hospital in Cambridge with belly pain and a fever. Did I want to visit her? A real patient! Of course I did.

Madeline looked like a gypsy queen in her hospital bed. She had black curly hair, gold hoop earrings, and a velvet bathrobe. A fancy old quilt lay over the white hospital blanket. Flowers were everywhere, and there were drawings taped to the walls. We talked about gypsy migrations and rutilated quartz and the kidney block. The fluid from Madeline's IV bottle dripped in time to our conversation.

It was very well to sit and chat, but a burning question hung in the air: What was Madeline's diagnosis? I finally asked.

"I don't know," she said. "The doctor didn't tell me."

"Did you ask him?"

"Sort of. But I didn't get a straight answer."

"Well, why did he put you in the hospital?"

"He said he had to run some tests, and I had to have an intravenous."

My questions seemed to fan the flames of their latent physician phobia. What exactly *was* wrong with Madeline? Was the doctor hiding something? Doug and Madeline were counting on me, as an official representative of the medical establishment, to get some answers.

I brought all my fledgling medical skills into play. First, what exactly were her symptoms? She had had lower abdominal cramps and nausea and a fever, and maybe a vaginal discharge. Was she still febrile? I looked at her bedside chart. There were two wavy parallel lines, red and blue. I couldn't figure out which was temperature and which pulse. Next, what was she getting in the IV? "Aq. Pen G, $2x10^6$ U.," the bottle said. Not much help there. Finally I asked Madeline about what seemed to be the most likely diagnosis — was there any chance at all that she had some sort of V.D.? I avoided looking at Doug. Madeline shrugged and said the doctor didn't say anything about gonorrhea.

I thought back to the already dimming pathology course. Maybe she had pelvic inflammatory disease, PID. "Did the doctor say you had something called 'PID,' by any chance?"

"What's that?"

"It's a pelvic infection involving the fallopian tubes."

"No, I don't recall him saying that."

"How long will you have to be in the hospital?"

"He wasn't sure, but maybe four or five days, I think."

"Listen, Ken," Doug said impatiently, "we've got to find out what's going on. What are they trying to do to her?"

The pressure was on. I decided that the only way to get to

the bottom of Madeline's mysterious disease was to read her chart. The chances that they would actually let me see it seemed pretty slim. But on the other hand I *was* a medical student. I had to try, or risk shame in the eyes of my brother and his girlfriend.

I went to the nurses' station. Doug stayed right behind me; I guess he wanted to make sure I was really going to ask. We waited for a nurse.

"Excuse me," I said when a white-uniformed woman finally appeared. "I'm a friend of Madeline Hobbes in room 126, and I'm a medical student. May I please see her chart?"

"Sure, as far as I'm concerned," she said. I was incredibly relieved! I never expected it to be so easy. "But I'm just a nurses' aide," the woman continued. "You'd better ask the nurse."

Devastated, I waited some more. Finally a precise woman with all her ends tucked in came to the desk. I first made sure she was a nurse, then repeated my request. "No," she said, "I'm afraid we can't let unauthorized people look at patients' charts."

So I had gotten the humiliating answer I expected. My comeback was ready: "But surely the patient should have control over her own hospital record. If she says that someone she knows, especially a medical student, has permission to look at her chart, why not? Her doctor hasn't told her a thing and she's frightened. If I could see her chart, I'd be able to explain things to her."

The nurse said she was sorry but she couldn't let just anyone rifle through patient records. "There are legal considerations, you know."

"But I'm not just anyone. I'm a medical student."

"I'm sorry."

I stood at the desk, feeling impotent in my brother's eyes. Some medical student his brother turned out to be! I didn't know what to do.

Fortunately the nurse broke the silence. "If you like, I'll page Miss Hobbes's physician. I think Dr. Arnold is still in the building."

"OK, thanks. That sounds like a good idea." We waited in the patients' lounge. After about ten minutes a man I took to be Dr. Arnold appeared and began talking with the nurse. I smoothed my hair and went up to introduce myself. We shook hands, but even though we were in the same business I didn't feel much kinship.

"I'm very sorry to trouble you, Dr. Arnold, but my friend is upset," I said. "She doesn't quite understand what's going on and she's very apprehensive. I thought if I could review her chart I'd be able to explain things to her."

"Well," Dr. Arnold said, "let me tell you the story." He quickly went over the case. Unfortunately he was using unfamiliar words. He told me the details of the physical exam and went over the lab tests but it didn't make much sense. He kept using the word *salpingitis;* I was too mortified to ask him what it meant. After all I *had* said that if only I could read Madeline's chart I'd be able to explain everything to her. It wasn't until many months later, during the reproduction block, that I learned that salpingitis is simply an infection of the fallopian tubes — essentially PID.

I thanked Dr. Arnold for his time and his very helpful explanation, and Doug and I went back to Madeline's room.

"Well?" she asked. I told her that Dr. Arnold wouldn't say what was going on. I said I couldn't tell if he was being evasive, or if he wasn't certain of the diagnosis himself. I felt like a real fraud. I promised myself I'd study extra hard during the coming neurosciences block, and learn something, for a change.

4

Learning the Laying On of Hands

The Final Preclinical Courses

T HE NEUROSCIENCES BLOCK began appropriately with a section on anesthesia. During the long hot summer between the first and second year of medical school I came to feel that the study of neuroanatomy was one of the most potent anesthetics known to man. The curriculum committee that mercifully streamlined gross anatomy had clearly been deposed; the new regime condemned us to spend hundreds of hours laying down on the circuitry of our own brains the memory of the brain's minute twisty circuits.

Each part of the neurosciences block had its own laboratory session. In anesthesia lab we murdered mice. The anesthesia lab was held on a balmy afternoon in early summer. On arrival we were greeted by hundreds of little mice swarming in a big wire cage at the front of the room. The lab instructor explained that we were going to observe the effects of varying doses of anesthetic agents. He divided us into groups of four. One person was the timekeeper, one the recorder, and the other two the observers. A representative from each experimental squad collected a handful of mice while the instructor handed out the anesthetics.

Our group got chloroform. We measured out the first dose and soaked it into a big piece of cotton. Then we set the soggy white wad on the bottom of a five-gallon bell jar, dumped in the mice, and replaced the heavy lid. Through the jar's thick glass we watched the little mice become agitated, wobble, fall, twitch, and die. The observers narrated the deaths while the timekeeper droned out the minutes and the recorder got down all the facts. Then there were more experiments, each with a higher dose of chloroform and a fresh contingent of mice. After each run we removed the dead mice by the tail and dumped them into a big paper bag at the front of the room. By the end of the morning several hundred scampering mice had been transformed into still little bundles of fur, piled high in the paper-bag grave.

Once, when we removed the mice at the end of an experiment, one came alive. We watched it gasp for breath with its feeble anesthetized lungs. Mike, our group's timekeeper, held the mouse in his cupped hands and gave artificial respiration with his thumbs. When it became more lively he put it down on the table. The mouse jerked and staggered forward, first to the left and then to the right. Mike watched its desperate drunken walk for a while, prodding it away from the edge of the table. Then he picked it up and tossed it back into the chloroform jar, this time for certain death.

At the end of the lab session we arbiters of life and death assembled at the front of the room, next to the dead-mouse bag. The instructor asked each group for its data and plotted it on the blackboard. We determined that anesthetic agents vary in potency, and that the higher the dose of a particular anesthetic the more quickly it takes effect. These startling conclusions had cost several hundred mice.

Some of us weren't happy with anesthesia lab. If it were really important that we see mice anesthetized to death, why not make a movie or a videotape that could be shown every year? The instructor said something about there being no substitute for seeing anesthesia work in person, and besides, making a movie would probably be too expensive.

After the anesthesia section there were several lectures on pain medications. Next, neurophysiology, my original but waning motivation for going to medical school, was dismissed in a few lectures. Then for most of the rest of the summer we wallowed in neuroanatomy, the anatomy of the brain and spinal cord and nerves. The mornings were spent in a hot bell jar of a lecture hall. Classes were taught by a neuropathologist, a chubby elf named Dr. Fuchs. He had a red goatee and wore bright yellow bermuda shorts. But despite his flashy getup and lively lectures, neuroanatomy was a bore. By ten minutes into a lecture half the class had been anesthetized into a deep sleep.

There were hundreds of compulsive little neural connections to be learned. And it was brute-force memorization — there was no apparent logic to neuroanatomy, no Newton's Law of the Brain to help organize all the facts. Once again I thought back to my old nemesis, organic chemistry. Medical schools did indeed seem wise to use the grade in organic chemistry as a predictor of how well pre-meds would do. I thought ahead — how would I ever have room to cram three more years of dense memorization into my poor little brain, already teeming with *E. coli* and polypeptides and Medical Facts of the Day?

One day Dr. Fuchs tried to impress us with how much we were learning: "I want you to know you're getting the same lectures I give to the neurology and neurosurgery residents," he said. But rather than comforting me, the remark confirmed my hunch that we were being fed far more neuroanatomy than we really needed to know.

The Endale Rest Home broke up just as the neurosciences block began. There was little holding the motley group of housemates together. Our weekly encounter sessions had gotten to be a burden; just as with neuroanatomy, we were learning more about each other than we wanted to know. So when the lease expired we decided not to renew it; we'd each go our computer programming and Montessori and medical ways.

I needed a new place to live. For months Phyllis and I had talked about living together. She had been at school for most of the spring, but was now again in town for a double work-study term. She'd be in Boston for most of the year — should we get an apartment together? Like applying to medical school, it was a major and traumatic decision. And as with medical school, we decided yes.

We found a cheap apartment in the slums of Cambridgeport. While Phyllis painted the walls I sat anesthetized on the mattress in the living room, memorizing neuroanatomy. Sometimes I'd look up from my books and watch her on tiptoes on the stepladder, touching up the molding around the ceiling. I marveled at her cerebellar balance centers.

Each morning we got up, had breakfast, and rode away on our bicycles. Phyllis rode north to the nursing home where she was now working, and I went south across the sizzling B.U. Bridge to Dr. Fuchs's lectures. In the afternoons I went to neuroanatomy lab. The lab rooms had closets stacked with tan ceramic crocks. Each held a human brain bathed in a savory preserving fluid. We'd take out these anonymous dripping globes and study all their little dips and ridges and get to know them by name: the sylvian fissure, the precentral gyrus, the cerebellopontine angle. We were learning the geography of a new world.

After several weeks of studying the surface we went subterranean. The instructor showed us how to cut the brains into neat, quarter-inch-thick slabs; it was like cutting a squat gray salami. We traced the subtle shadings of tissue that were revealed, pink and brown, gray and beige. We learned which areas controlled speech and vision and movement. While cutting one brain we came across a dark little crater in the left hemisphere — it was an old stroke! We worked out that the owner of this brain must have had a weak right arm and probably some trouble speaking. The instructor looked up the clinical history and yes, we were right! For the first time I caught a glimmer of the excitement that could come from memorizing Dr. Fuchs's endless wiring diagrams.

One day in lab I realized that in addition to speech and vision and movement, all the person's memories must be stored somewhere in the brain too. As I plunged the knife down through this meaty loaf of memories was I cutting through the first kiss? The smell of a steak? How to pitch a curve? After that realization I always felt reverent when I opened the crocks that held these amazing anatomical specimens, these brains.

The summer passed quickly. In the breezy evenings we often sat out on our little porch, on the old bus seat we used for a couch. I pored over my neuroanatomy while Phyllis practiced her guitar and wrote essays for school. As the sun went down we ate Italian bread and sausages from the North End and drank Cribari wine, the cheapest.

"Hey, let's go to a movie," Phyllis would say sometimes after dinner. Or to a bar, or out dancing.

"I'm too tired. Today was a really exhausting day" always seemed to be my answer. "Besides, I need to read some more before I can think about going out." As our studies grew more directly related to patient care little threats and warnings were injected: our case histories sometimes told the sad story of a doctor who blew a diagnosis because he overlooked a key symptom or failed to order a certain lab test. Disastrous consequences followed for the patient, and the physician was roasted over the coals. I still had little idea what it was really like to be a doctor, but a steady undercurrent of fear seemed to be part of it. So how could I indulge in a Bergman film when I wasn't sure about the anatomy of the seventh cranial nerve? Seeing Liv Ullman tonight might mean missing a case of Bell's palsy next year.

But why should doctors be expected to know everything? They were no different from other mortals. Couldn't they look things up in books when they weren't sure? Ask a colleague? Refer patients to a specialist? This seemed reasonable until I thought how I'd feel if Phyllis got sick. The doctor that would take care of her damn well *better* know everything. So we didn't often go to movies. I stayed home and studied against future disasters.

Finally autumn came. When I looked up from my neuroanatomy the apartment was all painted and the leaves were once again browning. I had been a medical student for over a year. It had been exactly two years since I'd begun applying to medical school. I thought back to my fire-escape talks with Phyllis. "I can't understand why anybody would want to be a doctor," she had said. I still wasn't sure that I could either.

After the neurosciences the rest of the organ blocks passed in quick succession — the digestive system, hematology, the endocrine and reproductive systems. The days were long and rich with facts: we learned why the urine turns dark with hepatitis and how birth control pills worked, and what those Geritol commericals meant by "iron-poor blood."

In a lab session during the hematology block we passed a historic milestone. We learned to draw blood. After a demonstration by the instructor we paired up. Half the class became vampires and the other half victims. Tourniquets were cinched tight, needles flashed, and the room filled with cries of both pain and triumph. Then we switched roles, the bloodletters becoming the bloodgivers. One student in the lab didn't participate in all the activity. He had worked in a blood bank for the past year; he was a blood-drawing expert. He yawned conspicuously as the rest of us excitedly lost our hypodermic virginity.

One night I took Phyllis to the lab to show her my blood. I had her strap the tourniquet on my arm nice and tight and showed her how to hold the syringe. After several minutes of saying she didn't want to do it I got her to plunge the needle into my juicy worm of a cephalic vein. It popped just right and blood shot back into the syringe. "Phew," Phyllis said, "that was worse than getting my *own* blood drawn."

I smeared the blood out into a thin film on a glass slide. After it had dried, I stained it and put it under the microscope. Twisting the lens into focus resolved the orange blur into the rich little world of my blood. There were the red cells, like little pink life-preservers bobbing on some microscopic sea, the tiny purple smudges that were the platelets, and the elegant white corpuscles. I found one of my eosinophils for Phyllis, a shimmering sphere filled with bright orange jewels. We looked and we looked. It was exciting—we weren't just looking at a blood smear; we were looking at me!

During the endocrine block I developed Hodgkin's disease. I read through my textbooks, searching for other explanations for my symptoms. Finally, though, it became clear that there could be no other possible diagnosis; I realized I had to face the truth. So I made an appointment at the Health Services.

"I've been feeling lousy for several weeks now, Dr. Daley," I said. "I'm tired all the time and I think I've been having night sweats, and I have a little lymph node in my neck."

"Interesting," Dr. Daley said. "I've bet you've already made the diagnosis."

"Yes. I believe I have Hodgkin's disease."

"That's what I figured. Before we start radiation therapy, though, let me ask a few questions and look you over."

Fifteen minutes later he'd finished his questions and had done a physical exam.

"Well, Kenneth, you're right about one thing — the diagnosis is quite clear. What you have is a bad cold."

I left Dr. Daley's office relieved but, unaccountably, a little disappointed.

In late winter the organ blocks drew to a close. Our classroom days were almost over. After just a few more courses, virtually the rest of medical school would be spent in "clinical work": that is, in the hospitals, taking care of patients. Stints on the surgery and internal medicine wards were required. Apart from these we could pick ward rotations from a huge list of specialties, including obstetrics and gynecology, pediatrics, and psychiatry. There were only a few preclinical hurdles left before reaching the seventh heaven of the hospital wards: surgery lab, learning to do a physical examination, and a course called Introduction to the Clinic.

Surgery lab was like being back in kindergarten. We learned how to scrub our hands and how to dress. "This is the last time anyone is ever going to check how well you wash," said Dr. Samuelson. He was a bored chief surgery resident who had been pulled from the operating room to teach us how to do a surgical scrub. He began by spraying a mysterious solution onto our hands. "Let this stuff dry," he said; "I'll explain later." Then, like a fussy grandmother, he showed us how to wash away all those nasty germs that infested our skin.

The surgical scrub is an elaborate business. It begins with a general lathering of the hands and forearms. Then you ream out all traces of dirt from under the fingernails with a special plastic stick. Finally there's a ten-minute scouring of every square millimeter of epidermis below the wrist. After Dr. Samuelson's demonstration we each popped open a little plastic bag that held a scrub sponge and went furiously to work.

When everyone was done we lined up for inspection. Dr. Samuelson pulled out an ultraviolet lamp and told us his secret: the solution he sprayed onto our hands fluoresced under ultraviolet light. He flipped on the lamp and turned off the room lights. I was aghast — there were little glowing spots all over my outstretched hands! So my grandmother was right; I never washed well enough. I got a surgical scolding along with everyone else, for not one of us had managed to scrub away all the fluorescent germs. The prospect of doing surgery began to seem overwhelming — I couldn't even wash my hands right.

Next we were taught how to get dressed. The cap and mask were simple, but putting on the gown was traumatic. Again we found that germs lurked everywhere — if we so much as brushed the sleeve of the gown against anything, the precarious barrier of sterility was broken, condemning our theoretical patient to a postoperative infection.

"Watch it, doctor!" Dr. Samuelson yelled as I pulled on my gown. "You've just contaminated yourself. Your left sleeve touched that table; start over." The stakes for careful dressing were never higher; getting on a tux for the senior prom was nothing compared to this.

After the gowns were on it was time to glove up. This was no simple matter: to preserve sterility the hands had to remain retracted within the sleeves until the gloves were on.

The idea was to slip the glove over the sleeve, then slide the fingers out into the fingerholes. The fingers of the other hand manipulated the glove through their protecting sleeve. Like double amputees we all struggled to put on the wily gloves. Everyone seemed to end up with two or three fingers in one fingerhole. A roomful of green-gowned beings seemed to be growing rubber udders from the ends of their arms as they grunted and twisted to get on the gloves.

After we had mastered washing and dressing we advanced to the cub scout stage — we learned to tie knots. "You may wonder why we're teaching everyone how to tie surgical knots," Dr. Samuelson said. "After all, some of you will go into radiology or public health or research and never need to tie a knot again. Well, it's because knowing how to tie a good surgical square knot is part of being a doctor, just like owning a stethoscope or being able to deliver a baby. Once you learn to tie knots you'll never forget. Even psychiatrists remember. They often tie knots under their desks while they're talking to a patient on the couch." I liked Dr. Samuelson. He was one of the few instructors who seemed to appreciate the historical significance of all the things we were learning for the first time.

He began the demonstration with some stout nylon clothesline. We sat at our little knot-tying stations and fumbled as Dr. Samuelson repeated the knots for us, over and over. I looked around the room and thought how ridiculous this was — here were grown men and women, all with college degrees, who sat struggling to tie a piece of clothesline into a knot. We had spent four years as undergraduates studying Plato and Freud and quantum mechanics for this? I thought of my old college cronies who had gone on to graduate school in physics and linguistics and economics — how embarrassed I'd be if they saw me now!

In the evenings my homework was tying knots. It became almost a nervous tic; I was continuously fiddling with my knots on the arms of chairs, on doorknobs, on Phyllis's fingers. Lengths of rope and nylon suture material hung everywhere, tinsel for a surgical Christmas.

When we had all earned our knot-tying merit badges we were ready to operate. Surgery took place in the animal research building of one of the hospitals. We worked in a big room with five or six surgery stations, each with its little operating table, overhead light, and anesthesia equipment. Four students took turns assuming each of the positions on the operating team: scrub nurse, anesthesiologist, assistant surgeon, and surgeon. We were going to learn how to operate on dogs.

When we came in for the first day of surgery we found the animals had already been set up by the lab technicians. Our patient, a black and white mongrel, lay belly-up on the steel table, strapped in place. An IV was running into a vein in the left front paw and an endotracheal tube protruded from his mouth. With help from Dr. Samuelson, we hooked up the tube to the respirator and deepened the anesthesia. After the surgeon's assistant shaved the abdomen, the anesthesiologist gave the go-ahead. Then as scrub nurse, I handed the scalpel to the surgeon, self-consciously re-enacting dozens of operating room scenes from TV and the movies.

Our junior Ben Casey poised the knife over the smooth-skinned belly and prepared to cut. But he hesitated. Cutting living flesh is very different from cutting dead, chemical-soaked cadaver tissue, and even that's hard enough. He wasn't able to bring himself to do more than nick the skin. Finally he asked Dr. Samuelson for help. "I don't remember where I'm supposed to cut," he lied. The real surgeon took the scalpel and plunged it into the dog's abdomen, slicing a deep bloody incision eight inches long. The entire operating team winced. "Do it like you mean it," Dr. Samuelson said. "Remember, it doesn't hurt the mutt — that's what anesthesia is for."

Each week we would do a different operation on our dog; in the course of a month we'd experience each of the positions on the operating team. If the dog survived all the surgeries he'd be put to death at the end of the month. If he didn't pull through the whole course we'd get a fresh animal; there were plenty.

For my surgical debut I removed our dog's spleen. This was the third week, so I was operating on a dog who was missing half of his thyroid gland and part of his bowel. The next day I visited him in his little cage. He lay on his side, wearing the big dressing I had taped to his belly as if to hide my dirty deed. Even though he obviously hurt, he wagged his tail wildly and tried to get up to greet me, his tormentor. The harder he wagged, the guiltier I felt. By all accounts real patients were the same, worshipping their doctors, the very ones who caused them pain.

We were being propelled toward the hospital wards with increasing speed. After dog surgery it was time to learn the laying on of hands — we were going to be taught to do a physical examination. So it was time to acquire the tools of the trade: a stethoscope, a reflex hammer, an ophthalmoscope, and a black bag. Drug companies traditionally gave medical students these instruments as gifts, "Eli Lilly" or "Upjohn" discreetly stamped on the side. Most of us refused to accept these pharmaceutical bribes. Instead we banded together and ordered in quantity, right from the wholesalers.

The day my instruments arrived I rushed home and accosted Phyllis. I spent the next hour listening to her captive heart and looking in her eyes and testing her reflexes. I must have done the knee jerks fifty times each; we both giggled gleefully each time her leg kicked. "Well, doctor," she said when I had at last had enough, "what's the prognosis? Will I live?"

"I'm afraid I have bad news, my dear," I said in a deep doctorly voice; "your case is difficult and puzzling. It could be something serious. I'll have to call in a specialist for help, maybe a third-year student." Then I let Phyllis hear my heartbeat and knock my knees.

The following week we'd begin to learn how to do a physical examination. We would learn on each other. Our instructor was Dr. Conn, an infectious-diseases specialist just finishing his training at the Beth Israel Hospital. He was an intense man, skinny with red hair, a beard, and wire-rim glasses. He really seemed to know his stuff. On the first day of the course he led our group of five students across the Beth Israel parking lot to the old student nurses' quarters. We proudly carried our black bags, filled with shiny new instruments. On the elevator up to the room we'd be using I wondered if we would have to do rectals on each other. It was very quiet — was everyone else wondering the same thing? Only Dr. Conn knew what was going to happen.

"This is where you come to screw the nurses," Conn said

suddenly as the elevator came to a stop at the third floor. No one smiled. He sure knew how to take the majesty away from the occasion of our first physical exam! He was at the end of the long path of medical training that we were just beginning. Was he trying to make it seem even longer by flaunting his experience?

In our little room was a bed, a desk, and two chairs. Someone sat uncomfortably on each piece of furniture. As Conn began talking about the physical examination, his manner grew serious. "A careful physical exam is worth a hundred laboratory tests," he said. "I can't emphasize enough the importance of a complete, compulsive examination. When you're an intern and you've gotten your fifth admission in the middle of the night, you'll be tempted to skimp on your exam. Don't. I'm warning you, you'll miss things. Remember, the physical exam is one exam that's not graded, but you still can't afford to make any errors. If you get something wrong, it's the patient who suffers. When you assume the care of a patient by doing a physical exam you take on a tremendous responsibility. His life is in your hands." Yes, Dr. Conn's manner had changed. He was no longer the swaggering nurse-screwing stud of a doctor. Instead he was now the wise and experienced one, passing on to his apprentices the ancient creed of service and responsibility and, therefore, specialness. I squirmed uneasily in the hot, crowded room.

"Now to get down to specifics," he said. The demonstration began. He showed us how to take the pulse and blood pressure and how to visualize the retina with the ophthalmoscope. We paired up and began to examine each other, playing doctor at the highest possible level before doing it for real.

Over the next week we worked our way through the entire body. We listened to hearts and lungs, looked into ears and throats, tapped out livers and spleens. I learned that there were a whole slew of reflexes to test in addition to the knee jerks. I heard my first official heartbeat, which didn't sound at all like "lub-dub." I found out why the doctor percusses the lungs. But to everyone's relief, we skipped the rectal exams.

Carrying my black bag home from these sessions, I felt very powerful. I now had the tools to divine the secrets of the human body. Soon I would learn how to heal the sick. Research in neurophysiology paled in comparison.

After we'd learned how to examine each other we were ready to try our skills on real patients. We met on an internal medicine ward at the Beth Israel Hospital. Like white-coated puppies we stumbled after Dr. Conn as he confidently led us from room to room. He had picked out patients with abnormalities on physical exams. The first few were easy. We felt a cancerous liver, enormous and knobby, hard as concrete. Then there was a case of severe psoriasis that almost glowed in the dark. Next we saw an old man, blue and bubbling with pneumonia. The pneumonic right lung crackled and wheezed into our stethoscopes under its burden of inflammatory fluid. It didn't seem hard, physical diagnosis.

But that feeling evaporated with the next case. Dr. Conn tried to convince us to hear a heart murmur that wasn't there. "This is a two out of six early diastolic murmur," he said at the patient's bedside. "It's classical for aortic regurgitation. Listen carefully; it's a good one."

I went first. The heartbeats came in loud and clear, but there was no murmur. Dr. Conn listened once more: "Yes, there is. Try again." I still couldn't hear it. He found the murmur again. "It's a fairly soft murmur, but very distinct. Here, try my stethoscope." He held the head of his stethoscope in the exact spot where he had just heard the murmur and handed me the earpieces. I still couldn't hear it! I was completely unable to account for the murmur's disappearance.

The sound was certainly getting through the stethoscope, for Dr. Conn had just heard it through the same stethoscope in the identical place. And I knew I wasn't hard of hearing. So where had the murmur gone? It must have gotten lost as it echoed around the hills and valleys of my brain. I tried to recall my neuroanatomy for a possible explanation, but none was forthcoming. I gave up: "Sorry, I just can't hear it."

A classmate named Jeff had the next turn. I was pleased when poor Jeff said he couldn't hear the murmur either. Dr. Conn sang it for him: "Listen, like this — lup bum-pss, lup bum-pss. There's S-1 and S-2, then the murmur, lup bum-pss." Jeff tried again, but in vain. This time Dr. Conn found the murmur with *Jeff*'s stethoscope. As before, he held the head of the stethoscope on the patient's chest and gave the earpieces back to Jeff. Jeff parked them around his neck as Dr. Conn once again described the murmur. "Remember, it's a fairly high-pitched murmur in early diastole, lup bum-pss."

"Oh yeah!" said Jeff, "I hear it now." I think I was the only one to notice that the earpieces still sat around Jeff's neck — he had forgotten to plug them back into his ears.

Our final bit of preparation before starting work on the wards was a course called Introduction to the Clinic. Each day we were assigned a patient to work up as if we were taking care of him or her. Then we'd present our findings, impressions, and theoretical plans to the instructor. A "workup" meant spending several hours with the patient extracting a complete medical history and doing a detailed physical examination. It was an excruciating process. We knew very little about the diseases the patients had; how were we to know all the relevant questions to ask? And often, even when we knew what we were supposed to ask, we forgot, in the frenzy of patient contact.

One of my first workups concerned a woman with congestive heart failure. After about an hour of questions I at last got out my stethoscope to begin the physical exam. "Wait," she said; "you didn't ask me how many pillows I sleep on and if I ever wake up short of breath. All the other doctors asked me that." These patients were pros. By the time we saw them they had already been examined by the ward medical student, the intern, the resident, and sometimes a consultant or two. They knew more about their diseases than I did.

I felt guilty making these often-uncomfortable patients endure my slow and fumbling history and physical. "There's no need to apologize," Dr. Conn said. "You're doing a very thorough examination. You might pick up something that the patient's doctors have missed." *Me?* I couldn't even hear a classical heart murmur. The only real justification for putting patients through the discomfort of my examination was simply that I had to learn on *someone*. The best rationalization I could come up with was that these patients, by being in a teaching hospital, were surrounded by professors of medicine as well as students, and therefore presumably got good care. Submitting themselves to my exam was the price they had to pay for the professors.

The wards were efficient bustling cities. There were nurses, nurses' aides, orderlies, secretaries, social workers, cleaning people, physical therapists, and dietitians. These people, we were told, were "ancillary personnel." Their collective job was to carry out the orders of the doctors on the ward team.

On the bottom rung of the ward team was the medical student. The student's work was surpervised by an intern, an M.D. in the first year of training after graduation from medical school. Over both the intern and the student was a resident. This was a doctor who was in the first or second postinternship year. Heading the ward team was the "visit," a staff physician who held an academic appointment at the medical school.

Each ward had two or three of these teams. In turn each was assigned newly admitted patients. After the patient arrived and the ancillary personnel had done all the paperwork and put the patient to bed, the medical student would do a history and physical. After the student finished, the intern, then the resident, would evaluate the patient. Then the three would huddle to discuss the case and decide what tests should be made and what treatments given. The student would write the appropriate orders, which had to be countersigned by the intern or resident. Then the next day, on "visit rounds," the student would formally present the case. The "visit" would see the patient briefly, lead a scholarly discussion, and make recommendations for further care.

During Introduction to the Clinic I wasn't part of a ward team. I was just plunked down on any ward that had a suitable case. Therefore I wasn't introduced to anyone, and I had no orientation. As a result I was often completely lost. Once it took fifteen minutes to find where the tongue depressors were kept. Another time I waited around for half an hour to ask a nurse for permission to give my patient a glass of water.

As I fumbled about the ward, things were happening all around me. Orderlies zipped patients to mysterious destinations, dietitians delivered obscure diets, and nurses' aides mixed up arcane enemas. Often I thought of the trip Phyllis and I had taken to Europe the summer before medical school began. Just as if I were in a foreign country I felt conspicuous and bewildered on the wards — the customs were strange and the language largely unknown. It was hard to imagine ever hobnobbing with the natives.

Once, as I sat at a patient's bedside extracting information about stool color and urinary frequency and exercise tolerance, a third-year student came into the room. She was on the ward team, doing her internal medicine rotation. She excused herself very professionally — she had to get some blood for a special test. Efficiently and painlessly she applied the tourniquet, drew the blood, put a Band-Aid on the little venipuncture site, and left the room with a brisk "thank you." How competent she seemed! And she wasn't just doing an artificial exercise that made both her and the patient uncomfortable. She was really taking care of him! I thought ahead just a few weeks to when I would gain citizenship on the wards. When Introduction to the Clinic was over I'd begin obstetrics and gynecology, my first ward rotation. How could I ever handle it?

The night of our workup we were supposed to read about the patient's medical problems and write a summary of the case. The next morning we'd stand at attention at the patient's bedside and recite the medical history and findings of the physical exam from memory. The audience would include the patient, one or two other medical students, and the instructor. It was often painful and embarrassing. The instructor would interrupt to ask questions, and the patient sometimes piped up to correct us on the facts. I never understood the point of this ritual, "presenting at the bedside." Its main function seemed to be to give the student diarrhea.

Once I presented a post-op patient to Dr. Rhodes, a surgeon. The patient was a diabetic who had just had his gallbladder removed. In the part of my recitation called the "review of systems," I mentioned that my patient occasionally had pains in his legs. "Well," cut in Dr. Rhodes, "what do you think that represents?"

"I don't know, sir, we haven't learned much about leg pains yet."

"That's no excuse. Why didn't you read about the differential diagnosis of leg pain last night?"

"Well, the pain didn't seem to be a major problem. I spent

my time reading about diabetes and gallstones and gallbladder infections."

"But I didn't ask you about diabetes or gallstones or gallbladder infections. I asked you about leg pain. I want to know the differential diagnosis of leg pain in this patient."

"The pain isn't bad, doctor, really!" my patient said. "I don't know why I even mentioned it." He looked guiltily at me, as if it were his fault that I was getting put on the spot. Dr. Rhodes ignored the patient and just stared at me.

"I'm sorry, Dr. Rhodes, I just don't have an explanation for the leg pain."

"Well, we'll just stand here until you come up with something." I twisted and squirmed and said a few ridiculous things about arthritis and poor circulation, and finally Dr. Rhodes let me off the hook. I couldn't wait to get onto the wards and be done with this sadistic surgeon. But then again, I thought, maybe the wards would be even worse.

5

"No Puja"

Obstetrics and Gynecology

"**N**OW TELL ME what you see."

"The mucosa is pink and moist. The vascular pattern is not unusually prominent and there are no masses, exudates, or other grossly visible lesions. The cervical os appears parous and the endocervical border shows the normal transitional pattern."

I was glad the other student had spoken up. All I saw was the inside of a vagina. It was my first view through a speculum and my powers of observation were not at their peak.

This was the first day of obstetrics and gynecology. I had survived a year and a half of medical school. Behind me were the basic sciences, the organ blocks, and even the final preclinical courses with their evil lurking surgeons. At last I'd made it onto the wards!

We were allowed to choose the order of our clinical rotations. I'd decided to begin with ob-gyn (as it's known in the trade) for several reasons. Most important, it was not a very demanding rotation. Gynecologists aren't generally recognized as the intellectual heavyweights of the medical world. They just like to get the job done, no questions asked. For my first rotation, that suited me just fine. Also, ob-gyn involves lots of work with the hands. Before I did rotations in the broader specialties of surgery and internal medicine, I wanted to feel more comfortable with the procedures that take up so much time in caring for patients. When I became facile with things like starting IV's and tapping body fluids, I'd theoretically have more time for reading about the diseases I was dealing with.

Obstetrics also appealed for the obvious reason that I'd learn how to deliver a baby. This, of course, is what distinguishes cab drivers and doctors from the rest of humanity — what could make me feel more like a bona fide physician-in-training? And the sooner I learned the better — as word got around that I was a medical student the time might come when I'd be called on to do an emergency delivery. What if one of our neighbors went into labor? What if a woman started having contractions on the MTA? I'd certainly *better* know what to do!

So for my ward debut, obstetrics and gynecology it was. My scheduling sheet told me to report to the gyn office at the Massachusetts General Hospital. There the secretary sent me to the operating room. I got into scrub clothes and met the gynecology chief resident and another medical student in O.R. Number 2. They stood between the spread legs of an anesthetized woman. A shiny metal speculum protruded from her vagina. My new instructor looked up. He was a short, muscular man named Dr. Meyer, with wavy black hair. The student was Joel Lindell, a fourth-year student taking a double dose of ob-gyn as one of his last courses before becoming a surgery intern at the Peter Bent

Brigham. He had been on rotation for six weeks already, dividing his time between obstetrics at another hospital and gynecology at the Mass. General. Joel and I would be a team for the next month and a half, tagging along with Dr. Meyer and other residents and staff members.

Meyer seemed pleased with Joel's description of the interior of his patient's vagina. "Very good, Dr. Lindell," he said. "Dr. Klein, do you have anything to add?"

"No, I don't. I agree with him completely."

"OK then," said Meyer. "Before you begin sounding the uterus, Dr. Lindell, why don't you tell Dr. Klein about your patient."

"Yes, sir," Joel answered briskly. "This gal is a fifty-five-year-old woman who reached menopause six or seven years ago. After mild estrogen withdrawal symptoms lasting several months, she was asymptomatic until four weeks ago, when she began to experience intermittent spotting. In the last week to ten days the flow has increased, becoming heavy enough to require several pads per day. We're doing the D and C, of course, to rule out endometrial cancer."

"Of course," I said. At the time I didn't even know that "D and C" stood for "dilatation and curettage," the scraping of the lining of the uterus. In this case the purpose was to look for malignant tissue.

"Now, Dr. Klein," Meyer continued, "tell me about the epidemiology of endometrial cancer while Dr. Lindell begins his procedure."

"I'm sorry, Dr. Meyer," I said, "but I can't tell you much about endometrial cancer. I'm just a second-year student and this is my first ward rotation."

"That," snapped Dr. Meyer, "is no excuse. OK, Lindell, tell Dr. Klein about the epidemiology of endometrial cancer."

Joel almost saluted, then recited several pompous paragraphs about geographical prevalence and peak age incidence as he manipulated the metal probe that measured the depth of the uterus. I wasn't listening. I had no idea what Joel was talking about, and very little understanding of the D and C. What am I doing here? I kept thinking.

The procedure was long and boring; Joel turned out to be much quicker with the facts than the endometrial curette. After he was finally done we went on ward rounds. I followed Dr. Meyer and Joel from patient to patient. They gave me a summary of each case, then we reviewed the chart for new lab data, and sometimes listened to the patient's lungs or felt the belly. The diseases each patient had, if I'd heard of them at all, were only faint ghosts haunting me from the endocrine-reproduction block of long ago. I filled up several index cards with things I needed to look up: the Stein-Leventhal syndrome, metrorrhagia, the fern test, hydatidiform moles.

After rounds there was the gynecology tumor conference. Then there was a lecture by a visiting professor, followed by a specialty outpatient clinic. Throughout the day Dr. Meyer constantly quizzed Joel and me about aspects of the cases we were seeing or hearing about. It was as if he were single-handedly trying to give the lie to the stereotype of gynecologists as easygoing nonthinking physicians; he was as high-pressured as they come. If Joel missed an answer, for example, Meyer would remind him that he was on the verge of becoming a doctor: "Get with it, Lindell," he'd say. "This is your last chance to learn this stuff before you start playing for keeps."

I cringed at the prospect of six weeks of Meyer and Lindell. But I was reluctant to try to back out. Doctors were supposed to be able to deal with any situation they faced. If interns could stay up for thirty-six hours without complaining and residents could take care of twenty-five sick patients without ever making a mistake, surely I should be able to endure six weeks with a sadistic chief resident and an ass-kissing senior medical student. But, on the other hand, why should I have to? If I could switch to a better learning situation, why not? Especially now that I was doing clinical medicine, learning seemed very important.

After a bad night's sleep I knew what I had to do. Instead of meeting Meyer and Lindell for morning rounds, I went to the registrar's office. I explained that I was mismatched with a senior student; it was hard for the staff doctors to find common ground from which to teach. It wasn't fair to the senior and it wasn't fair to me. Besides, the Mass. General usually dealt with esoteric cases, and at this stage in my training what I needed was to see lots of common problems. I asked to switch to the Boston City Hospital, where I'd heard there was plenty of basic obstetrics and gynecology.

The registrar mercifully agreed to the change. I said good riddance to Meyer and Lindell and made my way to the gynecology clinic at the Boston City. The senior resident in the clinic was a doctor from Nigeria, named Dr. Waziri. He giggled when I explained why I was a day late for the start of the rotation. "That's what you get for going to the Mass. General," he said. "Don't worry, we'll treat you well down here in the slums."

He looked at the clinic chart he was holding: "I'm just about to see a seventeen-year-old woman with a vaginal discharge. Not terribly exciting gynecology, but if it's common things you want, this is the place to start. Let's go."

I followed him into the tiny examining room. The patient was already lying on her back, her feet up in stirrups. As many times as I saw women in this position during the next six weeks, it never ceased to seem the height of inelegance.

Happily, Dr. Waziri introduced me as a beginning medical student; it was a pleasure not to be masquerading as a doctor. He explained how to insert the vaginal speculum, an instrument so hard and unfriendly it surely couldn't have been invented by a woman. We examined the vagina and took a sample of the discharge to look at under the microscope. Then Dr. Waziri removed the speculum and felt the uterus and ovaries. When he was done he asked the patient if she would mind if I did a pelvic too: "Kenneth is just starting out and needs to learn how to do these things."

She shrugged her shoulders under the sheet that covered her and said no, she didn't mind. I doubt that she thought she really had a choice. Dr. Waziri handed me a pair of gloves and I stepped up between the patient's legs. Why did she seem to be lying there so comfortably? She was the one who was half-naked and I was the one doing the exam, and yet it was I who was trembling. It just didn't seem right.

I went through the motions of a pelvic, but my fingers were numb — I couldn't feel a thing. I was amazed that this woman was allowing me, a total stranger, to explore her vagina just because someone said I was a medical student. I remembered a story in the paper about a crazy who came onto a hospital ward in a white coat. He went around to each room and did pelvics on all the female patients. Not even one woman questioned his authority! So I moved my hand around in this trusting stranger's pelvis and pretended to feel the cervix and uterus and ovaries. I thanked her when I was done and she thanked me, I don't know why.

I was right; there was lots of common gynecology at the Boston City. The clinic was rampant with irregular periods and menstrual cramps and urinary infections. I learned how to do a good pelvic exam. I became a connoisseur of vaginal discharges.

As the second week began I had settled into a comfortable routine. I'd arrive early in the morning, drink coffee and gossip with the nurses, and then start seeing patients. After lunch one of the staff gynecologists gave a talk for me and the other two students in the clinic. Then we'd see more patients for the rest of the afternoon. At first I tagged along with Dr. Waziri, but after a while he let me see patients alone. I'd get a medical history and do an exam. Then I'd present the case to him and we'd go back and see the patient together. He would do his own quick history and physical and finally we'd decide on a plan of diagnosis and treatment. If medication were needed I'd write a prescription for him to sign.

At night over dinner I'd announce to Phyllis all my discoveries that day. We celebrated my first fibroid with a toast of Cribari rosé. "At first I almost missed it," I explained excitedly. "It was off to the left and very posterior. But Dr. Waziri examined the patient and said I was absolutely right; what I felt was a fibroid!"

"What exactly *is* a fibroid?" Phyllis asked. I gave her an

authoritative explanation, recalling that day in pathology when we had seen the fibroid-bearing uterus in the carry-out box. Now I'd not only seen a fibroid in a box; I'd felt one in a patient. Some of the preclinical teaching was beginning to return to consciousness.

In the evenings after dinner I read. Since there was little formal teaching anymore, almost all my learning was from patients. If I'd seen a patient in the clinic that day with an ovarian mass, for example, I'd read about cysts and tumors of the ovary. This kind of learning sank in so much better than it had in the organ blocks — now I wasn't reading about a disease; I was reading about a person.

During the final week in gynecology clinic I both made and missed diagnoses. One day a woman came in because she couldn't feel her IUD string. She also had a heavy vaginal discharge and some cramps. Aha, I thought, another case of PID. I knew that women with IUD's were prone to pelvic inflammatory disease — maybe she couldn't feel the string because the IUD had become dislodged and somehow stirred up an infection.

The nurse set her up in stirrups and I inserted the speculum. Not only couldn't I find the IUD string protruding from the cervix, I couldn't find the cervix itself. Something seemed to be in the way. I asked the nurse for the ringed forceps, poked around, and pulled out a soggy white lump. "My God," said the nurse looking over my shoulder, "what's that?"

"I don't know; it looks like an old tampon," I said. Indeed it was, left over from the patient's last period.

"*What?*" said the patient. "An old tampon? That's disgusting!"

"No, no," I said. "It's common for women to forget to take out the last tampon of the period. We see retained tampons all the time. That's why you couldn't feel your IUD and that's why you had the discharge." Actually I'd never heard of a retained tampon before; I made it up on the spot.

After the tampon came out, it was easy to find the IUD string, properly in place. The entire pelvic exam was normal too. I went to present the case to Dr. Waziri.

"And on speculum exam I found an old tampon in the vagina!" I said.

"Oh yes," he said, "a retained tampon. We see that all the time." So something I thought I had made up turned out to be true. Usually in medicine it was the other way around.

The glory of my retained tampon discovery rapidly faded. The next day a woman came in because she hadn't had a period for over three months. "Usually I'm regular as clockwork," she said. "Something must be wrong."

I took a careful history. We went over the timing and duration of her periods. I asked about weight change, headaches, and blurred vision. We carefully went through all the medications she had ever been on and even talked about the stresses in her life. Then I did a complete exam.

I presented the case to Dr. Waziri with excitement. I knew I'd done a thorough job; I was anxious to impress him. "The patient is a twenty-six-year-old woman with a history of normal menarche and regular periods," I began, "who now presents with amenorrhea of three months' duration."

"Well done, Kenneth," Dr. Waziri said after I'd finished reciting the history and physical. "Now what do you think the diagnosis is and what would you do to establish it?"

"Well the differential diagnosis of secondary amenorrhea includes a number of endocrine and anatomical possibilities in addition to metabolic and psychic stresses. I'd order LH and FSH levels to look for ovarian and pituitary failure. Then I'd get a prolactin and growth hormone, and maybe skull x-rays, to rule out a pituitary tumor. The next step might be a hysterosalpingogram, or at least a D and C, to look for causes of obstruction at or above the level of the cervical os. If all that's normal, a workup for an occult systemic disease might be in order."

"Phew! That's a very nice differential diagnosis," he said, "but you forgot an important cause of secondary amenorrhea, in fact the most common one. Remember, Kenneth, in medicine common things are common. What's the first test to do before you get all those fancy hormone assays?"

I racked my brains, but I couldn't think of anything else. Dr. Waziri finally had to tell me what to order. Half an hour later, the pregnancy test came back positive.

Just as I was really beginning to enjoy myself in the clinic my three weeks were up. It was time to move on to the obstetrics ward. This was the first of many traumatic uprootings in the course of my clinical rotations. As soon as I began to feel comfortable on a ward or in a clinic, I was transplanted to a new setting.

On the obstetrics ward I had to learn a whole new routine. Taking care of a hospitalized patient is quite unlike seeing someone for fifteen minutes in the clinic. And a delivery is a very different sort of vaginal discharge from the ones I'd been dealing with!

The obstetrics ward wasn't much to look at. It occupied a dingy floor of a dingy building. There were high ceilings, dark halls, and peeling paint. The rooms were almost all four-bed "suites." Each patient was vaguely separated from her neighbors by flimsy beige curtains, torn and stained through years of being pulled back and forth. The beds were old and rickety, the iron bedrails encrusted with thick hospital paint.

Floating up from these creaking beds, through the beige curtains, were the screams of women. These women were young, mostly black or Puerto Rican, and alone. And they were terrified. The nurses said you didn't need to go into a patient's room to monitor her contractions — you just sat at the nurses' station and timed the screams.

Somehow all this didn't have much to do with childbirth as taught in the endocrine-reproduction block. Where were the loving husbands? What happened to the Lamaze classes? Where was the birthing room?

The two other students and I got a tour the first day. Mrs. Sullivan, the wiry, gray-haired head nurse, showed us the patients' rooms, the "clean" and "dirty" utility areas, the nurses' station, the staff toilets, and the delivery room. It was suggested that we ask her before we did anything. Mrs. Sullivan ruled the realm of childbirth with an iron fist.

"Now you fellows have to realize that a lot of the girls who come here to deliver are Puerto Ricans," she said back at the nurses' station. "Most of them don't speak English, but you must still be nice to them. You need to know just a few words of Spanish to get by. *Puja* means 'push.' *Dolor* means 'pain.' You'll hear a lot of that. *Profond* means 'much,' like *dolor profond* or *puja profond*. Get it?" We all told her we thought we could handle it.

The medical side of the ward was run by the chief resident, Dr. Dennis Adler. He was tall, thin, and balding. What hair that remained was already mostly gray. It was hard to imagine his ever having been less than thirty years old. He was in his last year of training in obstetrics and gynecology; in three months he'd be done. His mind seemed to be more on the details of setting up his practice than on teaching medical students.

Dr. Adler seemed to think that all members of the female species were weak creatures, at the mercy of their hormones. He was condescending, even for an obstetrician. He had a standard reassurance rap for women in labor: "It's not so bad, dear," he would say to a woman screaming with contractions. "I know just how it feels. We have two children and I was right there with my wife through the deliveries both times. I know exactly what you're going through." I hoped he was more convincing to his patients than he was to me.

Each day began with rounds. In addition to Dr. Adler, me, and the other two students there was John Tuttle, the junior resident. John didn't seem like a gynecologist. For one thing, he was young-looking. And for another, he had a sense of humor. We met at seven o'clock, gathered up our patients' charts, then trooped around the ward. A "hello" or *"buenos días,"* and a quick pat on the belly was the usual extent of each patient visit.

After rounds Adler and Tuttle disappeared to the operating room and we students waited for new admissions and deliveries. There was a lot of waiting. New admissions were mostly healthy young women in labor. It didn't take long to get a medical history and do a physical exam. After that there was nothing to do until they were "ready to hatch," as we put it. An occasional pregnant patient needed close attention: for instance, when she had diabetes or congenital heart disease. But since we students were just starting out on the wards, Dr. Adler felt these patients were too complicated for us — he and John Tuttle called all the shots while we looked on, bewildered and passive. Nonobstetric patients were admitted too, usually older women with possible pelvic tumors. They took more time to work up and look after, but the residents usually told us not to bother with them.

So we waited. We paced up and down the ward like expectant fathers. We read our obstetrics books in the on-call room. We spent a lot of time drinking coffee and talking at the nurses' station. One day while we sat and talked, a nurses' aide came by. "Would you doctors like me to make some more coffee?" she asked. We all flinched. We were still uncomfortable with the mantle of doctorhood starting to settle over us.

When we ran out of things to talk about we took turns negotiating a life-sized plastic fetus through a set of pelvic bones bolted to a board. After a carefully dramatized delivery, including clamping and cutting the imaginary umbilical cord, the deliverer would pull the plastic baby's legs apart and say, "Congratulations, Mrs. Smith, it's a girl!" It seemed easy enough, delivering a baby. But we worried about dropping it. Newborns always looked so slimy in the obstetrics books, and we knew how slippery the rubber gloves were, too. And you probably had to be careful not to hold the kid too tight because it was so fragile. We asked around, but even the old-timers had never heard of a baby being dropped. That made us feel a little better.

My first delivery was a typical Boston City mess. I was assigned a nineteen-year-old Puerto Rican woman named María. This was her first pregnancy — she was a primipara or "primip," as they're affectionately called. She had no husband and, it seemed, no friends. She didn't know the whereabouts of the man who had made her pregnant and didn't care. Even though she was a primip, she had come to the prenatal clinic only twice — she had had essentially no preparation for childbirth.

Labor had been going on for sixteen or eighteen hours. María was exhausted. She spoke little English, so I simply sat with her. I wasn't sure I was making any difference, though; I had little faith in cross-cultural comfort. Occasionally I'd check her mound of a belly, feeling the position of the fetus. Then I'd use the "fetusscope," a specially designed stethoscope, to listen for the accelerated ticking of the baby's heart. The sound-collecting part of the scope was a two-inch hollow cone. It was fixed to a curved metal band which sat over the examiner's head. Rubber tubing went from the apex of the cone to the earpieces. I'd lean over María and press my metal proboscis to her belly with my head. After a little maneuvering, her baby's heartbeats came into focus, saying tsk-tsk at 140 times per minute. I felt like a giant mosquito trying to extract the contents of her huge belly.

When her contractions seemed to be coming close together I called Dr. Adler. But when we examined her, the cervix was hardly dilated. "It will be hours yet," he said. He left the ward and I went to the nurses' station and began ritualistically passing my plastic fetus through the bolted pelvis. This was my final rehearsal before entering the ranks of the baby-deliverers.

An hour or so later María let loose an especially frightening scream and Mrs. Sullivan and I sauntered down to her room, expecting another false alarm. We helped her lift up her legs so I could feel her cervix. But I didn't even have to feel for cervical dilatation — we could see the top of the baby's head.

"Goddamn primip!" Mrs. Sullivan said. "They never seem to do it right. *No puja! No puja!*" She told me to call Dr. Adler; she'd wheel the patient down to delivery.

After paging Dr. Adler "stat." I started a frantic scrub — this was my baby. I arrived in the delivery room just as María was settled into position. She was screaming. Mrs. Sullivan and another nurse were screaming at her not to scream. In between screams they helped me get on my gown, and laid out the packet of sterile gloves.

"*No puja!*" the nurses shouted in vain, "*No puja* yet!" Magically I got all ten fingers into the appropriate ten holes in the gloves and stepped up to the space between screaming María's legs. I took a deep breath — at last this was the real thing. Gently I pressed my right hand against the emerging head to slow its passage through the birth canal.

Dr. Adler arrived. "Listen, Ken," he said breathlessly, "I don't have time to scrub. This one's all yours." He stood to my left and Mrs. Sullivan moved in on the right. The baby's hairy head slowly made its way from one world into another. Dr. Adler's hands shadowed mine in guidance, hovering a few inches above them so as not to break the invisible barrier of sterility. The head suddenly popped out with a rush of white curds and blood. The sexless face was still.

"It's not breathing!" I whispered to Dr. Adler. "What should I do?"

"That's OK," he said. "The kid's still attached to the cord."

"Oh yeah. I forgot."

Dr. Adler and Mrs. Sullivan kept telling me that things were going well, that I was doing a good job. I hoped someone was giving María encouragement too. I heard occasional grunts and cries but didn't really know how she was doing. It seemed so far from where I stood up to her head.

I put a hand on either side of the baby's head and hooked my trembling fingers around the jaws. Almost by reflex I guided this little creature first down, then up and to the left. The slippery hunched torso shouldered its way out of the vagina. Soon the rest of the body, umbilical cord trailing, followed with another shower of warm bloody fluid.

Before I had time to drop the baby Mrs. Sullivan grabbed it. Another nurse handed me two Kelly clamps, which I attached to the cord. I cut between the clamps with a scissors, and the baby became a separate person. It began to cry.

"It's a girl! A *señorita!*" Mrs. Sullivan told María triumphantly. I had forgotten to look.

From then on things were easy. I wound the umbilical cord, like a huge piece of rubbery spaghetti, around the clamp and tugged the reluctant placenta from the womb. Dr. Adler massaged the uterus to help it contract.

Meanwhile María's daughter was washed, weighed, and given the routine eye drops and vitamin K shot. Someone did a quick exam, then the baby was wrapped in a blanket. Finally a nurse showed María her child. She smiled faintly.

Dr. Adler and Mrs. Sullivan both congratulated me on the fine job I'd done. "Congratulate the mother and baby," I said; "I didn't do anything."

For the next few days I kept going past the newborn nursery to see María's baby. It amazed me that I had had something to do with this pink little being's presence in the world. I was proud of my connection with this beautiful baby. Occasionally, all through medical school, I wondered what ever became of María and her child.

The evening after María's delivery Phyllis and I had Dave Rappaport over for dinner. Dave and I didn't see much of each other these days. With the coming of the clinical years, our class had been scattered to the winds. We were dispersed among five different hospitals, doing countless different ward rotations. It was frustrating, this fragmentation. The 140 of us had gone through so much together during the first year and a half of school, but now we were all rapidly losing touch.

David was doing surgery. Like me he was growing interested in internal medicine, the branch dealing with diagnosis and treatment of nonsurgical diseases of adults. His strategy was similar to mine: getting surgery and a few other rotations under his belt would give him a chance to master the basics of patient care. Then he'd do internal medicine and have more time to concentrate on both learning and getting a good grade. Rumor had it that the internal medicine grade was the single most important part of our record when we applied for internships. The pre-med preoccupation with grades didn't end with acceptance to medical school.

Dave and I spent almost the entire dinner talking about what it was like to at last be on the wards. He was impressed when I told him that I had just delivered a baby. I was impressed to learn that he had sewed up the belly of a patient who had had his gallbladder out.

"Did they let you take out the gallbladder too?" Phyllis asked.

"Oh no, they'd never let me do that. While the belly's open the most they let a student do is hold retractors, and maybe cut the ends off a tied suture. The gallbag is the resident's property. Medical students just get the skin."

"That makes sense," Phyllis said. "The only thing they let students do is sew up the skin, the one part of the operation that shows."

I pumped David about his experiences — surgery was my next rotation. Did the interns and residents do much teaching or did they just use students as slaves? When he was on call in the hospital did he get enough sleep? When he came home on his nights off did he have enough energy to read about his cases that day? Even though I'd gotten my clinical feet wet with ob-gyn, each new rotation held its own potential hazards.

Phyllis was very indulgent with all this shoptalk, but finally over dessert she declared a medical truce: she loudly cleared her throat and said, "Hey, David, seen any good movies lately?" We stayed away from medicine for about five minutes, then veered right back to ob-gyn and surgery and internal medicine. Deep into our first ward rotations medicine had become the central fact of our lives. It was easier to talk about medicine than any other subject. Once again I heard my father say, "Doctors are the most parochial of professionals," and I shuddered.

My next delivery didn't go well. With María things had happened so fast there was no time for spinal anesthesia and an episiotomy, both standard at the Boston City. This new patient, though, a better-behaved multipara named Mrs. North, would escape neither. Dr. Adler had plenty of time to scrub, and ran things from start to finish.

The anesthesiologist sedated Mrs. North into silence, then did the spinal. Then we put her legs up in the special holders and draped her with sterile sheets. As the baby began to crown Dr. Adler slipped two fingers into the vagina and pulled the vaginal wall away from the head. "Your last girl was lucky not to get a bad perineal tear," he told me. "It's always safest to make a bigger hole for the kid by doing an episiotomy. That way we have a clean incision to sew up rather than a ragged tear." He spread his fingers apart and cut the tissue between them with a sharp scissors. I winced, but the patient of course didn't feel a thing.

For the rest of the delivery my hands sat passively against the baby; Dr. Adler's hands lay over mine, doing all the actual manipulating. There was no fear of dropping the goods this time.

The glistening pink baby emerged. This time I noticed its sex and had the privilege of informing Mrs. North that she had a boy. She beamed. "Thank you, doctor. Thank you!" she said much to my embarrassment. The idea that it was the doctor who "delivered" the baby bothered me. In fact, by the mighty effort of pushing it out into the world, it's the mother who delivers her child to the doctor.

After the placenta was out it was time to sew up the episiotomy. Dr. Adler said I could do it. I was excited at the chance to keep even with Dave by stitching up a person. Adler sewed together the muscle layers and explained that we'd close the skin with a continuous stitch, culminating in a single knot. He warned me that the suture material was a little stiff and brittle; it had to be handled with care.

He did the first few stitches to show me how, his dragonfly hands darting and resting with incredible speed. Each movement seemed so inevitable. This will be a cinch, I thought. As Adler handed me the instruments, though, a sinister transformation occurred — they stopped working! The forceps wouldn't grasp the tissue where I meant it to. The needle suddenly became wobbly in its holders. And when the needle finally managed to settle in on one side of the wound, it had trouble burrowing through to the tissue on the other side. Dr. Adler and I both grew irritable. Neither of us could understand why I was having so much trouble.

He showed me again. I fumbled even more. Several times he had to take over in mid-stitch to set the misbehaving needle right. But I persevered. At last, in the time Adler could have done a Cesarean section, I approached the final pass.

"Now remember," he said, "since this is a continuous stitch the final knot is key, it holds the whole thing together.

Whatever you do, don't pull it too tight; that will break the suture material."

"Don't worry, I won't," I said; "I don't want to go through *this* again!"

With some effort I guided the needle in its last trip through the skin. I'd done it, the episiotomy was repaired! I carefully tied the knot and snugged it down tight.

As I breathed a deep sigh of relief the suture snapped.

Aside from suturing, nothing looks simpler but turns out to be more treacherous than starting an intravenous. The day after the episiotomy disaster the ward was quiet. A patient was about to be wheeled off to the O.R. for a hysterectomy.

John Tuttle asked me if I'd like to start her IV. I'd seen him do three or four so far. It was time for me to take the intravenous plunge.

"Sure," I said, scared to death, "I'd love to start an IV." I went down to the patient's room and introduced myself: "Hello, Mrs. Herrera. My name's Ken Klein. I'm a medical student. Dr. Tuttle asked me to start an intravenous before your surgery. I'll be back in a minute with all the supplies."

Twenty minutes later I hadn't yet returned. The obstetrics ward was still a foreign country. I was at the mercy of the natives, and the natives weren't very friendly. The nurses made it clear I was on *their* ward; they had to defend it against invading medical students. So it took a good twenty minutes of drawer-opening and closet-searching to get what I thought I needed.

Then I had an inspiration — I'd show my cache to the head nurse: "Is this all I'll need to start Mrs. Herrera's IV,

Mrs. Sullivan?" Asking turned out to be a wise move for two reasons. First, Mrs. Sullivan noticed I'd forgotten the adhesive tape and showed me where to find it. Second, she was flattered that a medical student had recognized her expertise and asked for help. After this little episode Mrs. Sullivan and I became good buddies. I rarely felt uncomfortable asking nurses for advice. It was just acknowledging the fact that they knew a lot of things I didn't. Many nurses, especially veterans like Mrs. Sullivan, resented medical students strutting onto the wards like little doctors and barking orders right and left. But if their skills and experience were recognized, nurses could be incredibly kind and helpful. I learned a lot from Mrs. Sullivan.

Finally at Mrs. Herrera's bedside I had accumulated all the necessities. I tore the tape to size and laid out the sticky strips on the bed railing. Then I uncapped the bottle, plugged in the plastic tubing and hung the bottle upside down from the stainless steel gallows of an IV pole. I brought over a chair, remembering John's pearl of advice the day before: "There are two keys to a successful procedure: one, have everything ready before you start and two, make yourself as comfortable as possible."

So I was all set. I went into the on-call room where John was watching TV and announced that I was finally ready for him to preside over my IV starting. "Jesus, you went to get the IV stuff half an hour ago," he said. "Where've you been? I thought you got mugged in the basement."

"The IV supplies were in hiding."

We went back to Mrs. Herrera's room. "Before I begin," I said, "I want to explain what I'm going to do so you wouldn't be frightened."

She stuck out her arm: "Let's just get this over with, OK?"

"Sure," I said. "Somehow I get the feeling that you've had IV's before."

I strapped the tourniquet around her upper arm and held my breath, praying for veins. It was my lucky day — several prime vessels sprouted gloriously under the arm's burden of extra blood. I savored them with my palpating finger, then picked an especially succulent specimen on the lower forearm. After cleaning the skin with alcohol I poised the IV needle just above the spot I meant to stick. I looked up at John for the all-clear sign.

"Fine, fine," he said impatiently. "Let's go already."

"OK, Mrs. Herrera, grit your teeth," I said, gritting my teeth. "Here we go." I stabbed the needle into the innocent vein. Mrs. Herrera's arm jerked, but the needle held its ground. Blood began to trickle out from its plastic hub.

"Good!" said John, "I think you've got it." I grabbed the tubing which dangled down from the IV bottle and plugged it into the end of the needle.

"OK to turn it on now?" I asked John.

"Let 'er rip!"

I loosened the plastic screw that controlled the flow of fluid through the tubing. A rush of air bubbles passed under my hand which lay on Mrs. Herrera's vein, just above the needle site. Somehow I had injected air into her veins! I squeezed her arm tight. Neither she nor John seemed aware that anything was wrong.

"My God, what did I do?" I asked John.

"What are you talking about?"

I leaned toward him so Mrs. Herrera wouldn't hear. I still had her arm in a death grip to prevent more air from passing. "The bubbles," I said. "I felt air going through her vein."

John checked the IV bottle. It was dripping normally, despite my stranglehold. "It looks fine," he said. "Hey, I bet I know what happened. You probably forgot to flush the air out of the tubing before you attached it to the needle."

"Yeah, I guess I did. Jesus, John, what are we going to do?"

"Don't worry, dummy. Nothing will happen."

"But I thought you could kill a person by injecting air," I said. "Everybody knows that."

"Is that so? What course did you learn that in? I suppose if you injected a lot of air right into an artery you might cause trouble. But the tiny bit of air you put into her vein surely dissolved before it even got back to the heart. It would never get as far as the arterial circulation. Don't worry."

"*I* wasn't worried," said Mrs. Herrera, smiling at me. "In fact, you did a pretty good job, Dr. Klein." I realized she had heard our entire whispered conversation.

"Well I'm glad you weren't worried," I said, " 'cause I was scared to death."

"I know. You doctors can't hide things nearly as well as you'd like to think. We patients aren't stupid, you know."

I taped the tubing in place, and a few minutes later an orderly came to take her off to the operating room.

Diseases of the uterus seemed to be a very common affliction of women, perhaps second only to vaginal discharges. The ward was always brimming with hysterectomies. In many cases, though, the reason for surgery was obscure, at least to me. To be sure there were cases of cancer. It was exciting to see patients cured by an operation after a Pap smear or a D and C picked up an early tumor. But the most common indication for hysterectomy seemed to be irregular or heavy periods. Patients and gynecologists alike apparently felt that menstrual abnormalities were a malignant nuisance.

Some of the women in my class told me that unnecessary surgery was going on. They said that a gynecologist-in-training needed a certain number of hysterectomies under his belt to become fully certified. Also, they said, to a male gynecologist the uterus of a woman done with childbearing was a useless organ. It just sat in the pelvis, waiting to develop a cancer. So why not cut it out?

What my friends said made sense. But I couldn't quite believe that a physician could cynically remove a woman's uterus without good reason. From our pathology course I knew there was a controversy about which microscopic changes in endometrial scrapings were premalignant. Maybe the gynecologists were just being conservative in interpreting the histology from the D and C that was a prelude to almost every hysterectomy.

I was assigned a woman named Mrs. Gleason. She had had two children and was just entering the menopause. Her periods were irregular and there were sudden episodes of heavy spotting. A D and C was done in the clinic. Dr. Adler said the pathologist reported precancerous changes. So Adler admitted her for a hysterectomy.

Shortly after Mrs. Gleason arrived on the ward I went down to her room. I introduced myself, then began my medical history by asking her why she was in the hospital — I'd already learned that the patient and doctor often have different stories. She told me she had come in to have her uterus taken out because she had cancer.

I decided to see for myself. After I'd done my workup I went to review the D and C slides. The route from the ob-gyn ward to the pathology department was long and circuitous; I was passing from the land of the living to the land of the dead. As I got farther from the ward things became quieter, and somehow more certain. A sign that said "Pathology Department" appeared. Then there was that familiar acrid-sweet smell, harking back to the days of autopsies and cadavers.

I traveled down the River Styx of formaldehyde to the histology section and asked the secretary for Mrs. Gleason's D and C records. She sat me down at a two-headed microscope and in a few minutes came back with the slides, shiny glass rectangles impressed with flat little chips of Mrs. Gleason. I put one in place on the microscope stage and focused down on intricate pink and purple mountain ranges, meteor craters with fantastic twisted borders, and wild red rivers streaming out in all directions. I used the low-, medium-, and high-power lenses. The focus was perfect, the details were sharp. But unlike my textbooks, there were no labels. I couldn't make any sense of it all.

Then Dr. Mertz, the pathologist who had given me and Phyllis the pop anatomy quiz at the autopsy, happened by. "Hi there," he said. "What brings you to pathology — still looking for that thymus?" Unfortunately, he remembered.

"No, I gave up. Actually I'm taking care of a woman who's going to have a hysterectomy and I wanted to review the histology of her D and C."

"I'd be delighted to go over it with you," he said. "We

don't get many people who bother to come and look at their patients' slides."

"That's because it smells so bad over here." Fortunately, he laughed.

Dr. Mertz scanned the slide while I looked through the teaching head of the microscope. Individual cells and groups of cells unjumbled as he spoke. My histology came flooding back. He explained that there was a spectrum of precancerous changes, and admitted that there was disagreement over precisely where to draw the line. "But," he said, "in my opinion there's very little concern for a malignancy here. To me, this is simply not a precancerous endometrium."

"Then why are they doing a hysterectomy?"

"Well, if I were to be unkind I'd say it was simply because there was an empty spot on the surgery schedule. On the other hand, your resident could be extremely conservative in interpreting premalignant histology. Also it could be that your patient is so bothered by her symptoms that she wants the uterus out even if cancer isn't an issue. Why don't you simply ask your resident exactly why he's planning the surgery?"

"That's a good idea," I said. "I'll really pin Dr. Adler down." But somehow I never got around to asking him. As a student fresh on the wards, I just didn't feel comfortable challenging a chief resident.

Fortunately, Mrs. Gleason had an uneventful postoperative course.

The police called. A prison ambulance was on its way in with a pregnant heroin addict. The prison nurse said the woman was beginning to withdraw and, she thought, was going into labor too. She was apparently in bad shape.

The call jolted me back into the present. It was the next to the last day of ob-gyn; I was psychologically severing myself from the rotation and preparing for surgery, which would start the next week.

"Those fucking cops should be shot," John Tuttle said. "Putting a pregnant junkie in jail to cool!" He explained that the fetus would probably be in big trouble; the woman would probably need an emergency Cesarean section. He alerted the obstetrics staff and the pediatricians.

By the time we got to the operating room the nurses were already setting up. Soon a pediatrics resident and a neonatal specialist arrived with an incubator and a huge tray of tiny instruments. They looked like toys from a fancy play-doctor kit. I went over and started talking with the pediatricians. They told me a little about the neonatal withdrawal syndrome: since heroin crossed the placenta into the fetus's bloodstream, the child as well as the mother would suffer withdrawal. The key to salvaging the baby, they said, was getting it out as quickly as possible.

Dr. Jorgenson, head of the obstetrics department, strode in; I knew for sure this was serious business. He went over some technical details of the procedure with John.

John told me to get an IV started as soon as the patient arrived. "We've got to go as soon as she hits the table," he said. He and Dr. Jorgensen went off to scrub. I'd only put in four or five IV's by then. How could he trust me?

The scrub nurse, the pediatricians, and I stood in the shiny sterile room. It was very still. I looked at the intravenous equipment laid out on the anesthesia stand and kept starting the patient's IV in my mind. I had already flushed the air out of the tubing but checked it again, just to be sure.

There was a deep rumbling in the distance. It was a stretcher, moving very fast. The noise grew quickly louder. Then the O.R. doors burst open and in rolled a small black women writhing in the leather restraints which bound her to the stretcher. She was screaming.

"My baby, oh dear God, my baby!" she wailed. Pushing the stretcher were a nurse from the emergency ward and Dr. Waziri, who had intercepted the ambulance as it pulled in.

"Let's move, *now!*" he said with a voice on the line between authority and panic. "The fetal heart tones are very slow!" John and Dr. Jorgenson rushed in from the scrub sinks. Their hands were still foamy with soap.

"Dear Jesus, my baby!" the woman wailed. Dr. Waziri, the nurse, and I unbuckled the leathers, scooped her up off the stretcher, and practically threw her onto the operating table. Waziri grabbed some iodine scrub solution and poured the entire bottle over the bulging abdomen. There would be no ten-minute skin scrub.

"Get that IV in, Ken. Fast!" said John. He was in his operating gown and had the scalpel already in hand.

I caught a flailing arm, pinned it to the armboard, and picked up the IV needle. I had already decided to forget about the alcohol — I'd just find a vein and go.

"My God!" I said when I saw her arm. It was covered with dark knotty ropes where veins used to be. This was the first time I'd see what shooting heroin did to blood vessels.

"Oh dear Jesus," the woman screamed, "help me!" I thought the same thing, for both of us.

There was suddenly a hand on my shoulder: "This is going to be a little tricky; why don't you let me do this one." It was the anesthesiologist, who had just arrived. I gratefully gave up the IV needle and steadied the patient's arm for him. He explored up and down the forearm with a quick and delicate finger. The needle floated momentarily above where his finger had come to rest. Then it zeroed in on an unscarred vein, invisible to my eye. I turned on the IV and the fluid poured in full blast.

"Incredible!" I said.

"Luck," he said with a smile, but I knew it wasn't so.

The pentothal went into the vein and the abdominal skin was cut almost simultaneously. The patient's last wail trailed off into a bright aseptic corner of the room.

I had never seen John move so fast. Once through the skin he occasionally used instruments, but mostly just his hands. He tore down through the layers of the mother's abdomen that sheltered her baby from the outside world. Dr. Jorgenson occasionally shouted orders, but mostly just gave John encouragement and endorsed his speed.

Just as incredible as John's pace was that his frantic tearing and cutting remained purposeful and precise. How could he possibly do it? Usually he was slow and easygoing, but now he was a hectic genius.

Suddenly, with a wake of water, a blue rubbery creature exploded from the belly like a fish coming up for a taste of air. John and Dr. Jorgenson clamped and cut the cord in a matter of seconds, and somehow sent the baby floating across its mother's open belly to the pediatricians. The pediatricians worked like a multilimbed robot controlled by a single computer brain. Four flapping hands grasped and transferred instruments with inhuman speed. The robot suctioned out the nose and throat, gave oxygen, connected tubes and electrodes, and in a few moments had transformed the blue fish into a pink crying child.

They worked over the infant for a minute or two and then looked up. "This kid is going to do OK," said one of them. "Good work, you guys."

To my surprise, I started to cry.

6

"A Chance to Cut Is a Chance to Cure"

Surgery

ONCE AGAIN the leaves were turning; it was early fall. I'd just finished ob-gyn and surgery was about to begin. I called up Dave Rappaport for moral support.

"Hey, Ken," he said, "do you realize that we're third-year medical students now? Medical is already half over!"

"Yes. But on the other hand, Dave, do you realize that medical school is *only* half over? We still have two whole years to go."

I'd chosen to do my three-month surgery rotation, like ob-gyn, at the Boston City. The wards were brimming with common diseases, and medical students were given the chance to do a lot. The rotation began with three weeks in the emergency ward. There I became an expert at sewing up the lacerated scalps of prisoners and drunks. Also I learned how to diagnose broken bones, what to do for drug overdoses, and how to treat dog bites, rat bites, and human bites. It was during my fourth day in the emergency ward that Mr. Hastings with the subdural hematoma arrived, beginning the long night of terror that ended with his dead heart lying in my hands.

After my stint in emergency I moved to the surgery wards. There, under the supervision of an intern, I began to learn how to take care of patients.

The crowning triumph of my surgery experience was the case of George Boileau. Mr. Boileau was my patient through most of the time I spent on the surgery wards. When he was first admitted he was sick, deaf, and almost blind. No one could have predicted that this unappetizing patient would become a stunning medical success story.

The nursing home sent Mr. Boileau to the hospital because he "didn't look right." "He used to be a real firecracker," the head nurse told me over the phone, "but for the last week he's been really withdrawn. He doesn't eat a thing and won't even keep his glasses on. We know something's wrong with George." She made me promise not to send him to another nursing home once we fixed him up. Since nursing homes rarely want patients back once they get sick I knew this lump of a patient must be somebody special, at least to the head nurse. It was hard to imagine why. I thanked her for the information and said good-bye. "Now you take good care of George, doctor, and be sure to talk loud," she said. "He's pretty deaf, you know."

Mr. Boileau wound up on surgery because a resident in the emergency ward thought his belly was a little tender: "80 year old nursing home resident with one week history of malaise and anorexia," the EW sheet read. "Physical exam normal except for possible right upper quadrant guarding. Rule out surgical abdomen." The surgeons on my ward weren't thrilled.

"Jesus, what a dump," my intern said. "We're here to do surgery, not babysit old geezers." My intern's name was

Gregg Wolfe. He was short and chubby, with curly light brown hair and muttonchop sideburns. He was an uncomplicated person with strong opinions about everything — he was a typical surgeon. Gregg turned me loose on poor Mr. Boileau: "He's all yours, Ken. Take your time and don't page me till you have a diagnosis."

Despite Gregg's feelings about our new patient I went into his room with enthusiasm. It was exciting to have my own fresh case. If a patient was medically interesting or really sick, the interns and residents were all over him as soon as he hit the ward. They made the diagnosis, decided on therapy, and left all the scutwork for me. This meant doing the cardiogram, drawing blood for tests, taking the patient to x-ray, and writing a detailed note in the chart repeating what everyone already knew. So I didn't care that my patient was a feeble old man. What mattered was that he was all mine.

When I first saw Mr. Boileau I knew the nursing home was right — he clearly wasn't the life of the party. In fact, it was hard to tell if he was alive at all. He lay perfectly still under the bedclothes, staring at the ceiling. He had a small round face capped by a shining bald head. The gray bristles of a week-old beard roamed over his cheeks like emissaries from his tight little moustache.

He didn't move when I entered the room. I strode over to the bed, smiled, and in a booming voice said, "Hi! My name is Ken Klein, your medical student. I'm going to look after you while you're here in the hospital." I reached out to shake his hand. He looked vaguely over my right shoulder and grunted.

"Can you hear me?" I yelled.

"What?"

"Can you *see* me?" I said, louder still.

"No, I can't see without my glasses."

"Where are they?"

"Glasses? They must be in the top drawer of my night table." I opened the drawer of his bedside stand but all I found was a denture case and an old pouch of Bugler's tobacco.

I leaned down and shouted in his ear, "They're not here."

"No, no doctor, at home. My night table at the rest home."

My enthusiasm was fading. This patient was so deaf it was impossible to carry on a conversation, and since he was without glasses I couldn't even write down questions. This, I feared, was going to be another case of veterinary medicine.

I decided on an efficiency drive. I got a big syringe and a fistful of test tubes to collect blood samples. This way I could at least have some lab tests cooking during the hours it would take to work up this decrepit patient.

He didn't even wince when I poked the needle into his vein. After I'd withdrawn about 30 cc's of blood Mr. Boileau stirred. "By the way, doctor, which species of vampire are you?"

"Born and raised in Transylvania," I said. I ran the blood down to the lab, excited by the spark of life my patient had shown.

When I returned to Mr. Boileau's room he was lying just as I'd left him. The victimized arm was still hanging over the side of the bed, the hand still in a fist. Poor old guy, I thought.

I decided to dope out the hearing. Into his right ear I said, "How long have you been hard of hearing?"

"What?"

Then to the left ear, "Can you hear me now?"

"Can I what?"

The left ear was the winner. After this I always addressed his left ear. But several questions later I gave up in frustration.

It had cost me a sore throat just to find out that he was allergic to penicillin, had had scarlet fever when he was twelve, and took no medicines. Old people, I decided, were a pain in the ass.

I ditched the rest of my questions and began the physical exam. The ear canals were blockaded with hard plugs of wax. And I agreed with the EW resident, the right upper quadrant did indeed seem tender. The rest of the exam held no surprises; it just showed what happens to the body when it grows old.

While waiting for Mr. Boileau's blood test results I went on afternoon rounds with Gregg. Our ward was a Madame Tussaud's of horrible surgical diseases; each bed held its own depressing display. There were infected knife wounds, raw stumps of amputated legs, and bellies that wouldn't stay shut after surgery. "There's not a single clean case on the whole damned ward," Gregg said bitterly. He lusted for a simple case of appendicitis or a healthy young gallbladder, ripe with stones. All they would need was surgery, and an early discharge. None of our patients were that simple. They were all sick and stayed forever. Half were too sick to *have* surgery and the rest were so sick *because* of surgery. This was not an inspiring collection of cases for a surgeon-in-training.

The ward itself looked as sick as the patients — Marcus Welby wouldn't have let his patients be caught dead in a place like that. The halls were pastel green and the rooms a peeling beige. "They painted the walls with bile and feces," one of the orderlies claimed. The astounding smells that were always in the air made that seem a possibility.

Most of the rooms on the ward held four or more beds. There were plenty of windows, but the view was obscured by dirt, and in some cases by a rusty cross-hatching of thick iron bars. The heating was primitive and the plumbing squealed and shook.

My job on rounds was to push along the old metal chartrack as we strolled out among our charges. At each patient's bedside I'd flip open the chart and look for new lab results and consultants' notes. Then we'd say hello if the patient could talk, check the temperature curve, and take down the surgical dressing. This old building must have been infected with bad vapors that prevented wound healing — every patient's incision site was red and soupy. Drug addicts and diabetics were the worst healers. We despised the addicts and pitied the diabetics. No matter what the diagnosis, though, our patients all seemed to be falling apart. I told Gregg how frustrating it was to work so hard on these people and see no evidence that what I was doing made any difference.

"Well, Ken," Gregg said philosophically, "you have to realize you just can't polish shit."

Mr. Boileau's lab tests still weren't back after rounds so I decided to poke around in his ears. Even though Gregg said that earwax seldom plugs so tight that it affects hearing, I wanted to be 100 percent sure that this wasn't why my patient was deaf. Digging wax out of patients' ears seems to satisfy some deep inner need — I must admit that I was looking forward to retrieving some nice chunks.

I asked a nurse for a cerumen spoon, a stainless steel stick with a thin wire loop on the end, and set to work. With sign language and shouting I got Mr. Boileau to lie on his side. When he finally understood what I was about to do he said, "If you find anything worth mining, I'll split it fifty-fifty."

I started in on the right ear. First I placed the tip of the otoscope in the ear canal. Then I sighted the wax plug, slid the lens aside, and carefully inserted the cerumen spoon through the instrument. Several rounds of exploratory digging yielded only a few tiny orange chips from the mother lode. A reconnaissance mission to the left ear showed it to be just as hard to work as the right.

It was clear I needed a new plan of attack. I started asking around for advice on how to remove impacted cerumen. Everyone seemed to have their own remedy. A medical student friend swore her Italian grandmother stuck a candlewick in the ear canal and lit the protruding end. As the flame drew near the ear, the wax would supposedly warm and loosen. One of the residents recommended an eardrop recipe of one part hydrogen peroxide with one part water, and a nurse gave a testimonial for a commercial earwax remover called Ceruminex.

Since I wasn't sure the hospital's insurance policy would cover me if I set a patient on fire, I decided to resort to chemical warfare — it would be hydrogen peroxide in the morning and Ceruminex in the afternoon.

By eight o'clock that night Mr. Boileau's blood tests still weren't done. So I went home and read about right upper quadrant pain and earwax. The next morning the lab results finally came back. Mr. Boileau's white blood count was high and the alkaline phosphatase and bilirubin were up too. Could he have cholecystitis — infection of the gallbladder? Might he need surgery?

"You know Ken, that's a great idea," said Gregg. "I think you're on to something." He had taken a sudden interest in Mr. Boileau. We went down to his room and Gregg carefully poked his abdomen, especially the right upper quadrant, where the gallbladder lives. Mr. Boileau was now very tender there.

On the way out of the room Gregg slapped me on the back. "Well, well," he said, "looks like a hot gallbag, my man."

The abnormal lab tests seemed to give Mr. Boileau the right to get sicker. He stopped eating entirely and the next day he spiked a fever and began to vomit. Gregg ordered antibiotics. "If the dude doesn't cool off in a day or two, we go after it," he said with a scalpel's gleam in his eyes. He told me to draw blood cultures, start an IV, and write a note in the chart. As usual, the intern made the decisions and I did the scut.

I think Gregg enjoyed being an intern for two reasons: he got to operate and he got to order medical students around. "Stud," he'd say (all medical students were "studs"), "that new admission in 213 needs a cardiogram. And while you're down there grab some urine on Jeffries — his last urinalysis had some red cells, so we better check it again." We studs were slave labor not only for the intern and resident on our team but for other interns and residents as well. Even the nurses sometimes asked us to run errands. I was apparently paying $3000 tuition for the privilege of drawing blood, carrying specimens to the lab, and restarting IV's in the middle of the night.

But how could I refuse? I wanted to stay on the good side of these people, and there was no doubt they were overworked and could use the help. Also, of course, I worried about my grade.

At one point, though, the volume of scutwork became unbearable. I had no time to read or even keep up with my patients. I called the staff surgeon who directed the rotation and complained. "Listen, Ken," he said, "you should think of scutwork as an investment. The more you do for your intern, the more time he'll have for teaching."

The next day on rounds I decided to collect some of the teaching Gregg owed me. We were writing IV orders on an old man named Mr. Marinelli. "OK," said Gregg, "let's give this joker Ringer's Solution at 75 cc's per hour."

"Sure," I said and wrote the order for Gregg to sign. "But tell me, Gregg, why give him Ringer's instead of just normal saline?"

"Because that's what I *want* to give him." I didn't seem to be getting a very good return on my investment.

The afternoon after Mr. Boileau's fever spike I discovered the heart of the hospital. I left the ward and went out onto one of the main corridors. In the dark hallway I mingled with the traffic. There were dietitians pushing food carts, pharmacists toting wire baskets, and orderlies with stretchers cruising for patients. I was practically the only one not pushing or carrying anything.

At one point on my journey I had to leave the building and cross a street filled with Puerto Ricans and blacks. In my white coat I felt very white.

I entered another wing of the hospital through a side door and trotted down a flight of stairs to the basement corridor. The air was cool and saturated; there could have been mushrooms. Thick soggy flakes of paint hung down from the ceiling. Arterial and venous pipes overhead carried fluids to the hospital's extremities. Some of them were leaky, slowly bleeding down the walls and onto the wet floor. Maybe it was this subterranean hallway that brewed the wound-perturbing vapors that seemed to hang over the surgery ward. I rounded a corner. In the distance I could hear the lub-dub of the laundry.

I used to think about the laundry as I lay between my starchy sheets in the on-call room at night. I conjured up all the patients the sheets must have sandwiched — the gall-bladders and drug overdoses, the broken hips and heart attacks. I wondered how many people had died between my sheets. Was the laundry thorough enough to bleach out the illness and death that had soaked into the fabric?

A short flight of stairs took me down to the room that was home to the hospital's dirty linen. It was a two-story concrete structure, filled with frantic activity. Washing machines worked over the sheets and towels within their giant ventricles; rows of dryers murmured cleaning tunes.

Precise workers pumped the presses that steamed out wrinkles, while their comrades folded pillowcases and packaged lab coats.

Every move was filled with certainty. These people must have known what to do for every possible stain; not a single piece of cleaning came to them that they couldn't handle. By comparison, our work on the wards seemed tentative and insubstantial. Half the time we couldn't make a diagnosis. Even when we could, the best way to treat the patient might not be clear. And it wasn't that all our problems were complex — I couldn't even figure out how to get the wax out of Mr. Boileau's ears! Also, our responsibility was merely for the patients on our ward. The laundry, on the other hand, was central to the life of the entire hospital. Dirty linen continuously streamed to it from every wing, and after being cleaned and pressed flowed back out, like red blood cells cycling through the heart and lungs.

I finally found what I was looking for — an area filled with clones of uniforms hung on long steel racks. "PHARMACY," "DIETARY," "PHYSICAL THERAPY," they were labeled. I humbly approached the mastermind behind the counter and told her why I was there: "Hi, I'm a medical student on surgery. I've come to trade my white coat in for a clean one."

She led me to a rack that said "MEDICAL STUDENTS" — yes, there was even a place for me. I told her my name. "Kenneth Klein, third-year medical student, 38 long," she said authoritatively. She read it from a list, but she seemed to know the facts without looking. I took the new coat she handed me, thanked her, and left the laundry with awe.

On my way back to the ward I ran into Eric Costello, the surgery chief resident from the Emergency Ward.

"Hey, Ken, how's life on the wards?" he asked.

"Oh, not bad. Say, Eric, what about removing earwax?" Mr. Boileau's cerumen was on my mind a lot.

"Oh I don't know," said Eric. "I usually dig it out with the cap of my Bic. If I don't have a pen handy I use a paper clip, but that doesn't work as well."

"No, not for you! What do you do when a *patient* has impacted cerumen?"

"What? You mean they actually admitted someone to the surgery service for earwax? Jesus, you guys must be hard up for patients!"

"No no, he has cholecystitis. But I'm the cerumen specialist on the case."

"Oh I see. How interesting."

As with everything else, Eric had the answer. He told me about the ear irrigation syringe. It's a big stainless steel syringe with a blunt tip that is inserted into the ear canal. You shoot in warm water and the wax softens and floats out. I returned to the ward and ordered one up.

I couldn't resist an immediate shot at Mr. Boileau's cerumen — he had stopped vomiting and looked a little stronger since the IV was put in. The nurse made a bib out of a bath towel and held a vomit basin under Mr. Boileau's right ear; I loaded up the syringe and fired away. The water bounced off the cerumen and fizzed and gushed back out, cascading over his earlobe to the basin below.

"Hey," Mr. Boileau said, "it feels like the water's leaking

out my other ear!" It's hard to think of sick people as having a sense of humor; I took him seriously. I went around to look in the left ear.

"I don't see any water," I said. Mr. Boileau cracked up. For the next few hours he kept giggling and pointing to his left ear.

"Some gratitude!" I said.

After an extensive hosing out of both ear canals all I had to show for my work were a few dark flakes. Even Eric Costello wasn't wily enough to outwit the earwax of Mr. Boileau! The cerumen crusades were at a standstill.

That afternoon was the last time Mr. Boileau laughed for a long time. Overnight he got much worse. When I came in for rounds the next morning he was soaked with sweat, and he was really hurting. I leaned down to his left ear and said, "Mr. Boileau, how are you feeling? You look terrible."

"Yes, you're right," he said softly.

Gregg was ecstatic. Since the antibiotics hadn't controlled the infection, he'd get to do his surgery. He skipped into Mr. Boileau's room with the consent form. After handing it to Mr. Boileau he shouted, "George, read this and sign your name down here. We have to cut out your gallbladder to make you better."

"Sorry, son, I'm blind as a buzzard without my glasses." He turned to me: "Doctor, this intern here seems to want me to sign my life away. What do you think?"

I smiled smugly at Gregg, then said to the left ear: "Well I think the young fellow has the right idea. You really do need surgery. I advise you to sign."

An hour later Gregg sliced a long red line across the famous right upper quadrant of Mr. Boileau's surgical abdomen. I stood next to Gregg. Across the anesthetized body from us were Frank Stevens, the junior resident, and Dr. Raya, a staff surgeon. Everyone was anonymously gowned and masked, as if to escape undetected after we had stolen the patient's gallbladder.

Gregg hummed contentedly to himself as he elbowed his way down through the layers of muscle that stood between him and the gallbladder. Tension mounted as he approached the peritoneum, the final covering over the abdominal cavity: we savored the moment when we would at last see the inflamed gallbladder everyone had predicted. There was always room for a little doubt, no matter how certain the diagnosis seemed. Entering the abdomen was like opening a giant box of Cracker Jacks; you could never be sure about the prize.

Dr. Raya handed me a retractor, a medical student's inevitable surgical appendage. It was like a huge stainless steel popsicle stick with a right-angle bend, used to hold the skin, fat, and muscles of the abdominal wall out of the way. Frank Stevens, opposite me, was honored with another retractor.

Together we parted the fleshy curtains that covered the peritoneum. Dr. Raya fussed with the tiny bleeding vessels in the retracted fat and muscle. This, it seemed to me, was an unnecessary delaying tactic. The purpose was apparently both to heighten the drama and to make it clear to everyone that he was running the show.

Finally Gregg got the go-ahead. He carefully snipped into

the peritoneal membrane which Dr. Raya had tented up with forceps. The abdominal cavity was at last exposed; Mr. Boileau's liver and intestines blinked in the bright lights of the operating room. Gregg then took the meaty liver in his hands and hoisted it up to expose the object of his desire, the gallbladder. It cowered, swollen and purple, under his predatory stare. So we were right, the gallbladder did it. "Whooee," said Gregg, "she's a hot one!"

After a learned dissertation on the pros and cons, Dr. Raya decided to let Gregg remove the gallbladder. The alternative, he explained, would be merely to drain it and then take it out at a second surgery, after the patient was in better shape. The rest of the operation went well. Gregg was a credit to the surgical race.

Mr. Boileau awoke from surgery sprouting tubes. An IV burrowed into his arm. A nasogastric tube went down his nose into his stomach, and a tube whose end sat in the bile duct exited from the abdominal wall in the right flank. There were two Penrose drains, enormous flaccid rubber bands, growing out of the lower part of the belly.

"This doesn't feel like heaven, so I must be in the other place," he said to me as he came out from under anesthesia. And he was right — the next week was hell for Mr. Boileau. He hurt all the time. Despite the stomach tube he vomited regularly. Each morning I'd follow Gregg into Mr. Boileau's room for the ritual torture session. Gregg would take down the dressings, poke at his belly, and advance the Penrose drains. Mr. Boileau rarely spoke, but his eyes were filled with pain. At first he was too fragile for ear irrigation, but I stuck faithfully to the hydrogen peroxide–Ceruminex one-two punch.

After belly surgery the bowels take a few days to resume their churning. During this period the tube in the stomach removes the gastric juice. The first sign that the intestines are working again is a gurgling heard with the stethoscope. As the intestines continue their reawakening the sounds grow louder and more frequent. Then the patient finally passes gas. After this momentous event the tube comes out, and feeding can begin. So I watched Mr. Boileau's bowels like a hawk. Twice a day I asked him if he had passed gas yet, then I put my stethoscope to his battlefield of a belly. He must have been asked about passing gas four or five times a day; the question is an automatic greeting on surgical wards. Mr. Boileau was amused by our interest in his flatus. "Where I come from, polite folks don't ask about things like that," he said.

The third day after surgery I thought I heard a few rumbles, and the next day there were more. "Get those bowels churning again, Mr. Boileau," I shouted. "I'm tired of looking at you with that stupid tube up your nose."

"You'd look stupid too with a tube in *your* nose."

On my way home that evening I popped in to his room to say good night.

"Doctor," he said, "please come here." Oh no, I thought. His IV probably came out again. Phyllis and I were going out to dinner and I was already late. I didn't want to stay another hour wrestling with the IV.

"Yes?" I yelled impatiently. "What is it?" I grabbed his arm, but the IV looked fine.

"Doctor, I have something important to tell you."

"Well for God's sake what is it? I've got to go."

"Doctor, I just farted."

The morning after Mr. Boileau's wildly celebrated flatus I took out his nasogastric tube. We toasted him as he drank his first postoperative glass of apple juice. Then, since the ward was quiet I decided to wander down to my old stomping ground, the emergency ward.

"Hey, Ken," said Tom, my favorite E.W. orderly, "what brings you down to the pit?"

"Oh, just sightseeing. What've you got?"

"We got a couple of hot ones. The docs are all really busy; watch it or we'll put you to work."

I was secretly hoping he'd make that offer. The only thing I'd really done with my hands on the surgery service was to hold retractors and try to hose out Mr. Boileau's earwax — I was anxious to get back to the sewing. I volunteered to help.

Tom set up a man with a juicy scalp laceration. He was so drunk he fell asleep as soon as his head was shaved; I began peacefully joining the torn tissue. Soon the universe was only me, my sutures, and the laceration. The needle burrowed in and out of the pliant skin and the silk knotted just as my fingers asked. I was making a nice closure. How wonderful, I thought, not to have pesty interns ordering me around. And there were no lab tests to track down, no IV's to restart, no blood cultures to draw. I began to miss the Emergency Ward.

That night I was on call with Gregg. It was just after 11:00.

We sat eating the dry sandwiches and mushy apples they set out for us in the cafeteria. I told Gregg how gratifying it was to see Mr. Boileau cured by surgery and well on his way to recovery.

"Of course," he said. "As opposed to you fleas we surgeons cure patients."

"What do you mean 'fleas'?"

"Internal medicine types are fleas. All they do is crawl around on the surface of the body."

"If you guys spent a little more time crawling around on the surface you wouldn't need to go inside so often to find out what's wrong."

"Whoa! That's a little heavy for this time of night. Listen, why don't you check up on that guy with the fever; I think I'll hit the hay."

"Sure, boss, anything you say." By this time I was used to being abused, especially when we were on call.

We were on call every third night. This meant spending the night at the hospital to take care of emergencies and late admissions. This was the pattern: every third day I'd come to the hospital with my razor and toothbrush and a change of underwear. I'd be there that day, all night, and the next day until evening. Then I'd get to go home. The following day I was like a normal person; I went to work in the morning and came home in the evening. Then the next morning I packed my overnight kit again and was off for another thirty-four- or thirty-six-hour stretch.

On the call nights time stretched like taffy. As it grew dark outside I began to settle in for the long evening ahead. In theory there were unlimited possibilities for catching up on chart work, reading, and tracking down lab tests. If things were quiet I relaxed and slowed down. I sat with patients and talked with nurses.

Sometimes Phyllis came to the hospital to have dinner with me, but it was hardly ever worth her while. As we sat in the dreary cafeteria I couldn't seem to ignore all the nagging things I suddenly remembered I had to do up on the ward. To Phyllis I seemed tense and preoccupied. To me she seemed like a foreigner, impossible to communicate with. "You know," Phyllis said one time, "you're almost a different person here." I bitterly resented the hospital for coming between us.

It was at times like this that I was sure medical school was a mistake. While my college friends were hitchiking around South America or writing their Ph.D. theses I was squandering my life in endless hours of holding retractors, writing detailed chart notes that no one would read, and playing errand boy for a jerk of an intern. I had so many options after college; how could I have possibly chosen medicine? I remembered something my friend Karen Grieves had said during our first year: "Medical school is intellectually the easiest but emotionally the most difficult of the graduate fields."

I usually got to bed well after midnight. I slept on the bottom level of a creaky iron bunk bed. Gregg slept on the top. "I'll let you answer the phone," he said to me our first night on call. "That will give you experience in dealing with emergencies. If you have any real problems, just wake me up; I'll be right here."

Even though I was exhausted from being on my feet all day it was always hard to fall asleep. The problem wasn't the swayback mattress, or even Gregg's snoring. It was the black plastic time-bomb on the chair next to my bed—the telephone. It sat silently ticking, ready to go off at any moment. Every ring was a potential cardiac arrest.

But even when the call turned out to be less dramatic, it usually meant the loss of at least an hour's sleep. And the nurses detonated the bomb all night long: Mr. Marinelli's IV is plugged up, Mrs. Berg can't sleep, Mr. Eklund has a tummyache. I would sigh, put my white coat over the green surgical scrubs that became pajamas at night, and trudge out to the ward.

Half the time I'd find the patient with the belly pain sleeping soundly, and the IV usually ran fine when I just straightened the patient's arm. Or worse, the IV really *did* need restarting and the patient attached to it was an old man with invisible veins. When I finally got back to bed I stewed, and couldn't sleep.

The night after being on call was in some ways worse than the call night itself. The hospital that had swallowed me up for thirty-six hours then spat me out into the fading daylight. On the way home I glared at all the people on the street; everyone looked at me as merely another person on his way home from work. No one seemed to be aware of how special I was for having spent a horrible but heroic day-and-a-half at the hospital. The traffic didn't part, and I wasn't ushered through red lights—it didn't seem fair.

I arrived home exhausted and selfish. I was too tired to feel guilty for not helping with dinner, but never too tired to be cranky if it wasn't ready. I didn't feel like talking to Phyllis about the hospital, but I also didn't want to hear that my brother had called, that the cockroaches were back, and that Art and Lynn asked us to dinner on Friday. I wanted only food and sleep.

After supper I usually dozed off at the table while trying to read in my surgery textbook. Phyllis would do the dishes and then gently sleepwalk me to bed. Sometimes I defiantly stayed up, not able to read but unwilling to admit that the hospital was ruling my life.

The second night at home was the only time in the three-day cycle when I had any chance of escaping from the medicinal bars that caged my life. With a good night's sleep under my belt I could talk, help cook, and even go to the movies. Out on the street, as Phyllis and I walked arm in arm, I felt as if I were on parole. But my freedom was brief. Even as I breathed the public air I girded myself for the morning when another thirty-six-hour incarceration in the hospital-prison would begin.

About two weeks after Mr. Boileau's surgery an event occurred that was even more momentous than the first passage of gas — I finally delivered his earwax. By this time Mr. Boileau was able to sit up and hold the plastic basin under his ears like a pro. I hosed them out daily.

One morning, halfway through the second syringeful something big and solid spurted out of the left ear. I looked down into the basin — bobbing just beneath the surface of the water was a sweet-potato submarine. "Yahoo!" I shouted. I held up the basin for Mr. Boileau to see.

He squinted at the awesome plug of wax. "My God!" he said. Then I turned the syringe on the right ear. Amazingly, a big chunk of cerumen shot back out of that one too.

"Whooee," I whooped again, "a doubleheader!"

The moment of truth had finally arrived. In an even voice I said, "Testing, testing. One, two, three. Come in, Mr. Boileau, can you hear me?"

"Of course I can hear you," he said. "All I needed was to get that damned wax out of my ears!" We solemnly shook hands, and the patient in the next bed cheered. Floating in the emesis basin, the earwax honkers sat on display at the nurses' station for the rest of the day.

Removing Mr. Boileau's earwax seemed to uncork all his memories. He turned out to be a fascinating person. He grew up in a French-Canadian family that had moved to the western provinces. As a young man he had busted broncos and rode in the rodeo. Later he became a lumberjack in the big fir forests of British Columbia. He had homesteaded and he had prospected for gold. I sat with him for hours, hypnotized by his stories.

He was so tickled to be able to hear again that he'd talk to anyone within range. He got to know all the other patients, the cleaning people, the kitchen workers who brought the meal trays, and even the mysterious nurses on the night shift. He charmed everyone. Even Gregg warmed up to the old guy, and I knew this was genuine, since he had already done his cutting. But despite his new loquaciousness, as Mr. Boileau got better he complained more and more of being bored. He said he missed being able to read. This was a call to battle for me.

Early one morning I drove to Mr. Boileau's nursing home. It was an old frame building on a side street in the Jamaica Plain section. A group of vinyl-covered chairs stood in the dingy lobby, filled with overstuffed patients. The lobby smelled of urine and stale coffee and cigarette smoke. These odors seem to be a feature of every nursing home, as if they were required for state accreditation.

I went up to the nurses' station, introduced myself to the nurses' aide, and explained that I'd come to pick up Mr. Boileau's glasses. She nodded and lumbered down the hall. After a few minutes she returned with a shoebox half-full of eyeglasses.

"I just started working here, so I don't know this guy," she said. "Whenever a pair of glasses turns up they just put them in this box. We have another box for dentures; want to see?"

"No thanks," I said, "mine fit fine. Hey, isn't there anyone here who knows Mr. Boileau?"

The aide went off down the hall again. This time she returned with a huge woman who huffed and puffed through flared hairy nostrils. This was the charge nurse on the day shift.

I introduced myself once again and asked her if she knew Mr. Boileau. "Yes, of course I know George. How's the old fart doing anyway? He's one of my favorites, you know."

I told her the dual sagas of gallbladder and earwax removal and assured her he was making an excellent recovery from each. "You know," she said, "I *thought* he had cholecystitis. He had just the sort of pain I've seen before with a hot gallbladder." It turned out that she knew quite a bit of medicine. She said she once even looked in his ears with the nursing home's ancient otoscope and saw the impacted wax, but regulations wouldn't permit her to remove it. This woman was really sharp. Overweight nurses always seemed to be the best.

We pawed through the shoebox together. "They all look

the same to me, doctor," she said. "In fact I could use a pair myself."

We picked out several pairs that looked like they might belong to an eighty-year-old former lumberjack and rodeo star. The nurse put them into a disposable paper slipper for me, and off I drove to the hospital.

I went to the intensive care unit, where we began morning rounds. While waiting for Gregg I leafed through some charts, enjoying the chance to sit down. In the stillness of the new day the intensive care machines fed on the sleeping patients. Parasitic tubes sucked vital substances from the veins. Monitor wires diverted energy from the beating hearts and the respirators collected and stored each breath. The patients were keeping the machines alive.

Gregg finally arrived. Our two ICU patients were doing well, so we went out onto the ward to continue rounds. The first patient, a middle-aged woman named Mrs. Chandler, looked terrible. I had worked her up the day before when she was admitted with right upper quadrant pain, fever, and elevated liver tests. She was a female version of Mr. Boileau; there was little doubt she had cholecystitis. We had started antibiotics, but they clearly weren't helping — her pain was worse, her fever was higher, and her blood pressure was dipping. We aborted rounds and whisked her off to the operating room. Since Gregg had just done Mr. Boileau, this gallbladder belonged to the junior resident, Frank Stevens. Like Gregg, Frank loved to wield the knife. "A chance to cut is a chance to cure," he used to say.

I stood at Frank's right, toward Mrs. Chandler's feet. Across the table were Ralph Sasaki, the chief resident, and Dr. Raya, the staff surgeon. As he dissected the rectus abdominis muscles with a flourish Frank said to me, "OK, Dr. Klein, since the Boileau case has made you an expert, tell me about gallbladders." Medical students call this sadistic exercise "pimping." Somehow academic physicians seem to feel that making students squirm is a good way to teach. I asked Frank if he wanted a speech on gallbladder anatomy, physiology, pathology, or what.

"Everything."

I took a deep breath through my soggy mask and began to ressurect all I knew about gallbladders. As I droned on, Frank opened the peritoneal membrane. The liver, much to everyone's surprise, lay in a pool of blood. I decided it was time to stop the gallbladder dissertation.

Dr. Sasaki said he'd better take over, so he and Frank changed places. The ritual of aseptically changing places in midsurgery involves clasping gloved hands together against the chest and do-si-do-ing around the operating table without ever facing away from it. Going sideways, Frank tripped over the electric cautery cables.

Dr. Sasaki suctioned out the blood and lifted the front edge of the liver. Everyone gasped: there was a large laceration on its under surface, oozing blood. The gallbladder was normal. "But there was no history of trauma!" Frank said, as if to deny the presence of the tear because the patient's story didn't fit. Dr. Sasaki told me to pull back harder on my retractor, and he dove deep into the belly.

"Jesus, what a mother!" he said. "Gentlemen, I'm afraid we're not dealing with a hot gallbag."

Dr. Raya elbowed him aside and looked at the "mother" himself. "OK, Ralph," he said, "this is a good-sized laceration. God knows how she got it. Get better exposure, and use the biggest needle we've got." Dr. Sasaki put some gauze cloth on the liver edge for a firmer hold and bent it way up and back.

While he and the others were absorbed with the laceration I noticed that Sasaki's grip had tightened. He was tearing the liver's surface just beyond each of his fingertips. I wondered if the same thing would happen if you squeezed a piece of liver from the supermarket.

I wanted to point out what was happening on the top side, but the others were very involved down under, and a medical student doesn't tell a chief resident how to operate. Finally though, as the tears began to ooze blood, I decided to step out of line. "Dr. Sasaki," I said meekly, "there seem to be lacerations developing where you are applying traction to the anterior surface of the liver."

"That may be," he said, barely looking up, "but you should see the gusher we got down here!" He stepped back; I peered over fat and muscle to see that the posterior laceration was now bleeding at a good clip. They began to consider removing the left lobe.

At about this time Dr. Randall, the head of the Surgery Department, arrived. Dr. Raya had told the circulating nurse to call him in when it first began to look as if there might be trouble. Dr. Randall, as it happened, was working on a chapter in his book on liver surgery when he got the call. Sasaki quickly explained how Mrs. Chandler's infected gallbladder had turned into a lacerated liver. Again Frank said pitifully, "But there was no history of trauma!"

"No need to fret, Frank," Dr. Randall said. "Liver injury

from occult trauma can be very tough to diagnose. She needed surgery and you *took* her to surgery — you did the right thing."

Dr. Randall dove into the abdominal cavity and rooted around with authority. His serenity as he sized up the situation reassured everyone. After carefully inspecting the liver he recommended suturing rather than lobectomy to control the bleeding, gave some pearls of technical advice, and left. Despite the confidence and calm he left in his wake, the bleeding continued. The sutures Dr. Sasaki put in were tearing the liver further rather than pulling the edges together again.

Dr. Raya took over. The ominous implications of surgery passing into the hands of someone yet another notch up on the surgical hierarchy were appreciated by everyone. The room grew very quiet. I began to feel that I was retracting the abdominal wall of a corpse.

Finally, though, a stitch held. The bleeding ebbed, and Dr. Sasaki took over again and even tried to tell a joke. Everyone smiled, not at the stupid joke, but because Mrs. Chandler would live.

After the closure of the peritoneum everyone left but Frank, the scrub nurse, and of course me. Frank sewed the abdominal muscles back together with obvious relief, then threw me the usual medical student's sop — I got to sew the skin incision closed. I couldn't wait to tell Dave Rappaport.

As soon as she awoke in the recovery room, we asked Mrs. Chandler if she had been hit in the belly. She said no. But her husband later let on that she had been drinking heavily two days before admission. He thought she had said something about falling down the basement stairs.

Several days later Mrs. Chandler's abdominal drains were out and she was doing fairly well. Then she developed a low-grade fever. Frank explained that this was due to atelectasis, the incomplete expansion of a section of lung. We tried to get her to reinflate the lung through coughing and breathing exercises, but she wouldn't cooperate; her incision hurt too much. Frank said she'd get pneumonia if we couldn't clear the atelectasis — we had to make her cough.

The solution was to force a cough by inserting a transtracheal catheter. This, he explained to my horror, was a thin plastic tube whose end sits in the windpipe: you punch a large needle into the trachea through the skin just below the adam's apple. Then the flexible tube is threaded through it and the needle withdrawn. So one end of the tube sits in the trachea, and the other end is capped and taped in place on the side of the neck. Several times a day you remove the cap and squirt in some sterile water. This causes a violent fit of coughing. My horror at Frank's description of this torture device was greater still when he told me that *I* was going to insert it. There's a popular saying among medical students in big city hospitals that goes, "See one, do one, teach one." But even this formula was being abbreviated.

How different this was from the way my friends in nursing school were taught! Even for things as simple as taking a blood pressure or giving an injection they had a whole series of lectures and demonstrations. Then they practiced on each other. Finally they had to pass a proficiency test before being turned loose on real patients. In contrast, we were often shown how to do something only once, then expected to do the next one on our own. It's not hard to understand how medical students could see their minimal training for complex procedures as evidence that they're special people who can do no wrong.

I carried the supplies to Mrs. Chandler's bedside with trembling hands, and our ordeal began. Frank told me where to inject the novocaine. "I'm going to inject the novocaine now, Mrs. Chandler," I said, trying to sound as if I knew what I was doing independently of Frank's instructions. I shared the terror this poor woman must have felt as her neck was assaulted by a medical student getting play-by-play instructions. I wanted to apologize: "I'm sorry, Mrs. Chandler. I don't like this either, but Frank's making me do it."

Fortunately things went well. Mrs. Chandler was periodically forced into spasms of painful but presumably therapeutic coughing, and she recovered without further incident.

The afternoon of Mrs. Chandler's surgery I finally had time to take the glasses to Mr. Boileau. He was lying in bed, humming a Sousa march in time to the beeping of his roommate's cardiac monitor.

"Mr. Boileau," I said, "I come bearing gifts." I dumped the glasses out on the bed. "Recognize any of these?"

"How could I, dummy — I can't see without my spectacles."

"Hey, let's have a little respect around here." I put a pair of bifocals on his face. "How are these?"

"No," he said, "the old codger who belongs to these is in even worse shape than me!" I put on a second pair, which turned out to be no better.

Then came some black horn-rims. "How do you like these, sir?" I asked. "I think they're rather stunning myself."

"Well, I don't think they're mine, but they see good. I'll take them."

"Very good, sir. Would you care to pay now, or shall we bill you?"

"I'll pay now. I always pay cash."

So Mr. Boileau was fully reconstituted. He read all the trash on the ward in a few days. I began bringing him books from home. Soon he was walking in the halls and eating like his old self.

The day came when he was finally ready to go. I called the nursing home and made the transfer arrangements. We had a little party for Mr. Boilcau the day he left. One of the nurses made a pumpkin cream pie. She called it "cerumen chiffon."

With Mr. Boileau's departure my time on the surgery wards drew to an end. I breathed a long sigh of relief and thought back over the last three months. Despite an extraordinary amount of wasted time, despite an unforgivable lack of sleep, and despite endless abuse at the hands of my intern, I had somehow learned a lot. It wasn't only about gallbladders and earwax and sewing up heads either. I was developing medical instincts: I was getting a feel for which sorts of symptoms could be watched at leisure and which needed immediate attention. I was beginning to be able to sense how sick a patient really was. And I was learning how to approach patients efficiently. Finally, as some of the terror and frustration in dealing with patients began to be forgotten, I was getting an inkling of how satisfying this business of caring for patients could be, even patients like those on the surgery wards at the Boston City.

Surgery ended on a Friday. I packed up my little overnight kit for the last time and said good-bye to the nurses and the patients and even to Gregg Wolfe, and walked out into the twilight of evening. On the way to the parking lot I sighed another long sigh and felt free. But almost immediately I began thinking about the next quarter year. It would be a time of stress, perhaps even more than surgery. First, the next rotation was internal medicine, another three-month blockbuster. Second, Phyllis was going back up to Goddard for winter term. It would be incredibly lonely. But on the other hand, with Phyllis gone perhaps I could completely give myself over to medicine without feeling so much resentment and guilt. Maybe I could drown my loneliness with work. I wasn't anxious to find out.

7

Dealing with Death
Internal Medicine

THE DAY AFTER Phyllis left for Vermont I made an expedition to the Stop & Shop. I bought four boxes of spaghetti, a dozen tins of sardines, and six frozen chickens. I was stockpiling for the long dark winter of my next rotation.

Internal medicine was the most demanding of the clinical rotations. There was an incredible amount to be learned. The hours were very long. The work was hard, both intellectually and emotionally. And there was tremendous pressure to do well. For two years it had been drummed into us that the grade was of major importance. Just as a good grade in organic chemistry was supposedly the key to getting into medical school, doing well in internal medicine was said to assure a good internship. Especially for those of us who planned to become internists, the stakes were high.

Over the last year it had become clear that I'd go into internal medicine, or simply "medicine," as it's known in the trade. The intellectual appeal of neurophysiology had lost out to the rewards of working with people. With its emphasis on careful diagnosis and treatment of internal disorders, medicine seemed to be the clinical field where I could best salvage some science.

The Beth Israel Hospital was my choice for the medicine rotation. It had the reputation as the friendliest and most humane of the teaching hospitals; I figured I'd need all the help I could get. The rotation was divided into thirds; a month on each of three ward services. On each one I'd join a ward team with whom I would live almost twenty-four hours a day. My principal partner in this group marriage would be an intern. Together we'd care for about eight to fifteen patients. Another student-intern pair would do the same. Supervising both pairs would be a medical resident. Over the resident, and acting as father figure to the whole team, was the staff physician called the "visit."

As it had been for surgery, the medicine rotation was really an apprenticeship — I'd learn the craft of patient care by working with the people on my team. Occasionally there would be formal lectures to the students, but the great bulk of learning would come from seeing and helping to treat diseases in the flesh. I knew that the people to whom I was apprenticed would teach me more than just facts. They would also transmit styles and attitudes and philosophies. They would be socializing me as well as educating me into doctorhood, like it or not.

The night of my Stop & Shop expedition, after I had stashed away all the provisions, I pulled out my typewriter and wrote a letter to Phyllis. When I had finished I decided to leave the typewriter on my desk. I thought I'd try to keep a record of the momentous and lonely time that was about to begin. I wanted to remember not only the medicine I would learn; I wanted to remember how I'd learned it. I wanted to remember the jumble of days and nights that lay ahead. I wanted to remember the confusion and stress, and the excitement and satisfaction that would all be a part of the experience. I knew I was being changed into a physician, perhaps slowly, but surely. I wanted to be able to look back and recall how it had happened.

To my surprise I was faithful to my typewriter. Every night or two, after I had eaten my spaghetti or my sardines, I'd type a few pages about what had happened at the hospital that day. When I was done, or sometimes before I was done, I'd sink into bed and fall fast asleep.

January 4

Today was the first day of internal medicine. All these months and what seems like years and years of medical school, I consoled my ignorance with the thought that if I didn't know something I'd learn it during the medicine rotation. Suddenly, this is it. When I finish these three months I'll be close to being an intern — a doctor. I still feel so far.

Compared to surgery, internal medicine already seems so stiff and formal. There's much more of a premium on what you say. Maybe that's because a surgeon can always cut, but an internist often can't do anything for a patient but stand around and talk. My new intern, Don Murphy, is a real internal medicine type. Everything about him is intense but under control — his manner, his clothes, even his compulsively trimmed black hair and beard. Don is such a contrast to my last intern. Gregg Wolfe was so simple and straightforward; Don, on the other hand, bubbles over with ideas and worries and equivocations.

For this first month I'll be on ward Four South. Twice a week the other student and I have to present cases to the visit. One of the visit's functions, I'm told, is to make students twist and squirm in front of the entire ward team. This somehow enhances learning. People say I speak well. But when I feel nervous I get all inarticulate and slobbery — I'm afraid this will happen when I present, and there goes my grade.

I'm worried about my grade. Even though I'm going into internal medicine, I feel so ignorant compared to my classmates — they already all seem to know how to read EKG's and do blood smears and interpret chest x-rays. Maybe I should simply resign myself to a C and just learn as much as I can.

The next three months will be a huge block of time sacrificed totally to the hospital. My entire life will be consumed by medicine; it's probably good that Phyllis is up in Vermont. I'm looking ahead to a bleak, tense, exhausting quarter of a year.

January 5

I was right. I've been on medicine for only two days and it has already taken over my life. Last night was my first night on call. I got three hours' sleep. At home now all that matters is food and sleep. And while I eat I read medicine, and when I sleep I dream about patients, confusion, worry.

Last night I worked up my first patient. John McMaster is a very pleasant old man who I think has a liver tumor. He was feeling fine but came to the hospital because he noticed a big lump in his belly. "It doesn't hurt," he told me, "but it doesn't seem as if it ought to be there — I thought I'd better get it checked out."

I sat down on the side of his bed and began asking questions: Was his appetite good? Had he lost any weight? What about his bowel movements? And then I began my exam, checking his eyes and ears and throat and lymph nodes. Finally I came to the abdomen. There was a rock-hard mass high up in the belly, over where the liver sits. It was a tumor.

My excitement grew. I asked more questions and poked some more, trying to understand this malignancy. Was it a primary liver cancer or did it arise elsewhere and spread to the liver? I was hot on the trail of a tumor.

Suddenly it occurs to me that this interesting diagnostic problem is a man with children and grandchildren and friends who love him. And it also occurs to me that this man will soon be dead. In my frantic effort to make a diagnosis, I forgot the meaning of that lump on the liver. I forgot that the tumor is not in a jar; it lives in Mr. McMaster's belly. He can't walk away from it at the end of the day as I can. To him it's not an interesting case at all — it's his death.

January 8

I'm home after my second night on call, exhausted. Once more I got only a few hours' sleep. Again and again I wonder why I'm doing this. At 3:30 in the morning my intern and I were walking down the long dark hallway of Four South. We'd just examined the urine of a patient who had spiked a fever, probably from a kidney or bladder infection. Don got on the subject of kidney stones. He explained the different types of stones and their causes. Then, with a real gleam in his eye he said, "Regular chemical analysis is really no good for figuring out the structure of a kidney stone because its surface gets coated with all sorts of crud. So what you have to do is x-ray crystallography; let me show you." But in the middle of the night I didn't care. I just wanted to sleep.

In a daze I followed Don to the library. To my amazement there were people up reading. He pulled out a book about kidney stones and showed me pictures of the various types. He turned to the section on x-ray diffraction and went over the different patterns. And then, despite my yawns, he began telling me about a patient he took care of once. She had kidney stones due to a rare metabolic disease called cystinuria. Don, thank you for all your knowledge and enthusiasm and interest in teaching. You're such a nice contrast to Gregg Wolfe. But don't you understand that at 4 A.M. my only interest is sleep? You are really a madman. Do I have to be one too to be a good doctor?

January 9

Today I presented my first case to Dr. Fine, our visit. It went pretty well, even though I had diarrhea all morning. The whole thing seemed so contrived and theatrical. The other medical student and the interns and resident gathered in the patients' dayroom and waited reverently. When Dr. Fine at last arrived, nervous smiles flashed all around the room, and we all said hello. Don actually called him by his first name! I was awed.

I bow, hand Mr. McMaster's chart to Dr. Fine, and take a deep breath. Then I begin a formal recitation of the case.

Almost every paragraph starts with a set formula. I just fill in the blanks: "THIS IS THE *first* BETH ISRAEL HOSPITAL ADMISSION FOR THIS *71* YEAR-OLD *man* WHO ENTERS WITH A CHIEF COMPLAINT OF *awareness of a mass in the abdomen* FOR *three* DAYS." I recall my brief time on the debating team in high school. I played one match, lost, and quit. We were judged on form and style, not on what we were trying to communicate. Saying things in the right way was key.

After visit rounds all the students doing medicine at the Beth Israel had a meeting with Dr. King, the professor who supervises the rotation. After a welcoming spiel he asked if anyone had anything they'd like to talk about. The room was still. Then, to my surprise, I blurted out a question: "Dr. King, everyone knows how tense students are made to feel on this rotation. Do you think that's a necessary part of the process of medical education?"

"Of course not," he said. "I'm distressed that you feel that way. Why should you feel tense? You don't have to compete to prove anything anymore — obviously you're all the cream of the crop or you wouldn't be here." Then he got off on a long harangue about how overrated grades were. "Ignore grades," he told us piously; "just work for the knowledge." He didn't explain, though, why we had been told for two years of the ultimate importance of the medicine grade. And he didn't explain why the patient dayroom was tight with tension when a student presented a case to the visit, and why you could always find medical students in the library in the middle of the night desperately reading for rounds the next morning.

January 10

Frances Morris is a miserable old woman. We don't know much about her, but she has apparently been demented for the last fifteen years. She was admitted to the hospital from her nursing home a month ago; they said she was getting weaker. Now she won't feed herself and she refuses to be fed by the nurses. She continues to live, rigid and moaning and crazy, because there is a feeding tube in her nose which goes down into her stomach. Every four hours a nurse squirts a syringeful of highly nutritious liquid into the tube. Frances never speaks, or even looks at you.

Today she pulled out the tube. I went down to her room with Don to help him replace it. Frances's husband and her daughter were there. The daughter was trying to feed her. "Now, dear, take just one little bite for me," she said as she shoved the spoon into her mother's sputtering mouth. It was a daughter's revenge.

Don cleared his throat and all three people looked up. Frances had a big growth of custard on her lower lip. Her daughter immediately began assaulting Don: "If you really want to know honest to God what's wrong with Mother, it's that she doesn't have her dentures. She'd eat fine if she had them; Mother was always embarrassed to be without her teeth." Don asked her where they were. "I think the lowers got lost in the sheets when they were making the bed the other day. You know, doctor, if the hospital wasn't so careless and insensitive, Mother would be fine." Don nodded and then asked her and her father to wait out in the hall while we replaced the feeding tube.

I held Frances's pitiful bony head while Don forced the

tube into her nose. She fought and gagged and rocked her legs. The tube wouldn't go down. I pried open her jaws and shone a flashlight into her mouth. Don spotted the tube curled up behind the tongue and guided it back to the esophagus. The beam of the flashlight lit up mossy patches of food on Frances's palate. Her breath had the odor of death.

She continued to fight Don off, grabbing for his tie and sometimes, it seemed, his balls. But it was the two of us against her and we won. Don looped the tubing up from her nose to her forehead and taped it in place. Then we made sure she wouldn't yank it out again. We wrapped her hands with layers of gauze and adhesive tape and tied her arms to the bedrails with twisted bedsheets. She looked like a punch-drunk boxer tangled up in the ropes. She was down for the count.

We left her room in a rush, striding brightly down the hall with all our equipment, leaving her daughter and husband in our wake to continue their visit.

January 11

Today we had a talk by a visiting cardiology professor named Dr. Heckman, a flashy character who really wowed the crowd. In front of an audience of 30 staff and students Don presented a complicated patient from our ward, a woman with three different heart murmurs. Dr. Heckman then examined her and analyzed the case. It was a brilliant performance. He was incisive and witty. And he was totally insensitive to the patient. He never introduced himself to her. While listening to her heart he pushed her around like a side of beef. And without a word of explanation in lay terms he talked about her "advanced valvular heart disease with a poor prognosis."

At lunch afterward I sat down next to the chief resident, Tom Wagner. "Well, Ken," he said, "how'd you like Dr. Heckman — pretty impressive, huh?"

"Yes, he knows his cardiology all right. But Jesus, Tom, he treated Mrs. Collins like shit!"

"Don't be so naive. Heckman was under tremendous pressure to dazzle the audience; he didn't come here to give a course on bedside manner. Besides, I'll bet Mrs. Collins was flattered to be examined by a famous cardiologist."

The others at the table agreed with Tom. He's probably right. I'm naive, I'm overreacting. My perspective seems to be so different; what's wrong with me?

January 13

I was just thinking how nice it would be to go to the midnight movie at the Orson Welles again, the way Phyllis and I always used to when we lived in Cambridge. Then I realized that of course I'm still here; it's *Phyllis* who's gone! This funny feeling of separateness from everyday things reminds me of coming home for vacation freshman year of college. I felt so alienated from all the familiar things around me — shopping at Snyder's, driving through Rock Creek Park, playing miniature golf. I felt superior to everything; after all I was a college student. Now, though, it's these normal everyday things that I respect and crave. I'm the inferior one, living in such a queer constricted world.

January 16

When Mr. McMaster needed some arterial blood drawn today I decided I wanted to do it myself, without help from Don. But as I was about to begin I realized I needed someone to compress the artery while I iced the specimen and sent it off to the lab. I fretted about what to do. Instead of grabbing the nearest nurse, as any doctor would have done, I kept wandering up and down the hall trying to get up the nerve to ask for help. But I didn't know which nurse covered which patient. And even if I got the right nurse I was afraid she'd be insulted by a mere medical student asking for a favor — the nurses always seemed so busy. I felt small and foolish wandering the halls with my syringe while the ice melted in the basin on Mr. McMaster's bedside stand. Finally after 10 or 15 minutes I saw Peter Mundy, the other student, come out of a patient's room. I asked him for help. "Sure," he said, "I'd be glad to hold the artery. But why didn't you just ask a nurse?"

January 17

Julie Stein is a tiny old woman. She was admitted to our ward with pneumonia two days ago. Last night she got confused and dove over the bedrails, trying to find her way to the toilet. I was called by the angry and embarrassed nurse. "Now why didn't that stupid patient just ring the call bell instead of trying to get out of bed by herself!" she said. The nurse didn't understand that Julie was not a stupid patient. She was an old confused woman who knew only that she was caged in her bed and needed to urinate.

I knelt down to Julie where she still lay on the floor; she wouldn't let the nurse help her up. "Mrs. Stein," I said, "how are you?"

"I'm fine, mister, I'm just fine. But I have to make pee-pee."

I helped her to the toilet, and when she was done walked her back to bed. Then I examined her for a head injury and broken bones. Everything was normal. "Goodnight, Mrs. Stein," I said and tucked her in. As an afterthought I tied a rolled bedsheet from bedrail to bedrail, across her chest.

When we saw her on rounds this morning something seemed wrong. Finally I realized she wasn't looking at us. I jabbed my hand in front of her eyes; she didn't blink. Don and I examined her in detail. Then we ordered some skull x-rays and tests looking for what might be causing the sudden blindness. There was no subdural hematoma. But as a result of the fall she seems to have suffered some sort of a stroke.

This afternoon when I went by to check on her I noticed a sign the nurses had put on the wall above her bed: "PATIENT IS BLIND." Jesus, I thought, couldn't they at least have said, "Patient can't see"? "Blind" seemed so cruel and final; it was horrible to read. Julie Stein came in with pneumonia and will leave without her sight. I'm learning that the hospital is not a safe place to be.

January 18

Last night I worked up a patient named Rose Levine, a 78-year-old woman with a bizarre disease called agnogenic myeloid metaplasia. The diagnosis had been made several months ago. She was brought in by her family last night because she was growing weaker.

She had lost weight, yet her abdomen was enormous. It was filled by the massively enlarged liver and spleen. They had grown trying to do the job of the bone marrow, which had been replaced by a mass of fibrous tissue. Mrs. Levine looked like she had been drawn by her five-year-old granddaughter: her stick arms and legs protruded out from a big round belly.

I was up late with this wonderful pitiful old woman, asking questions, examining her crumbling body, doing a cardiogram, taking blood. By the time I was done we were both dozing off. I said goodnight and headed for the library to learn about agnogenic myeloid metaplasia. Until I read the diagnosis on her chart I had never even heard of it.

I left Mrs. Levine's room and walked down the quiet hallway to the elevator. Outside several rooms heart monitors peeped to each other in the darkness. The soft green cardiogram tracings bobbed and dipped in time to the peeping, like athletic glowworms doing their exercises. Secure snores floated out into the hallway, and occasionally a patient said something in a dream. The whole ward was softly sleeping. I had an unexpected rush of maternal feeling. These were my babies, all peaceful and snug in their beds. I was a contented parent, responsible for their care. I said goodnight to my children, then stepped onto the elevator.

Even in the middle of the night the library was alive with white-coated ghosts poring over medical texts. I found the journal article on agnogenic myeloid metaplasia that Don had told me about — I'm convinced he knows everything — and sat down to read. I had to present Mrs. Levine's case to Dr. Fine in the morning; it was important that I knew my stuff. To my surprise, even in the middle of the night I was excited to learn more about this strange disease that had taken possession of my patient's body. As I read I began to understand why her arms were so thin and covered with bruises, why her belly was so big, and why she had had infections.

After tussling with the long article until 2:30, I went to bed, anxious for the dawn and the chance to wow Dr. Fine with my knowledge. Even though I was exhausted, it was hard to get to sleep. When I finally did, the operator called immediately to tell me that it was 6:30, time to get up.

An hour later I sat at attention with a cup of coffee in my hand, waiting for Dr. Fine in the patient dayroom. I was to present the first case. The others came and settled in. Then Dr. Fine appeared, smiling, vigorous, and immaculately dressed in a three-piece suit. I nodded, handed him Mrs. Levine's chart, and began my recitation.

Don nodded off while I was still on the medical history. By the time I got to the physical exam I noticed that Peter Mundy and the resident were peacefully dozing. Nevertheless, I trudged on: "The patient was edentulous and the buccal mucosa was pink and moist with scattered petechiae. The posterior pharynx showed atrophic tonsils. The tongue was red and smooth and the neck . . ."

" — Wait!" said Dr. Fine. Everyone jerked awake. "Tell

me, Kenneth, what diseases can cause a smooth red tongue?"

I mumbled something, I don't remember what. Then Fine began pummeling me with questions: How is the tongue in iron deficiency anemia different from the pernicious anemia tongue? What does the tongue look like in pellagra? In riboflavin deficiency? In beriberi? And, speaking of beriberi, what is the mechanism of edema in wet beriberi?

I squirmed, and I was angry. I'd invested a precious two hours in the middle of the night to become an expert on agnogenic myeloid metaplasia. Yet Dr. Fine was asking me lots of garbage about vitamins! I answered as best I could, impatient to get on to my patient's disease.

Finally we got off tongues and beriberi and he let me finish my presentation without further molestation. Then, at last, came the magic question: "Well, Kenneth, what *is* this entity 'agnogenic myeloid metaplasia'? Tell us about it."

I smiled and nodded. Then I gave a scholarly homily that seemed to please him. Afterward Peter Mundy congratulated me on my performance. "Jesus," he said, "I knew you must have read about myeloid metaplasia, but how did you know so much about tongues?"

"I don't know. I guess I faked it."

A few days ago at one of our EKG teaching sessions a similar thing happened. I got called on to read an EKG that was projected onto a screen at the front of the room. The jagged lines of the heartbeat were over a foot tall — it must have been the cardiogram of a whale. I went up to the huge tracing and mumbled what I thought was a pretty pitiful interpretation. But after I had sunk back down in my seat a classmate leaned over and whispered, "That was great, Ken; I don't believe how well you know this stuff!"

I was stunned. I'm never sure if compliments like this are deserved. Did I truly understand that cardiogram and did I really know the answers when Dr. Fine was speaking in tongues? Or am I just smart enough to guess what the instructor is after? I always wonder how deep my understanding really is. I compare myself to Don, and get discouraged.

January 19

Today I ordered a nebulized mist mask and chest physical therapy for rickety old Mrs. Levine with the bulging belly. I was afraid she was getting a pneumonia. After I wrote the order I went down to her room and sat with her and her omnipresent family and told them what to expect. They were so appreciative for the explanation. I felt good for the rest of the day.

But now I'm sad as I realize that doing something like this means so much less than quoting from last week's *New England Journal of Medicine.* Not that it's such a big deal to warn the Levines about the coming of physical therapy and the big plastic mask. But I feel bitter that no one teaches us to do things like that, or even seems to care.

January 20

They're deciding what to do about Mr. McMaster and the mass in his abdomen. Don thinks he should have an operation. I don't. Everyone agrees that it's a tumor of some sort, and the x-rays and scans show that it's in the liver. The question is what kind of a tumor is it and where is it from.

"What difference does it make?" I asked Don. "If it's a primary liver tumor there's no cure, and if it has spread from somewhere else there's no treatment either. Mr. McMaster is still feeling pretty good. Why subject him to an operation that might kill him just to find out what type of cancer it is? Why not send him home to be with his family, and give him pain medication when he needs it?"

"Hey, take it easy," Don said. "I think you're getting too emotionally involved with your patient. When you're taking care of someone you have to remain objective and do what's medically best."

"So why is an operation just to satisfy your curiosity medically best?"

"Put yourself in his place, Ken. Wouldn't you want to know what sort of a tumor you had? He's got to order the rest of his life, you know."

"What little of it he has left! No, I wouldn't care particularly if it was a hepatoma I was dying of, or a metastatic pancreatic cancer. I think *you're* the one who wants to know, Don."

"Ken, you're being naive. How can you take proper care of a patient if you don't know what's wrong with him? And what if he really doesn't *have* a tumor? What if it's something else?"

"But Don, you told me yourself the night Mr. McMaster came in that the only thing that feels like that is 'the big C,' remember?"

"Well, yes, it's probably cancer — that's true — but we

never know for sure until we have a tissue diagnosis. It would be terrible to be missing something else, especially something we might be able to treat. We can't take that chance."

We reviewed Mr. McMaster's case with Dr. Fine this morning on visit rounds. Dr. Fine cast the deciding vote: surgery is scheduled for later in the week.

January 22

Gloria Milner is a prima donna. She has staked out a two-patient room for herself. Today she insisted on a new mattress for her bed because last night she didn't sleep well. And she has a teenaged daughter who is always with her. Already today her daughter has given her three back rubs!

Gloria Milner is a 44-year-old economics professor whose doctor sent her into the hospital yesterday because of fevers for the last two months. She also has had joint pains and a heart murmur. She was admitted to Four South, so I'll help take care of her even though she has her own private doctor.

Things became uncomfortable from the minute I first met her. "Hi, Mrs. Milner," I said, "I'm Kenneth Klein. I'll be your medical student while you're here in the hospital."

"Please," she said, "my name is *Dr.* Milner. I have a Ph.D. in economics."

Getting a medical history was agonizing. She tried desperately to keep control of the conversation. She constantly mentioned her doctor and what he had to say about her case: "Dr. Hunter says I have a heart murmur. He thinks that my symptoms are due to an infected heart valve. It's called 'subacute bacterial endocarditis.'"

"Yes, I know all about SBE," I said. But we both knew I really didn't.

It was hard to get her to answer any questions. "Do we have to go over this again?" she kept asking. "I already told all this to Dr. Hunter." I tried to explain that I was helping. Dr. Hunter take care of her, so I needed to know her case too.

Finally it was time for the physical. Simply getting the bed flat was an ordeal. With the electric control she brought the head of the bed down only a few inches at a time. Then she'd stop and I'd have to readjust her pillow. "My joints hurt so much, Kenneth," she said. "You're probably too young to know what it's like to have real pain."

Finally I got her horizontal. I asked her if she would unbutton her pajama tops so I could examine her breasts and her heart. She unbuttoned the flannel shirt and threw it open. I checked her breasts and listened to her heart murmur. Then I tried to button her back together again. "Don't bother," she said.

Next, when I asked her to pull her bottoms down just a bit so I could examine her belly she pulled them halfway to her knees. I tried to hike them up above her groin for decency, but she said, "What's wrong, Kenneth? You *are* going to be a doctor, aren't you?" I felt so stupid and helpless sitting on the bed with this woman whose pajamas were practically off. What if a nurse walked in? What if Dr. Hunter walked in? The situation was out of hand.

I hurried through the rest of the exam. She finally buttoned her pajamas and then asked me to help her sit up.

While my hand was around her back, hoisting her up, she looked at my nametag. "Doctor Kenneth Klein," she said with a sigh, adding the "doctor" herself. "Your mother must be proud of you." Then she asked if I were married. I lied that I was. "Well, I suppose your wife must be even prouder. You know, Kenneth, you've been very kind to me. You have a very nice bedside manner. You'll make a fine doctor someday."

I was confused about what was happening. I didn't like not having things under control. I knew Gloria Milner was going to be trouble.

All that was yesterday. Today was the real disaster. The lab called to say that the blood cultures I drew from her yesterday were growing what seem to be two types of bacteria. This is very unusual — in SBE the heart valve is generally infected with only one bug, which it sheds into the bloodstream. Whenever more than one bacteria is cultured out, the suspicion is always that the specimen was contaminated. I would have to draw more cultures to be certain. Unfortunately, Milner has lousy veins and is extremely needle-shy. I wasn't anxious to stick her again. I went down to her room carrying the vampire tray, sat down on her bed, and carefully explained why I had to take more blood.

After I left her room with the precious vials, I began wondering if it was right to have told her all that. I asked Don what he thought. He didn't have to think long. He simply suggested that I say good-bye to my testicles because they would belong to Dr. Hunter as soon as he found out what I'd done. "Jesus, Ken," he said, "Milner's a private patient. You don't tell a private patient she might have bugs in her blood. You don't tell a private patient *anything*. The patient's doctor is the only one who gives out information."

"But, Don, I just wanted to explain why I had to stick her again. And Hunter has already told her he thought she had SBE; she *knew* that she might have positive blood cultures."

"I agree; what you did was very reasonable. Unfortunately, though, it was wrong. Always call the private doctor and have *him* tell the patient."

I still hadn't met Dr. Hunter, though I was taking care of his patient. But I knew his reputation. They say he is a very meticulous cardiologist who likes indirect methods. I decided to get it over with; the sooner I told him what I had done, the better. One of the nurses, who had agreed to be my spy, paged me when Dr. Hunter appeared on the ward.

I strode right up to him and introduced myself. "Dr. Hunter," I said, "I have something unpleasant to tell you." I told him exactly what I had done, then winced. I deserved everything I was about to get.

Dr. Hunter didn't blow up. He just frowned. But I could sense a seething behind his placid cardiologist's face. "You shouldn't have told her that," he simply said. Then he walked away.

I'm really scared. I came between a doctor and his patient, apparently a serious crime. If Dr. Hunter with his indirect methods tells Dr. King my grade is shot, and so is a decent internship.

I called up Phyllis in Vermont a few minutes ago. She said that what I did was right. She said it makes sense to tell patients the truth — they usually know something's going on anyway. And besides, it was only courteous to tell the patient why I needed to draw her blood again.

"But, Phyllis," I said, "I came between a doctor and his patient!"

"Big deal."

January 23

Lunch today was a truly nauseating experience. I ended up in the cafeteria line behind Dr. Fine and Peter Mundy; I had no choice but to sit with them. Dr. Fine's specialty is high blood pressure — guess what we talked about over our plastic ravioli. Peter did some really Olympic ass-kissing; he never misses an opportunity to butter up the visit. "Dr. Fine," he asked, "can you tell us about your research on the action of guanethidine as an antihypertensive agent?" Then, "Do you think reserpine currently has any place in the treatment of high blood pressure?" And, "In your experience, what is the long-term prognosis of malignant hypertension?" They blabbed on and on.

These people aren't human. Why can't they talk about anything normal — skiing, news, even the weather? For me the cafeteria is a precious refuge from the wards, a chance to regain a little contact with the outside world. How can they squander lunch over high blood pressure?

This isn't to say I don't like medicine. It's just that other things are important to me too; medicine isn't the core of my life. I don't know, though; if I want to be a good doctor maybe it should be.

January 24

I went to John McMaster's operation today. Even though I didn't think surgery should have been done, I was still curious about this tumor I'd been feeling these last weeks. What did it look like? Where was it from?

It was surprisingly pleasant to be back in the operating room, a privileged sanctuary where medical students are immune from pages and teaching sessions. After my stint on surgery I finally felt comfortable with the O.R. routine. Scrubbing was a cinch. I even got my gloves and gown on without a speck of panic.

The surgeons were really nice to me. I think they were flattered that even an apprentice flea wanted to watch. They patiently explained the anatomy they were traversing and took pains to make sure I got a good view. It was as if they were proudly displaying their own internal organs.

As they opened the peritoneum, though, they stopped talking. The solemn moment when knowledge is revealed was near. Soon the five of us in the operating room would know the nature of Mr. McMaster's tumor, information shared by no one else on earth.

The liver looked like a subterranean vegetable garden. The dark soil of its capsule was studded with little tumor-mushrooms, feeding greedily. Even where there were no obvious tumors there were ominous bulges and puckerings, suggesting sproutings beneath the surface. And growing out of the left lobe of the liver was the mass we had all felt, a big tough cauliflower of a cancer. Did all this exuberant growth originate in the liver, or was the cancer seeding from elsewhere? The surgeons prowled the abdomen for an answer.

The tumor, it turned out, was from the pancreas. The head of the pancreas was swollen and distorted like a hard ugly fist. The tumor within it had begun to strangle the duodenum and the common bile duct. If it cuts off either of these structures, Mr. McMaster will go fast.

There was nothing to be done. The surgeons took a few biopsies to confirm the obvious. Then they shook their heads and sewed up John McMaster's belly, sealing in the cancer.

So the surgeons will triumphantly announce the type of tumor that will kill Mr. McMaster. Don and Dr. Fine will have their curiosity satisfied. But even with this knowledge neither Don nor Dr. Fine nor anyone else will be able to do anything more for Mr. McMaster. I hope this mistaken surgery doesn't hurry his death.

January 26

Today was a good day. On call last night I admitted a medical disaster area. Her name is Elizabeth Bander, an elderly woman with sixteen different medical problems. She knows all the doctors and nurses at the Beth Israel; she's practically a professional patient. Her current job is being hospitalized for fevers and chills for the last two weeks.

I spent three hours going through the five volumes of her hospital records. I sorted out all her ailments and summarized the grisly history of each. There were the colon cancer and the TB, the diabetes and the kidney failure, her heart attacks, her mastectomy, her gout. I was the first one ever to attempt this masochistic task, but somehow it was worth it. I was undoubtedly the only person to ever have mastered the case of Elizabeth Bander. My write-up was fifteen pages long. When I finally finished at three in the morning I treated myself to a Reese's peanut butter cup.

I didn't get much sleep last night but today I was unaccountably perky. I'm looking after five patients now. I had time to sit and talk with each of them and I wrote good progress notes in each of their charts. What a prosperous feeling, to be caught up with all my patients! For the first time in my life I can actually imagine myself as a doctor. And I'm looking forward to it. Enduring medical school, it seems, may be worth it after all.

I even did a new procedure today; I tapped the effusion from Mrs. Oppenheim's lung. She's a sweet Jewish grandmother with breast cancer. Her first two questions when I admitted her three days ago were was I Jewish and was I married. What a loyal grandmother — even with her cancer she was on the lookout for the ultimate catch for her granddaughter!

It had been getting hard for Mrs. Oppenheim to breathe. Her tumor had spread to the lining of the left lung, causing an accumulation of fluid. We decided it had to be drained. I'd seen a lung tap done several times before; Don said I could do this one.

I found the correct spot on the chest and prepared the skin with iodine and novocaine. Then I slipped a needle between her ribs to the area of the fluid and took off several quarts of pale yellow liquid. It reminded me of chicken soup.

After I had finished, Mrs. Oppenheim felt a little irritation where the needle had gone in. She grew frantic. "Oy, oy, docta," she yelled, "I'm going to die! This is it, docta; pray for me!"

I listened to her lungs and took her blood pressure and

held her hand and gave her reassurance. I don't think she believed me when I told her that everything was OK. But when I pointed out that her breathing seemed a lot easier since we took off the fluid, she realized it was true, and calmed down. I stayed with her for a few minutes more, talking about potato kugel and matzoh-ball soup. Soon she was back to normal.

"Docta," she said as I got up to leave her room, "you're a real mensch. I should have a son like you! I'll take you home and treat you like a king. Come home with me, docta." It was hard to say no.

January 28

I finally got a young patient today. What a nice change it is to be taking care of someone near my own age! I'm weary of old people with cancer.

Ned Carney is a twenty-nine-year-old man who probably has regional enteritis, a type of inflammatory bowel disease. Even his disease is a nice change from all the old people's illnesses that surround me. But it may be harder to take care of this man who has a disease I could easily have too. It's impossible to imagine being a John McMaster or a Mrs. Oppenheim. But it's easy to identify with Ned. It really hurts to see him with fevers and belly pain, on the bedpan ten times day. Dealing with his wife will be different from dealing with my older patients' spouses too — she could be my friend or my lover, not my grandmother. This may be more difficult, but I'm looking forward to it. I think I'll learn a lot from Ned and his wife.

January 30

Today I made my first real diagnosis. The honored patient was Elizabeth Bander, the medical disaster area. With all her medical problems she had a Sears catalogue of potential causes for her fevers. I figured she'd be on Four South for weeks while we ruled out all the possibilities. But the day after admission her temperature fell to normal and she felt fine. Then this morning she asked me why she wasn't getting her new high blood pressure pill. I realized I'd forgotten to order it along with her six other medications.

"You're right," I said, "I did forget to order the Aldomet. But what do you mean, *new* blood pressure pill?"

"My doctor just started it a few weeks ago; didn't I tell you?" When she first came in she had given me a list of her medicines; I assumed she had been on them all for years.

Suddenly I had a thought. Could the Aldomet be causing her fevers? We sat down with a calendar and worked out that she was given the prescription just two days before her fevers began. I began to think I was onto something.

After leaving Mrs. Bander's room I went straight to the library. I found three journal articles with reports of fever due to Aldomet. Her case fitted the descriptions perfectly!

I raced back to the ward and convinced Don to let me give Mrs. Bander an Aldomet. She got the pill at twelve-thirty. At three her temperature was 104°! We gave her something to bring the fever down, and by evening it was gone and she felt fine. There was no doubt that the Aldomet was the culprit. How wonderful to make this diagnosis. I feel as if I've just broken a code, and the message is good news for both me and Elizabeth Bander.

February 2

The first month of medicine is over. Today I moved from Four South to Six South. The theory behind the move is that we should be exposed to a variety of interns and residents and visits. But once again I'm a displaced person. I must adjust to a whole new set of surroundings. And I've left all my old patients behind. I feel guilty for having orphaned them, but at the same time it's nice to be free of responsibility for their care. It was so depressing to see Mrs. Levine get worse day by day, so difficult explaining to her relatives why she grew sicker despite our care. And it's a relief to be done with seductive Gloria Milner. She did turn out to have SBE, after all. The switch to Six South saved me from being her medical student for the month and a half she'll need to be in the hospital on antibiotics. But I'll miss Mrs. Oppenheim, my fairy godmother, and Ned Carney, my precious young patient.

February 4

I was thinking today about this peculiar business of working in a hospital. People are constantly streaming in for care. They come in through the emergency ward or are admitted by their own doctor. Each has a story, always different, but always there is pain or discomfort or worry. We respond with a whole host of things — we ask questions, take blood, do x-rays and scans. Then we feed them drugs and diets, give IV's, and maybe do surgery. Eventually they get better and go home, or else they die. Each room in the hospital contains a person somewhere along this sequence of diagnosis and treatment. The hospital is prepared to take care of anyone who comes through the doors, no matter what their complaint. How audacious!

February 6

I haven't gotten used to Six South yet. I still miss my old ward. So today I went back to visit my former patients. Mrs. Levine looked terrible. In five days she has somehow aged five years. Her voice was even weaker, and her arms and legs seemed as thin as the IV pole standing by her bed. Her abdomen, though, had grown bigger, as if it were feeding on the rest of her body. Her kidney failure is getting rapidly worse and the nurses say she now vomits all her food. I don't think she'll leave the hospital.

I saw one of her daughters in the hall. "Doctor Klein," she said, "I wish you hadn't left. Mother really misses you, you know." I told her that Don was an excellent doctor, and would continue to take good care of Mrs. Levine. "Yes, yes, I know," she said, "but he's not you." I was very flattered, and very guilty.

Then I ran into Don. More bad news — Mrs. Oppenheim is dead. The day after we tapped her lung she was up and tooting around the ward; she looked great. Originally the plan was to send her to a care center. But since she had perked up so much Don proposed that she go back home. Mrs. Oppenheim was ecstatic, but her husband balked. "I know my wife, doctor," he said. "She gets excited at the littlest thing. And I know her health is going to get worse. I don't think I can take care of her at home anymore." After thinking things over for a few days, he sadly decided she would do better in a nursing home.

Mr. Oppenheim began spending all day with his wife. He trailed behind her as she trudged up and down the halls. He sat beside her bed as she napped, holding her hand and staring at the floor.

The day she was finally ready to go to the nursing home, the nuclear medicine department asked to repeat her bone scan with a new isotope for a research study. She agreed, so her discharge was delayed until the following day. That night, though, she got a fever, and a few days later she was dead from pneumonia. Don told me she kept pulling out her IV. And she stopped eating and wouldn't take her medications. The nurses say that Mr. Oppenheim thinks he killed her.

February 7

A lousy day. I probably spent three-quarters of it as a messenger boy and a secretary. Endlessly running up and down four flights of stairs on two hours' sleep: delivering specimens to the lab, tracking down urine cultures, reviewing blood smears. Endlessly on the phone: scheduling x-rays, checking lab results, talking to patients' nursing homes. And all the writing: progress notes and insurance forms and social work referrals.

It's hard to make time to talk with my patients. There's almost never a chance to read about the diseases I'm seeing, or even to ask questions. There are always a million trivial mechanical chores screaming to be done; the din they produce makes learning impossible. They tell us we have to do all this scutwork so we'll be prepared for internship. But I thought I was in training to become a practicing physician, not an intern! It seems to me that we should be working for that ultimate goal, not just for the next step on the way. I'm supposedly paying tuition to get an education. In fact, it appears that I'm giving the medical school money so that I can be a hospital servant.

February 8

My God, it's impossible. Ned Carney is going to die. It had been such a treat to be taking care of someone my own age back on Four South. What a relief it was to be able to talk about politics and photography instead of grandchildren's bar mitzvahs! Ned told me about his work as an electrical engineer. I talked about what it was like to be a medical student, even though Dr. Fine would have said it was unprofessional. Ned and I grew close.

After some x-rays and blood tests, we decided he indeed had regional enteritis. He seemed to have a bladder infection as well. With steroids and antibiotics he improved dramatically. How nice it was to see a patient get better instead of die!

But Ned didn't really get better. Ten days after we sent him home, he was back. He had begun passing gas and feces through his penis — a fistulous track had developed between his intestine and his bladder. This is a fairly common complication of regional enteritis. It would have to be treated with an operation. I visited Ned every day on the surgery ward, where he was being prepared for his operation with intravenous medicines.

He finally went to surgery this morning. I decided to look

at his chart before I saw him, just to make sure everything went OK. It didn't. We were wrong—Ned doesn't have regional enteritis at all. He has cancer!

I am stunned. It turns out that even my friend Ned Carney is an old man. He has a cancer of the colon that is worming through the bowel wall into the bladder. And the operative note says they found metastases in the liver. His cancer is already far advanced.

So I am to be a voyeur of Ned Carney's death. This so-recently vigorous man will soon wither and die. And just as his wife is so closely involved with his life, I will be involved with him in his death. But unlike Debbie, I can go home and eat my dinner and drink beer and listen to records and think of other things. I am moved to be able to witness this intimate and dangerous thing, death, and yet pay so small a price.

When I came into Ned's room after reading the fatal words in his chart Debbie was there, very still, holding his hand. I whispered hello and Ned woke up and we all smiled weak smiles. The room seemed very dark but their faces both glowed the color of sliced apples. Debbie let go of his hand and stroked his black hair and then she fingered the sleeve of his bathrobe as we talked. Ned tried to talk, too, but he was still groggy from surgery, and dozed. I'm sure he doesn't know the truth yet but Debbie must have been told, Debbie with a three-year-old daughter.

February 9

Every minute is medicine. Almost all my time is spent in the hospital. In the precious few hours at home, all I do is study, eat, and sleep. And while I eat and while I sleep and even while I sit on the toilet, medicine is on my mind. I taped a diagram of the arterial circulation to the bathroom wall, above the toilet paper. Now I can memorize the branches of the aorta even while I take a crap.

It's frightening to see how easy it would be to be sucked into this way of living forever. There are no decisions to be made; medicine is everything. At times this could be handy. Medicine is a great excuse for avoiding responsibilities. Having extra work to do at your business is never a legitimate reason for not meeting other obligations. But medicine is *always* a reason. If I don't want to spend time with friends or relatives, for example, I need only invoke my work. These people will just have to understand that my time is precious. The more time I spend with them, the less I'll have for my patients. And also the less time I'll have to read, to learn how to heal the sick. Lives could be lost.

Not only is there little time for anything else, there's no leftover energy. I used to like to do photography, read novels, take hikes. But now, even if I had more free time I don't think I'd be able to print a roll of film. I don't even have the pep to start a crummy book. I can see how medicine could come to control my entire life. Maybe that's the way it has to be.

February 10

We actually cured a patient! What a wonderful feeling, especially after the endless succession of deaths on Four South. Rena Walton is a nice woman in her fifties. She came into the hospital a few weeks ago with high blood pressure and headaches, feeling weak and tired. Her potassium level was low, so we screened her for hyperaldosteronism. After a long series of tests we found that she indeed had a tumor of the adrenal gland. This little knot of perversity which sat above her right kidney amused itself by making aldosterone all day long. This hormone is what gave Mrs. Walton her high blood pressure and her headaches. It's also what caused her potassium level to drop. We sent her to surgery several days ago. It was a real treat to both discover the cause of all her symptoms and have a cure at hand.

Today I went up to the surgery ward to see her. She's doing great! She's already up and walking around. Her blood pressure and potassium level are back to normal and she says she feels better than she has in years. "You know, Dr. Klein," she said, "you're like a brother. You've been so good to me through all this."

Well, Mrs. Walton, you've been good to me too. You've shown me that we can cure patients occasionally, not just help them die. What a wonderful feeling!

February 11

I visited Ned Carney again today. His hair was combed and the shock of surgery was gone from his face. He lay covered by an antiseptic white bedsheet. The urine bag connected to his bladder catheter was discreetly hidden at the foot of the bed. There were precise vases of flowers on the windowsill. Everything on his body and each object in his room was clean and orderly. It was as if the doctors and nurses these last four days had scrubbed away all evidence of the cancer, to protect him from its knowledge.

They haven't told him yet, but he knows. The dressing over his incision was changed today. They removed the original bulky dressing and replaced it with a lighter one. Yesterday they had him walk for the first time. With the big dressing bulging out from under his bathrobe and the IV pole at his side, "it was like I was walking around with a shield and a sword," he said. "But today, after they took the big dressing off and put on this little one I feel sort of vulnerable and exposed."

Yes. Slowly the secret of your death is being revealed, Ned. You are very vulnerable, and soon you will be exposed.

February 12

Just when I think I'm making progress something happens to set me back. Today I admitted a two-hundred-pound patient named Mrs. Davis. She was sent in because her diabetes was out of control.

Mrs. Davis loves to talk. She told me all about her husband, her two daughters, and her little poodle, Perky. But her main interest seemed to be her hemorrhoids. She described in detail the times they hurt, the times they bled, and when they itched. Once they even popped out while she was shopping and she had to go into the restroom at a Brigham's and push them back in. "Frankly, doctor," she said in that husky voice of hers, "they're a real pain in the ass." I had to laugh, just as I'd laughed when three of my last five patients with hemorrhoids used the same line.

When Mrs. Davis had at last run out of hemorrhoid stories it was time to begin the physical. Things went well until I got to the rectal exam. She rolled over on her side, and I pulled her bathrobe up around her waist. Then I put on the examining gloves and tried to hoist up the top buttock to view her piles. It was hard to get much leverage though; I couldn't see in far enough. I decided that getting a good feel of the little devils would be sufficient, so I greased up my glove and dove in. I searched and I searched, but I just couldn't feel them.

"Doctor," Mrs. Davis finally said, "are you sure you're in the right hole?"

I turned red and thought fast: "Why, yes, Mrs. Davis, we always do a pelvic exam along with the rectal."

"Oh I see. It's funny, though; I don't remember ever having a pelvic done in this position before. Is this something new?"

"Mrs. Davis," I answered quickly, "would you please help me spread your cheeks so I can examine your hemorrhoids?"

February 13

Today I saw Ned Carney for the first time since he was told he has cancer, and I learned something more about his surgery. The operation was done by Dr. Sid Rose, an excellent surgeon who also does research. It turns out Ned worked for him as a lab technician a few years ago. That's why Ned came to the Beth Israel when he first got sick. He trusted the hospital and he wanted Dr. Rose to be the surgeon if he should need an operation.

The surgery, everyone thought, was to remove the section of bowel involved with the regional enteritis and to repair the bladder fistula. When Dr. Rose opened the abdomen though, he found a huge tumor, already spread to the liver. He was very shaken. He removed a small bit of tissue and called a pathologist for an emergency reading.

"But, Dr. Rose," said the resident assisting him at surgery, "it's obvious that it's a tumor. Nothing else looks like that."

"You can never be sure!" Dr. Rose snapped. "Maybe this is just intense inflammation from the regional enteritis."

So the pathologist came and prepared the specimen in the special pathology room next to the O.R. He needed to look under the microscope for only a few seconds. Then he called over the loudspeaker to the room where Dr. Rose was operating: "Whooee, it's the Big C, all right. It's very anaplastic. This poor bastard won't last more than a month or two." The pathologist didn't know that Ned had been Dr. Rose's lab technician.

How hard it must have been for Dr. Rose to tell Ned his diagnosis! I can imagine that Rose feels some responsibility for the cancer. In a way everyone regrets that the operation was done. One can almost believe that there would be no tumor if there had been no surgery. And I think there are hidden feelings that Dr. Rose somehow *caused* the cancer by operating. It doesn't help to know that these feelings are completely irrational. They're still there.

I went down to see Ned just after I'd heard the story of the operation. After knocking gently, I entered his room. Ned and his wife were both very still, he in bed with morphine, she in a chair with makeup. The atmosphere was hazy with narcotics and perfume. There was so little to say. I tried to talk to Ned, but nothing seemed relevant. I wanted to acknowledge that I knew he had cancer, but I couldn't think how to do it.

For Ned the past is over and there is precious little future. The present is only his increasing pain, and I didn't want to dwell on that. Talking to Debbie was much easier; both of us still live in the world of snow flurries and supermarket sales and traffic jams. I tried to include Ned as I talked with Debbie, but it was hard. How horrible it must be for him to see a healthy young man talking quietly with his pretty wife as he lies in bed with a tumor growing in his belly.

I realized how much his tumor had changed everything when Debbie at one point said, "I've always tried to get Ned to take me to California, but he never wants to go."

You mean he never *wanted* to go, I thought.

February 15

Rose Levine died today. She was the woman with agnogenic myeloid metaplasia, whose belly got bigger as her arms and legs shrank. I hadn't seen her for a few days, so I decided to stop by Four South on my way home. Several of her relatives were going back and forth between her room and the dayroom with fleeting inner expressions on their faces. I retreated to the nurses' station and confirmed the obvious — Mrs. Levine had just died.

I went out to the dayroom, where I had presented Mrs. Levine's case to Dr. Fine a month ago. Her family had gathered there, all posed like quivering statues. There were her children, her grandchildren, and, wearing his familiar soft brown sweater, her husband. He was sitting in the chair in the corner with his head in his hands, minutely rocking. I went up to one of the daughters and put my hand on her shoulder and said how sorry I was. Then, the same to one or two more of the children. I knew them all.

Mr. Levine suddenly got up and walked toward his dead wife's room. The children said, "Dr. Klein, don't let Dad go in there again," and I followed him across the hall, not really knowing why. The tan curtains were tightly drawn around Mrs. Levine's bed. He kept scratching at them and feebly shuffling one way, then the other, trying to see his wife. Finally he found the part in the curtains. He went up to her and bent over her and kept kissing her forehead with quick gentle kisses, rocking on his heels. Then he lifted her right arm, which was still connected to the IV tubing, and kissed her wrist. Then he laid the arm across her chest and his body shook and he turned and walked back out to the dayroom.

February 16

Death is the ultimate simplification of patient care. There is always worry in looking after sick people. As with Mrs. Levine, there were so many things to stew about. Should I call a dermatologist to look at her rash, or isn't it important enough? Should I check another uric acid level? What else can I do to ease the pain of her swollen belly? How much should I push the nurses to help her to eat? What should I tell the family about her condition? Are all her medications right? Am I missing anything?

But suddenly she's dead. Suddenly there are no more physical exams or lab tests or IV orders. There is only the solitary fact that she's dead. There is absolutely nothing more to be done; nothing more *can* be done. What wonderful simplification is death. How clean.

February 17

These days there is a great heavy steady tiredness. It's like being under a thick rug that is always there. Once every three weeks is a weekend off and I peek out from under the rug. But for most of the time I don't even know which way to move to get toward the edge. There is just a dull aimless wandering. I lurch from one thing to the next, trying to keep up with my work. I crave sleep.

February 21

I went to Mr. McMaster's autopsy today; Mr. McMaster is dead. His surgery merely documented the tumor we already knew he had. And as I suspected, it led to nothing new that could be done for him. And also, as I feared, he didn't do well after the operation. In the intensive care unit he had three cardiac arrests. Amazingly, though, he survived. But this man who came into the hospital feeling fine left for home weak and thin, with a painful incision in his belly and defibrillation burns all over his chest. He lasted at home about two weeks. Then a few days ago he came back to the hospital, jaundiced and vomiting blood.

Today I saw his tumor for the second time. The yellow shell of his body lay bare and wet on the autopsy table. The ribcage had been removed. It lay up against his left thigh, like a shield. His taut face held two jellied eyeballs which stared at the overhead lights, unblinking.

The pathologist presided over Mr. McMaster's internal organs, which were splayed out in front of him on a big wooden butcher block. He sorted through the entrails to divine the cause of death. The tumor had closed off the common bile duct, accounting for the jaundice. It also held loops of intestine in its gristly grasp. And the liver was chock-full of tumor. In the few weeks since I had seen them the greedy liver metastases seemed to have grown wildly.

The pathologist found the immediately fatal lesion in the stomach. It was a huge ulcer that had eroded down to an artery. The cancer's bid for a slow demise by organ strangulation had lost out to the ulcer's quicker technique — Mr. McMaster had bled to death.

Was surgery wrong? He surely didn't have long to live, in any case. But all our meddling made the last month of his life worse than it might otherwise have been. Who knows, though; Don says that surgery might have done poor Mr. McMaster a favor. He says that dying slowly from biliary and intestinal obstruction is one of the worst ways to go. The operation, which probably gave him the stress ulcer in his stomach, might have been merciful in speeding his death. But what a peculiar way to justify surgery!

I still believe the operation was wrong. But I have no great bitterness toward the doctors who decided to go ahead with it, just sadness that a very nice old man is dead. And his is just one of all the deaths raining down around me now. The bulk of internal medicine, it seems, consists of watching patients die.

I feel strength in being able to see these deaths not as terrible tragedies, but as simply what must happen to us all.

There is no dulling of feeling, but rather a sad resignation to what must be. I rejoice at being able to look at death so evenly, at being able to give some comfort to patients and their families. We will all die.

March 2

I've just made the last of my monthly switches; I'm now on Four North. The medicine rotation is two-thirds over. I've learned a lot these past two months. I can do a good history and physical. I feel pretty comfortable reading EKG's. Even presenting to the visit is getting to be routine. But there is still so much I don't know. It's frightening to realize I have only a month more to master the basics of internal medicine.

For the first time in my life learning is entirely up to me. No one is telling me how, or even what, to study. At the hospital in my little snatches of free time, and at home when I'm not exhausted, I read. I read textbooks and medical journals about my patients' diseases. What an unorderly way to learn! I now know a great deal about agnogenic myeloid metaplasia because I took care of Rose Levine. But I may never see another case. Meanwhile, since I haven't yet had a patient with pulmonary edema, I know practically nothing about this much more common condition.

My new intern is a woman, Maggie Hess. It will be nice to have a change from the usual all-male ward team. Unfortunately Maggie will be on Four North for only a few more days — the interns are on a different schedule from ours; they are just about to switch. I'll have to try to get to know the patients on our ward quickly. Then maybe I can give Maggie's replacement some help when he takes over.

March 5

The Krantz died last night. His real name was Sidney Rosencrantz, an old demented man who sat in a chair in the hall all day. His little waxy body was draped with white blankets and a tiny blue plastic feeding tube poked out of his nose. He was a male Frances Morris.

The nurses really seemed to like this old codger, though he couldn't talk or even feed himself—there must have been something special about the Krantz. They diligently washed him and turned him in bed and squirted food down his feeding tube. But he got weaker, and last night he died.

Maggie rang me awake in my on-call room. Did I want to see how to pronounce a patient dead? "Sure," I said, still coming out of an already-forgotten dream, "I'd love to." So I staggered out of bed and hitched up my size-large scrub pants and walked out onto the dark quiet ward. I asked a nurse if Dr. Hess had yet arrived.

"Yes. She was here half an hour ago. She said she figured you decided not to get up after all, so she pronounced the patient and went back to bed." I never figured out what had happened. I must have fallen asleep as soon as I hung up the phone, then awakened a half-hour later without realizing it.

As long as I was up, I decided I should practice intubation. I explained to the nurse that I needed to learn how to put a tube down the windpipe so I could handle an emergency respiratory arrest. I asked her if it would be OK. She said she didn't like me fooling around with poor old Krantz, but I might as well go ahead. "I guess it's better that you learn on someone already dead," she said.

"Yes. Don't worry, I'll be very gentle with him."

When I went down to his room with the intubation tray I found the Krantz sitting up in bed, leaning on three pillows. Air was leaking from the oxygen tank by his nightstand; for a moment I thought he was breathing. And he looked so realistic — the incredible detail of the body was amazing. There were the fine eyelashes, the pores of the skin, and the delicate cuticles. I guess I was surprised because a dead person is immediately a body, an object. There is astonishment when it still looks like a real human being.

Carefully I laid Mr. Rosencrantz down and tilted back his stiff head. Then I placed the laryngoscope under the tongue and maneuvered the endotracheal tube down between his vocal cords. Finally I connected up the Ambu bag and squeezed. Air sizzled through the tubing, the dead lungs expanded, and the chest shivered and rose. Yes, the tube was in proper position.

In the stillness of this death I thought of that frantic night in the Boston City emergency ward. Mr. Hastings had stopped breathing and Eric Costello deftly inserted the endotracheal tube, beginning my evening of horror. How I've grown since then! Not only have I learned how to bag patients properly, now I can even put in an endotracheal tube. I still feel infinitely below the interns, but somehow I know I'll be able to make it.

March 9

I inherited my new intern a few days ago. His name is Henry Fogelman. Henry is an efficiency expert; he hates to waste time getting supplies. Hooked to his belt is a hemostat, a blood-drawing tourniquet, a roll of adhesive tape, and a pair of scissors. His pockets bulge with alcohol swabs and syringes. In his hospital whites he looks like a zany Good Humor man going off to war.

Henry is very organized. The breast pocket of his white coat always holds a deck of index cards. They seem to contain every known fact about each of his patients — they must have microfilm inserts. On rounds someone wonders, "How long has Mrs. Horowitz been here?" Or perhaps, "How high did Mr. Leonard's CPK go with his heart attack?" Or, "Does that old goat Davenport have anybody to look after him when we send him home?" We all turn to Henry. He whips out his magic cards and tells us that Mrs. Horowitz came in on the afternoon of February 16, and that Mr. Leonard's CPK peaked at 942 on March second, and that Mr. Davenport has a son in Dorchester; do you want the phone number?

Henry is compulsive and efficient, but he's caring too. We talked about how one of our patients is dealing with her approaching death. And amazingly, he even asked me if taking care of this dying woman has been hard for me. Almost never does an intern have the perspective to worry about something like that. Henry is incredible. If I get sick I'd want him to be my doctor. I could never be as good an intern as he is.

On his first day on the ward we sat down to go over the patients on our team. Though I was officially taking care of only four, I knew them all from rounds with Maggie. So I helped Henry learn about these sick people for whose lives he was suddenly responsible. I liked these intern switches. For two or three days *I* was the expert on the ward and the intern had to ask *me* questions.

"Would you feel comfortable if I didn't see Mrs. Hayes today?" he asked that first day. "I've got a lot of real sickies to get to know, and you seem to have things well in hand." It was fine with me; I was flattered.

Mrs. Hayes is in the hospital because of a pulmonary embolus; she formed a blood clot in a leg vein which came loose and traveled to her lung. A few days before Henry came, we switched her from intravenous anticoagulants to Coumadin, an oral blood thinner. I've been examining her legs and her lungs every day, and monitoring her level of anticoagulation.

Henry didn't get around to seeing Mrs. Hayes the next day, or even the next. So I would see her by myself in the morning. Then in the afternoon I'd get that day's blood test results, decide on the next dose of Coumadin, and have Henry countersign my order.

Finally today, his fourth day on the ward, Henry went in with me to meet Mrs. Hayes. "Mrs. Hayes," I said, "I want you to meet Dr. Fogelman. He's your real doctor."

"No, no," Henry said to me, "*you're* her doctor. I'm just an observer."

I suddenly heard a two-year-old echo. It was Robert Siegel, now a fourth-year student. We were in the Vanderbilt Hall cafeteria discussing medical students who introduced themselves as doctors. I said I thought that was arrogant and deceptive. "Well, you know, Ken," Robert had said, "I used to believe that too. But now I disagree. When you're taking care of a patient you *are* the doc. Even though you have supervision *you're* really running the show, and the patient knows it." I finally understand what Robert meant. I still introduce myself as a medical student, but I no longer flinch when a patient calls me "Doctor Klein."

March 13

Mrs. Poe is getting weaker each day. She has completely lost her appetite. She even vomits when she tries to put in her dentures.

They found a tumor in Mrs. Poe's left breast three years ago. She had a mastectomy, but the cancer recurred. Then came a series of palliative operations, and several rounds of chemotherapy. The malignancy was controlled for a time. Now though, there's a recurrent tumor on her chest wall with a deep ulcer on its edge. It has spread to her bones and her liver. Her kidneys are failing too. The ureters, which connect the kidneys to the bladder, are blocked by tumor. When Mrs. Poe came in she had a urinary tract infection, which we have treated. Unfortunately there is little else that can be done now except to keep her free of pain and nausea.

Every day I remove the bandages which cover the ulcerating tumor and clean it and apply a fresh dressing. The nurses were repelled by this task, so I said I would do it. I want to show Mrs. Poe that her tumor doesn't disgust me; I want her to know that I care about her. I think I also want to prove to *myself* that the tumor doesn't disgust me.

We had planned to send Mrs. Poe back home. Her dressings would be changed by a visiting nurse service. But Mr. Poe, who drives up from Cape Cod every day to see her, is becoming frightened as his wife grows sicker. He has decided he can't take care of her at home. He's arranged for her to go to a nursing home on the Cape. Mrs. Poe tells me she doesn't like nursing homes.

She asked me for the first time today how much longer she has to live. She says she'd like to fall asleep and not wake up. I sit with her, and sometimes we talk. Mrs. Poe is getting ready to die.

Henry tells me that I've been taking good care of Mrs. Poe. He's pretty much letting me run the case. But it's so hard. I'm playing a big part in determining when she will die. It's mostly the kidney failure that is making her weak and nauseated now. It's the kidney failure that will cause her death. Peritoneal dialysis could make her feel better for a time. We would put a tube into her abdomen and run special fluids in and out to remove the toxins no longer filtered by her kidneys. But it would have to be done every few days, and it's uncomfortable. I don't think Mrs. Poe would want peritoneal dialysis; I think she's ready to die. But how can I be sure? I can't ask her, "Do you want dialysis, yes or no?" And I can't ask Mr. Poe, "Should we prolong your wife's life with dialysis, or should we let her die?" So it becomes my decision. They say doctors shouldn't play God by deciding when patients should die. But giving dialysis to prolong life is playing God too. When doctors say they refuse to play God they're usually just avoiding difficult decisions.

I think the next few days will make things clear. How Mrs. Poe is doing and the messages I get from her and her husband will say whether dialysis is right. I have to watch for clues from them, but in the end it's my decision.

March 19

I'm beginning to be able to make jokes on myself. Things aren't always so grim and serious any more. George Matthias is a thirty-five-year-old diabetic who is losing his eyesight. He came from Kentucky to the Beth Israel for an experimental treatment which they hope will arrest the diabetic deterioration of his eyes. The treatment involves the surgical destruction of the pituitary gland.

It has been hard taking care of him. Like Ned Carney, he's young. It's much easier to feel his suffering than the pain of pitiful old patients like Frances Morris.

George's surgery was today. They asked me to start an IV just before he was to go off to the operating room. The only IV's on the ward happened to be Angiocaths, which I'd never seen before. I knew that they're supposed to be harder to put in than the type I was used to. Oh well, I thought, I have to learn to do it sooner or later.

George was tense about surgery and tense about the IV. Like many diabetics he was very needle-shy, in spite of (or perhaps because of) his daily insulin injections. I got everything set up and checked that the tubing was flushed out. "George, you're going to have to be especially still for me now. I've never put in one of these before," I said with exaggerated menace.

George chuckled. "Very funny," he said. "That's OK, though, I really enjoy being a guinea pig."

That broke the tension. We both relaxed, and the IV went in fine. "George," I said as I taped the tubing in place, "I have something to tell you."

"What's that?"

"I wasn't kidding — this really was my first time."

"Why, you sneaky son of a gun; fool me by telling the truth!" We both giggled. I never would have been able to pull that one off even a few months ago.

March 24

Yesterday was a sunny Sunday. Beautiful weather was guaranteed since I was on call, quarantined to the hospital. The morning had been quiet. While I was in the middle of a long letter to Phyllis, a nurse called. It was about one of those really depressing stroke patients, an old woman named Mrs. Baxter. She had lost her gag reflex. Whenever she swallowed, food would shoot down the trachea to her lungs. Eating was torture; every bite of food or sip of water was punished by a violent spell of coughing. So, like Frances Morris and Sidney Rosencrantz, she was kept alive by tube feedings. And, as often happened, the tube came out. Or, perhaps, it was pulled out in a feeble declaration that she had suffered enough.

But the hospital gives patients no choice — the nurse asked me to replace the tube. I brought the tray of equipment to Mrs. Baxter's room and apologized for what I was about to do. She looked at me and grunted — because of her stroke she was unable to talk, but she understood. I greased up the tube and threaded it into her left nostril. She winced and she sputtered. Since she couldn't help me by swallowing, passing the tube was difficult. It kept coiling up in the back of her throat. When she coughed it uncoiled and sprang out at me through her mouth, like a slimy jack-in-the-box. Time after time I pulled the tube back and tried again. It was a degrading assault on this feeble old woman. She coughed in my face and tried to push me away with her limp, stroked-out arm. I grew angry.

After several more passes, each done more roughly than the last, the tube finally seemed to have gone down the right pipe. To make sure I filled a big syringe with air and connected it to the end of the tube. Then I placed my stethoscope on the belly. If the tube was indeed in the stomach I could expect to hear loud gurgles as air percolated through the gastric juice.

Just as I was about to squirt in the air I heard a shuffling noise behind me. Mrs. Baxter's face made a huge lopsided smile. I took off my stethoscope and turned toward the door. A small man with white hair, wearing a tweed sportscoat over a cardigan, had just come in. His twinkly eyes looked upward to compensate for his stoop. There was no doubt about who this was; I recognized him instantly from pictures I'd seen. It was Paul Dudley White, the famous cardiologist.

"Hello, young man," he said and shook my hand. "My name is Dr. White. How is our patient doing?" He told me that he first met Mrs. Baxter as a young cardiologist when she came to him with acute rheumatic fever. He had just stopped by now to check up on her. "I don't like to lose track of my old patients, you see," he said.

He explained that he first found a heart murmur about thirty years ago. "It's a very interesting mitral insufficiency murmur," he continued. "About eight years ago the second heart sound began to split more widely, and in the last few years a loud S-3 has developed."

I was paralyzed. This was how it must be to meet the President — after you shake hands there's nothing to say. So I just nodded and smiled stupidly and stood there, mute. Finally I excused myself and went back to Mrs. Baxter's feeding tube. I leaned over and put my stethoscope on her belly and squirted in the air. There was a gratifying gurgle — yes, it was placed right. From where Dr. White stood, he apparently couldn't see the syringe connected to the tube. He tapped me on the shoulder. "No no, young man," he said, pointing to our patient's chest, "the heart is up there."

"Oh yes," I said, "of course." And I listened to the murmur of mitral insufficiency.

26 March

Mrs. Poe will leave for the nursing home tomorrow. She is very weak. Her tumor and its ulcer continue to grow. Her kidneys have stopped working almost entirely. I indirectly broached the subject of dialysis to Mrs. Poe and her husband at different times. As I expected, they both made it clear that she's had enough. It's time for her to die.

She's frightened and depressed at the thought of leaving the familiar Beth Israel for a nursing home. And she will miss me a lot, I think. And she'll miss all the nurses and the incredible social worker who have all done so much for her. I feel guilty sending her away to die, but it makes sense that she be nearer her husband and children. It's nice too that a lot of leaving is going on at once. Her roommate, who became a good friend, left yesterday and I'll be leaving in four days, the end of my medicine rotation. I think Mrs. Poe will die very soon, probably within a week. Henry, though, says it could be a month or more. I hope I'm right, for her sake.

March 28

This was a big day. First, my cholesterol level, for which I drew my own blood two days ago, turned out to be nice and low. Second, Dr. King, the head of the medicine rotation, told me he had just reviewed the evaluations from my visits. All three had given me honors grades! I've been excited all day; in the same morning I was pronounced sound in both body and mind.

I was very flattered by my evaluations. But now I find myself with the funny feeling that I don't deserve such good grades. I feel dumber than most of my classmates. I still don't understand basic things that people talk about all the time, like the anion gap and the significance of nystagmus. I surely learned a lot these last three months, but there's so much I still don't know. Internship is only a year and a half away, but I feel totally inadequate to do the job. There are only half a dozen or so minor rotations left. How can I ever learn all I need to know to bring me up to the level of a Don Murphy or a Henry Fogelman?

March 30

Today was the last day of the medicine rotation. At last I'm over the hump of medical school.

I'm ending these three months liking medicine even more than when I began. Part of the reason is simply that I'm getting better at it. Even though I know I still have a lot to learn, I realize I've come a long way since obstetrics and gynecology. I've even come a long way since I worked up John McMaster's liver tumor just three months ago. It's nice to begin to see the payoff after so many years of being a student. Doing a history and physical is no longer a painful chore. And the mechanical parts of taking care of patients that used to terrify me — drawing blood, putting down feeding tubes, starting IV's — are at last getting to be routine. When my turn came to take an admission these last weeks, I no longer felt a surge of dread. I was beginning to look forward to new patients for the chance to unravel and treat their medical problems.

I've found so much pleasure in understanding how the body works in health, and how it deals with disease. It's exciting to be able to change things for the better. Seeing a patient improve under your care is like passing an exam — it shows you understand the physiology of the illness. The rare patient who can be truly cured, like Rena Walton, is a bonus. But this isn't necessary. Improving symptoms as much as possible, and comforting, are enough.

8

The Human Pincushion
Getting My Hernia Fixed

O NE OF THE THINGS we learned in our first-year social medicine course was that people can put off being sick. When a man finally retires, for example, there is less of a premium on being healthy. Previously ignored symptoms blossom, and his heart disease or his emphysema or his renal failure becomes manifest. Another case is that of the mother who works long and hard in preparation for her daughter's marriage. Shortly after the wedding she falls ill. She is hospitalized and found to have metastatic cancer. Despite having been able to work so hard so recently, she rapidly deteriorates, and soon dies.

After medicine my next two rotations were radiology and endocrinology. Then came the summer, marking the end of my third year of medical school. The summer also meant a vacation, the first since the break just before the neurophysiology block. I was going to stay with Phyllis in Vermont. Then when her semester was over we planned to do some hiking in the Green Mountains.

But during the last week of endocrinology, just as I started packing for Vermont, I became aware of a dragging sensation in my left groin. I realized I'd felt a fullness there ever since the middle of the medicine rotation several months ago; I'd been unconsciously pushing it back in with my discreetly pocketed left hand. But I'd ignored it. There wasn't time to think about my health during these last hectic months. Now, though, I had the leisure to attend to the nagging little things in my life. I became conscious of my symptoms and realized what was going on — I had a hernia!

Could I go hiking with a hernia? Was there danger of strangulation? Should I wear a truss? I went to see Dr. Daley at the student health services to find out.

"Well, Kenneth," he said after the examination, "you seem to be better with hernias than Hodgkin's. This time your diagnosis is correct. You indeed have a hernia, an indirect inguinal hernia, to be exact." There was little satisfaction in being right though; Dr. Daley said I'd need surgery.

"But how can I have surgery? I'm just about to go on vacation!"

"Great. What better time to have it done! You can recuperate over your vacation, when you don't have to worry about missing school. And by the time your next rotation begins you should be just about healed. Funny, isn't it, how things seem to work out like that?" He sent me to see Dr. Moss, chief of surgery at the Beth Israel.

Dr. Moss, a tall, thoughtful man with thinning black hair, examined me and agreed that surgery was indicated. "The operation is very simple," he said. "The anesthesia, if you have a general, actually carries greater risk than surgery itself."

"Well, are there alternatives to a general?"

"Sure. I'd personally favor a spinal, or perhaps a local. Otherwise there are the fringe methods of anesthesia like hypnosis, and, of course, acupuncture." This half-joking reference to acupuncture, as it turned out, began a fateful train of events that culminated a week later with me writhing in pain on a hard operating table.

Dr. Moss had mentioned acupuncture because the anesthesiologists at the Beth Israel had recently begun experiments with it. Indeed, Dr. Moss had already done a hernia operation with this technique. It had gone well, but he was still a skeptic.

I was intrigued with the idea of acupuncture anesthesia. Would Dr. Moss consider it for my operation? He said no. But I persisted, and he finally agreed. "This is against my better judgment," he said. "Remember, Kenneth, acupuncture is still an experimental technique. No one can guarantee success."

"I'm willing to chance it," I said bravely.

So, on the day when I'd been scheduled to leave for Vermont, I solemnly marched back to the Beth Israel Hospital, suitcase in hand. As I walked through the door to the admissions office I underwent a miraculous transformation. One moment I was a medical student and the next, a patient.

I sat uncomfortably in the little waiting room, watching the crowded hallway. There were kitchen workers and cleaning people and lab techs, all marching briskly in color-coded uniforms. And there were the doctors, big and handsome, loud and quick. Each was a flying wedge, parting the crowd, touching no one. Finally, marked by their flimsy striped bathrobes were my brethren, the patients. They rode on stretchers or in wheelchairs, or walked slowly in the teeming traffic. Their lost faces broadcasted private pains.

It was hard to sit. I decided to go to the library to read medical journals; I'd leave a note for the admissions clerk to page me when my turn came. But I didn't go. I just sat immobile in my chair.

Eventually I was called in. After answering a hundred questions and signing my name a dozen times, I became a certified patient.

"Now then, Mr. Klein," the clerk said when all the paperwork was done, "you are to go to your ward on the eighth floor. You go out this door, turn to your right . . ."

"— Yes. I know."

"Well, enjoy your stay."

I rode the elevator to the eighth floor and entered the door labeled "Clinical Research Center." Jane, the head nurse, was waiting for me. I followed her down the hall to my room. "I'll try not to be an obnoxious patient even though I'm a medical student," I said obnoxiously — I wanted to be sure she knew I was a medical student.

My new home was big, bright, and carpeted. There was a picture window. Two color TV's hung down from the ceiling, one at the foot of each bed. And in a large sturdy armchair sat Ronald, my new roommate. He was huge, about 350 pounds. Jane introduced us. "Ronald will be with us for three months," she said. "He's on a total fast." Ronald told me his goal was to lose at least a hundred pounds.

"So what are *you* in for?" he asked after Jane had left. "You don't look like you need to lose weight."

"No. I'm getting my hernia fixed."

"So how come you're in the Clinical Research Center? That's a pretty common operation, isn't it?"

"Yes. The research part is the anesthesia. They're going to use acupuncture."

"Acupuncture! Is your surgeon Chinese or something?"

"No. I just thought it would be interesting. Besides, I'm afraid of general anesthesia. I saw what it did to some mice once."

"Well, I think you're nuts. But I guess it will be more interesting than not eating for three months."

I unpacked my little suitcase. Nelson's *Textbook of Pediatrics* and Harrison's *Principles of Internal Medicine* went conspicuously on my bedside table. I figured that while I was in the hospital I'd have plenty of time to read. My pediatrics and cardiology rotations were coming up, and there was lots to learn.

Just as the last pair of socks settled into their new drawer the anesthesiologists came. They were both in their mid-thirties, thin, and quiet. One was a blonde woman from Vienna, the other a swarthy man from Karachi. They glided into the room on noiseless anesthesiologists' feet. In the softest of voices the woman said, "Hello, we're from the anesthesiology department. I'm Dr. Weber and this is Dr. Ahmed. May we talk with you?" They stood over me as I sat on the edge of my bed.

"Well," Dr. Ahmed said suddenly, "what type of anesthesia would you like to have?"

I was startled. "I thought the whole point of my being here was so I could have acupuncture."

"Do you want it?"

"Of course." They told me I had to formally request acupuncture since it was still experimental. "OK," I said dutifully, "I wish to have acupuncture analgesia for my herniorrhaphy."

"Good." They smiled.

Dr. Ahmed explained their technique. When he was done I asked him how acupuncture worked. He tried to explain the gate theory of pain, but it made little sense to me. Dr. Weber lent me a book about acupuncture. They said they'd return in the morning for a practice session, then they glided out of the room.

My next visitor was the Research Center dietitian. I think she was excited to finally have a patient who could eat normal food. She wanted to know my likes and dislikes so she could plan my meals. Poor Ronald sat in his oversized armchair trying to read as we talked about baked salmon and artichokes and peach flan.

Then came a psychiatrist; apparently I had to be certified psychologically fit to undergo acupuncture. I was unaccountably nervous in his presence. I said things I didn't mean. I stumbled over my words. I apologized. What a distorted picture he'll get of me, I thought. I'm not really like this. I'm just a little self-conscious and intimidated face-to-face with a shrink. How can a psychiatrist hope to know what a patient is *really* like, I wondered. I remembered back to the medicine rotation. When I'd sit down to talk with newly admitted patients they often seemed so inarticulate and nervous. I always figured it was because they were sick. I never considered that it might have been because of *me*.

Maybe even a medical student could be intimidating!

The psychiatrist and I talked for ten minutes. "Well, do you see any reason why you shouldn't have acupuncture?" he finally asked. It was as silly a question as the anesthesiologists'.

"No," I said, but the "no" carried less conviction than I thought it should have.

After his visit the psychiatrist wrote this note, which I later copied from my chart:

Psychiatry Staff

Problem: To evaluate this 25 year-old male medical student for acupuncture anesthesia for herniorrhaphy.

Subjective: Mr. Klein had knee surgery under general anesthesia as a kid — no traumatic hospital experiences. He is curious about but not devoted to acupuncture. He has greater faith in Dr. Moss than in the gate theory of pain. He is relieved that the option to switch to general anesthesia will be there. He has fair trance capacity as judged by his experiences in the student hypnosis course at the Mass. General. He has achieved relaxation with meditation for several years.

Objective: Eager, bright, but skeptical young man.

Assessment: I can give no prognosis for the success of acupuncture but I see no contraindications to its use. I'll be happy to answer any other questions.

After lunch the next in my endless stream of hospital dignitaries appeared. It was Dr. Moss's junior resident. He had come to do a history and physical. I recited the story of my hernia, then he did a quick exam. "Nice to meet you, Ken," he said on his way out the door; "I'll be back in an hour with the whole team."

Three hours later a twitching mass of surgeons entered and surrounded me in my bed. There were Dr. Moss, the junior resident, one or two other residents, and a woman about my age, with long red hair. "Hello, Kenneth," said Dr. Moss, "I just wanted to introduce you to the team." They all nodded. I said hello. Everyone immediately turned around and began filing out. "By the way," Dr. Moss said, nodding toward the woman, "this is Nancy Aarons, the medical student on our team. She'll be back to do a workup."

I spent the rest of the afternoon trying to neutralize my patienthood by reading medicine. It was impossible, though — I couldn't concentrate. Jane came in with some pajamas for me to put on. "But I'm not sick," I said.

"But you're a patient," she said. I put on the PJ's.

That evening Ronald and I watched the sunset through our picture window. After dinner (beef stroganoff for me, pills and water for Ronald) we succumbed to TV. A rerun of the Phil Silvers Show was disturbingly funny. Sergeant Bilko led to Sea Hunt, and then there was a John Wayne movie. Somehow it was easy to see myself in an army barracks, under the ocean, or in the wild west, but it was impossible to imagine reading pediatrics. I started to nod off during the eleven o'clock news.

Ronald's 350-pound snores were serenading me to sleep when I felt a gentle hand on my shoulder. "Ken. Sorry it's so late; I got delayed." It was Nancy, my medical student. "I hate to wake you up, but I need to do a history and physical. OK?"

What could I say? What can a patient ever say? I yawned, moved over, and offered her a seat on the bed.

"So you're starting your fourth year?" she asked.

"Yes. How about you?"

"Third year." She giggled. "Tell me if I do anything wrong." Then she got down to business: When had I first noticed my hernia? Was it painful? Did I have trouble reducing it? But we kept getting off the medical track. She asked me about people in my class that she knew. I asked her what it was like to work with Dr. Moss. We gossiped about professors; we could have been talking at a medical school party. We were both uncomfortable.

Finally it was time for the physical. Nancy went to get her black bag, and I ducked into the bathroom to pee and dry off my pits.

When I emerged Nancy was already arranging her instruments on my bedside stand. She moved stiffly, trying to act like a doctor. I sat down stiffly, trying to act like a patient. We both knew that the roles could just as easily have been reversed.

"Ready?" asked Nancy.

"Yep." She took my arm and pressed her fingers to my wrist. Her head nodded with each beat of my nervous pulse as she timed it with her watch. Then came the blood pressure, the eye exam, the ears. Her hands were steady; she was doing a good exam. But she was tense. Every few minutes she would pause, sit on the bed, and tell me about the time she broke her arm, or when she had had her appendix out. Somehow, I enjoyed her nervousness. Do patients like to see their doctors squirm, I wondered. Does it confirm their mortality?

"Well," she said, "would you mind taking off your shirt so I can do a pulmonary exam?" Off came my pajama tops. Only the skimpy bottoms remained between my hernia and this classmate with the long red hair.

"In and out now; in and out," Nancy said. I had barely noticed the stethoscope on my back. "Breath in and out through your mouth." Next she asked me to lie down, and she leaned over to examine my heart. The ends of her hair lay in little orange loops on my chest. They tickled.

She listened to my heart for a long time. She asked me to take a deep breath and hold it, breathe all the way out and hold it. Then she had me roll first on one side, then the other. It was disturbing. I was a year ahead of her, yet she was doing maneuvers for the cardiac exam that I didn't even know.

After she finished with the heart she put her stethoscope on my belly, eavesdropping on my bowels. Next her fingers crawled over my liver and spleen; she was getting to know me inside and out.

Finally it came: "Um, do you mind if I feel your hernia now?"

"Of course not; that's why I'm here." She delicately unbuttoned my PJ's and folded the edges down to where the pubic hair began to thicken. Then she put her finger into my groin just above the scrotum, and pushed up. Quickly she said, "Now let me know if I'm doing this right and if it hurts." She wasn't, but it didn't. I kept quiet. Nancy averted her face and went into a sort of trance. She kept pumping her finger in and out of my groin, missing the hernia entirely. As she pushed, the PJ's rubbed up against my penis. I began to get an erection. Soon, I realized, it would come up hard against her hand. I had to stop it.

"Nancy," I said.

"Yes?"

"You're giving me an erection."

"Oh!" She jerked her hand away. "I'm sorry."

"No no, *I'm* sorry," I said. "It was *my* fault." There was a long and awkward pause which Nancy finally broke by asking permission to do a rectal. I was impressed that she had the poise to continue examining her crude patient.

As my penis deflated my guilt grew. I wondered if women medical students and doctors often had to deal with their patients' erections, or just their colleagues'. I felt rotten.

After the rectal Nancy packed up her instruments and started to leave. I decided I couldn't let her go without giving her another chance to feel my hernia.

"Listen, Nancy," I said. "You did a super job, but the proper way to examine a hernia is with the patient standing. Here, let me help you feel it." I stood up and carefully muzzled my penis with the flap of my pajamas. "Just push your finger up into the scrotum and find the inguinal ring." But again her timid finger missed the mark, and again she didn't really feel the hernia. I was too uncomfortable to try and teach her how to do it properly, and she was too uncomfortable to have understood what I was saying anyway. Oh well, I thought, there would be lots of other hernias in her future. Better to start with a nonclassmate.

Nancy thanked me and said goodnight. I thanked her back and crawled into bed. "Sleep well," she said. She turned off the lights and gently closed the door.

I lay between the fiercely clean hospital sheets, wondering what it would be like to do a physical on Nancy. I couldn't sleep. Weird gurgles and breathings emanated from Ronald's enormous dieting body. The night nurses with their inverted circadian rhythms gossiped and giggled out in the hall. I heard traffic noises.

Finally I must have slept, for the next thing I remember is being awakened by the rumbling of a portable scale. The night nurse rousted me out of bed. She was anxious, it seemed, to get her devilish work done before dawn. I stood on the scale in a vertical stupor. The balances chattered up and down the metal arm, seeking the niche that told my weight. "Isn't it terrible how they wake you up so early for this!" she said.

"Yes, it's terrible how *you* wake me up so early for this."

"Don't blame me, kid; I didn't write the order."

I mumbled my way back to bed, and somehow got to sleep again.

I was awakened from a dream by a stern surgical voice: "Shield your face, Kenneth." The overhead lights shot on. My squinting light-stung eyes saw Dr. Moss, flanked by his surgical army.

"Oh, my goodness," I yawned, "I was dreaming I was on rounds." They all laughed. I yawned again and stretched myself awake, a sprawling horizontal surrounded by upright pillars of white.

"Well how are you today, Kenneth?" Dr. Moss asked.

"Fine."

"Good."

They left. No one looked for my weight, dutifully recorded as ordered on my bedside chart.

I tried to drag myself down into unconsciousness. At about seven-thirty, though, I was awakened once again. It was the newspaper man. He threw open the door without knocking and in his weary mechanical voice said for the hundredth time that day, "Newspaper? Paper this morning?" I remembered him from my medicine rotation. Occasionally I lent a patient money to buy his precious link to the outside world. But I never realized how intrusive his nasal newspaper chant could be to a sleeping patient. I decided I'd talk to him about being more thoughtful — at least he should knock. I wouldn't speak to him *now*, of course, not while I was still a patient. I'd wait until my next rotation at the Beth Israel. Then, in my white coat, with a stethoscope in the pocket I'd have a word with him. *Then* he'd listen.

I gave up all claim to a good night's sleep after the newsman's rude awakening; I got out of bed to begin the day. But what was on the schedule? After I had showered and put on clean pajamas I realized that all there was to do was wait. So I just sat. I didn't feel like reading even though the big fat pediatrics book by my bed was staring me in the face. "You'd better get cracking," it warned; "pediatrics starts in a month." But I guiltily ignored its advice.

Half an hour's hard fidgeting finally brought breakfast. The meal was over all to quickly, though, and I didn't even have to do the dishes afterward. I decided to write a letter to Phyllis. After it was done I had a stroke of genius — I'd go down to the lobby and mail it.

I told Jane I was going to go to the mailbox. "I'll have to page your medical student to ask if it's OK," she said.

"My God," I squawked, "this is bizarre! A fourth-year medical student has to get permission from a third-year student to take a walk!"

"Calm down. You have to remember something — you're not a medical student now. You're a patient."

The anesthesiologists woke me up from a nap. Dr. Weber held a package of needles and Dr. Ahmed carried a contraption which generated electrical impulses. The labels on the machine were all in Chinese. I wondered how they knew how to use it.

"Hello, Kenneth," said Dr. Weber. "Do you still want to go ahead with the acupuncture?"

I sat up. "No. I changed my mind. To tell you the truth, it seems like a pretty silly idea."

"*What?*" The anesthesiologists looked at each other with panic.

"That was a joke," I said. "I was kidding."

"All right. Are you prepared to have a practice session now?"

"Well, I do have a busy schedule this afternoon, but I think I can squeeze it in." I flopped down on my bed and lay with arms outstretched, a martyr to medical science. Dr. Ahmed drew the curtain.

"OK," said Dr. Weber, "let's start with one of the small ones." Ahmed handed her a vicious-looking six-inch needle. It had a thin silver shaft that broadened into a golden base.

"Wait a minute," I said. "Didn't you say that you were going to start with a *small* needle?"

"Yes. This *is* a small one."

"Oh."

"We're going to put the first needle into the 'large intestine point,'" Dr. Weber explained.

I unbuttoned my PJ tops to expose my belly. "No, no," she said, "the large intestine point is in the webspace between your thumb and first finger."

"Oh."

She cleaned my hand with an alcohol swab. The long sharp needle that was somehow supposed to eliminate pain approached. Despite my clinical interest, I became a patient at the last second — I closed my eyes. Dr. Weber threaded the needle in for several feet and then began twirling it between her thumb and first finger.

"How does it feel?" she asked.

"Not too bad," I lied. Another needle went in, this time on the back of my wrist. "Dr. Weber," I asked between clenched teeth, "is it really necessary for there to be barbs on the shafts of these needles?" She didn't smile at my heroic attempt at a joke. She never smiled.

"You seem to be having some discomfort," she said. "Don't worry. I expect we'll begin to get some analgesia soon." Dr. Ahmed handed his colleague yet another needle. "Now this one will go in what they call the gallbladder point." It settled in the skin above my right knee, on the outside part of the leg.

All three needles began twirling simultaneously. My eyes were tightly shut so I'm not sure if Dr. Weber was using both hands and a foot, or if Dr. Ahmed was helping out too. Or maybe the needles only *felt* like they were being twisted.

After a time the stinging grew more bearable. I opened

my eyes to see Dr. Weber connecting wires from the electronic box to each of the needles. She nodded gravely to Dr. Ahmed. He flipped a switch. I jumped — tiny stinging currents pulsed through my limbs. The conspiring anesthesiologists looked at me with concern.

"I sing the body electric," I quoted bravely.

My finger and thumb suddenly began twitching in time to the current. Dr. Weber said not to worry, it was normal. But she kept looking over at Dr. Ahmed. Finally they decided to move the large intestine needle to a different site, and the thumb stopped jumping.

The pain from the electrified needles gradually subsided. Instead of endless electric shocks the current seemed to be pulsing tiny parcels of novocaine under my skin. Then my right hand grew cold and heavy and numb. My right leg went funny too — the pajamas felt wet and rubbery against my skin. Every few minutes my assailants asked me to describe these peculiar sensations. It was tough; they were just vague enough that I didn't know for sure if they were real. But each time I mentioned rubbery PJ's or cold heavy skin they looked knowingly at each other, as if they fully expected these strange reports.

"Well," Dr. Ahmed said after fussing a bit more with the machine, "I think we've done enough for today." He turned off the electricity and Dr. Weber pulled the needles.

"Things seem to have worked quite well," Dr. Weber said. "For surgery we'll probably use the same points plus a few in the chest for reinforcement. Now please note your sensations for the next hour; I'll be back to check on you." They packed up the needles and the electric torture machine, and left.

"Well, how was it?" asked Ronald from the other side of the curtains.

"Weird."

"Hey, you're crazy. Why don't you just have them knock you out and be done with it?"

"Like I said, I'm scared of general anesthesia. Besides, that wouldn't be very interesting."

"So you think *pain* is interesting, eh? That must explain why you want to be a doctor."

My hand remained cold and sweaty for about ten minutes, then abruptly felt normal again. Dr. Weber returned two hours later. "Well, Kenneth," she said, "since the practice session went so well there's no reason for you not to go home for the weekend. By the way, Dr. Ahmed and I have decided to use Innovar to supplement the acupuncture. It's a fairly new neuroleptic agent; I presume you know about it from pharmacology." I didn't. But I was embarrassed to say so.

Nancy appeared a short time later and ordered a pass until early Sunday evening. "Be sure to get back on time," she said. "You'll be the first case Monday morning and you need a good night's sleep."

"Yes, Mommy."

I took the elevator to the ground floor and headed toward the entrance. But I hesitated. It seemed too easy to just walk out the door. When I did my medicine rotation at the Beth Israel leaving was always traumatic: did I get Mrs. Hayes's orders countersigned? I'd wonder. Had Mr. McMaster's blood been drawn? Should I check up on Mrs. Poe one more time? Especially if it were Friday and I had the weekend off I was nervous — a lot could go wrong in two whole days. But now, as a patient on pass, all I had to do was walk out the door. I was responsible for no one else. I was hardly responsible for myself! I wondered if Nancy would be fretting about me all weekend.

"Hi Ken! I didn't know you were at the Beth Israel — what rotation are you on?" It was Dave Rappaport. I hadn't seen him in several months.

"Hi Dave. I'm on surgery."

"I thought you did surgery at the Boston City."

"Yep, that's right. Like I said I'm *on* surgery. A patient. Dr. Moss is going to fix my hernia Monday morning."

"Wow. How does it feel to be a patient?"

"Lousy."

"Listen, Ken, I'm on my way to liver rounds. Want to come?" It was the perfect suggestion. Every Friday afternoon the medicine department had liver rounds, a get-together with beer and snacks at the medical school. What better way to feel like a medical student again!

It was awkward to be back among these people. I felt inferior somehow, and diseased. But I quickly drank three beers, and felt much better. I asked about that drug Innovar that Dr. Weber had sprung on me. It turned out that it was really two drugs, a narcotic combined with a powerful tranquilizer. It often made patients very wacky and disconnected and drowsy. I was alarmed. Part of the reason I wanted acupuncture was to avoid all the disorientation and loss of control that went with general anesthesia. Also, esthetically it didn't seem right to use a narcotic — either acupuncture would work on its own or it wouldn't.

So why had the anesthesiologists decided to use Innovar? Had they lost faith in acupuncture? Did the psychiatrist tell them I wasn't relaxed enough, or perhaps gullible enough, to succumb to the needles? I decided I had to read my chart to find out what was going on. Over the weekend seeing my chart grew to be an obsession. I decided I'd ask permission as soon as I got back.

On Saturday morning I took a long walk along the Charles River. The people I passed all looked so healthy — sunbathing, jogging, playing Frisbee. How I envied them!

After the walk I went back to the apartment and read about all the things that could go wrong during hernia surgery. Then I looked up Innovar in three pharmacology books. But since it was such a new drug, hardly anything had been written about it. I began attributing evil motives to my anesthesiologists.

On Sunday I read the paper, then had a marathon telephone conversation with Phyllis in Vermont. She wanted to be with me, but I said that was silly. After all, surgery would be trivial; I wasn't even going to have a general anesthetic. If she came to Boston she'd just be wasting bus fare and missing school. Secretly, though, I thought how nice it would be to have her near.

I was supposed to be back at the hospital by five o'clock. I made a point of cleaning up the kitchen very thoroughly, however, so I'd be a little late. But when the clock said four forty-five I hurried; I didn't want to get into trouble.

I arrived at the CRC at twenty minutes after five. Even so, it was two hours before anything happened. Then Dr. Moss came in while I was reading Dr. Weber's acupuncture book. He sat on my bed and explained the surgery. Then he asked me if I had any questions.

"Would it be OK if I read my chart?" I blurted out. "Not that I feel anything's being hidden or anything. Just so I can sort of keep in touch."

"Sure." He handed it to me. "I'm surprised you didn't ask sooner."

I was disappointed with what I found. Nancy's note began, "This is the first Beth Israel Hospital admission for this 25 year old male who enters for elective left inguinal herniorrhaphy." It was the standard opening sentence. The rest of the workup was equally ordinary. The anesthesia note, written by Dr. Weber, was just three lines long: "Healthy 25 y.o. man to have herniorrhaphy with acupuncture analgesia, which he requests. Plan to supplement acupuncture with Innovar." There were no surprises, no evidence of a conspiracy. It was just like any other patient's chart.

Another hour passed. Then a chubby man with graying hair came in. He wore a turquoise polyester shirt with "Beth Israel Volunteer" embroidered in red on the left chest.

"What are you doing in street clothes?" he demanded. He hadn't even introduced himself.

"I'm reading a book."

"Well, you'll have to get into pajamas. I need to shave you for surgery." It turned out that all the hair residing between my nipples and mid-thighs had to come off. This man had come to do the dirty deed.

I changed and lay spread-eagled on my bed. "OK, I'm ready," I said; "skin me." He unbuttoned my pajama top and pulled down the bottoms. Then he began shaving me with his fast little razor, raising a pillowy layer of hair.

"You're a volunteer, are you?" I asked, trying to make conversation.

"Yep."

"Enjoyable work?"

"Yep." He was now well below my belly button.

"Don't slip," I said. He didn't say anything. He just kept whisking away hair. I broke the silence again: "I bet you've heard that line before."

"Yep."

Soon he was done. He picked up fistfuls of hair and dusted me off with a big towel. My belly looked so smooth and white and naked; it was just begging for the slice of a scalpel.

"Boy, I really look strange," I said. "What will my girlfriend say?"

"I don't know." He turned and left. I pulled up the covers and went to sleep.

I was shaken awake by Dr. Moss's junior resident. It was still pitch dark outside. "I've got to start an IV," he said. He flipped on the lights, which drilled into my tender eyes.

"Oh Jesus," I mumbled, "can't we do it later?" There was a moment of horror as I remembered a patient asking me the same thing after I had woken him up to start an IV. The resident apologized, as I had, but said it had to be done. He grabbed my right arm and shaved off a wide band of hair above the wrist. "My God, I'll be another Yul Brynner," I said, but he didn't seem to appreciate the groggy joke. He efficiently started the IV and left.

A sleepless hour later a nurse came in with Dr. Weber's

Innovar. She unsheathed the needle, which reflected the malevolent gleam in her eye. "Oh so *you're* going to do the acupuncture today," I said. "Which point will you go for?" Like all night nurses, she had no sense of humor. She was used to dealing with babbling, half-asleep patients like me; she had learned to ignore what we said. So the Innovar went humorlessly into the pain-in-the-ass point.

Outside it grew light. A stretcher arrived, pulling an antiseptic orderly behind it. "Good morning," the orderly said. "I've come to take you to surgery. Scoot over on the stretcher, now."

"I don't know how to scoot."

"Huh?"

I crawled over onto this shining wheeled bier, ready to meet my destiny. The orderly transferred my IV bottle to a portable stand on the stretcher, then strapped me in. As I rumbled out into the hall I looked back to Ronald, lying in bed. "Good-bye, Ronald," I said. "Good luck."

"Huh?" he said.

The orderly said he'd leave me out in the hall while he called for the elevator. I lay on my back, staring at the ceiling. As I tried to decipher the messages in the textured tiles I realized that my eyelids had sprouted magnets — they suddenly snapped shut. This had nothing to do with sleep. My eyes had been drawn together by the mechanical attraction of opposites. So this is Innovar, I thought.

By pulling my eyelids apart with my fingers I was gradually able to overcome the magnetic force field. And what I saw! The ceiling was traveling down the hall at about ten miles an hour, in the head-to-foot direction. The white tiles moved, the fluorescent lights moved, and the phallic sprinkler heads moved. I had no sense of dizziness or revolving; there was just the steady unwinding of the ceiling down the hall. Again my eyes snapped shut. This time I decided to let the magnets have their way.

After several years the orderly returned and wheeled me onto the elevator. My eyes popped open. I saw myself in a white coat and stethoscope, standing next to my stretcher. I looked down at myself with mild interest. A white sheet covered my vulnerable body, and the IV tubing arched from under the sheet to the bottle suspended above the stretcher. Poor patient, I thought. Going to the O.R., it looks like. Why would someone so young and healthy-looking be having surgery? Testicular carcinoma, probably. Its peak incidence is in men in their twenties.

The elevator door opened and we again began horizontal movement. I must have slept, though it isn't clear how this was possible on the bucking stretcher with the clackety wheels.

Motion stopped and I woke up. Vertical people in green glided by, moving silently and effortlessly, as if on skates. With my magnetic eyes I followed them through a set of swinging doors. Those doors were familiar. Of course — I was just outside the operating room!

My stretcher began moving again. Sighting the trajectory between my bare feet, I saw that I was heading for the O.R. suite in the corner. It was the same one where I had learned the secret of Mr. McMaster's tumor. Mr. McMaster hadn't done well after surgery. There were three cardiac arrests in the intensive care unit. He went home with a chestful of electric tattoos from the defibrillations. "We'll put some needles in your chest for reenforcement," Dr. Weber had said.

I left the stretcher somehow and touched down on the hard operating table. Butcher block, I thought. Someone said, "Safety belt," and a thick nylon strap was snugged around my thighs.

There was a hand on my shoulder. My eyes popped open: fifteen feet above me was an enormous upside-down face — yes, it was Dr. Weber.

"Hello, Kenneth," her giant mouth said. "I guess this is it."

"Hey!" I heard myself yell. Someone was pinching me above the right thumb. It was the first acupuncture needle. Once it was seated in my skin the pain quickly left. Then came more needlesticks, a swarm of flesh-boring insects feeding on my arms and legs. "OK, Kenneth," I heard, "now we're going to put the needles in the thorax." I felt a tiny silver point on my right shoulder. It arced slowly across my chest, making a shiny wire from which hung three golden blobs. Were these three needles? I wasn't sure; there was no sensation of pain.

A huge pair of lips flapped into a waxy right ear, my right ear: "Now, Kenneth, we'll try a traditional Chinese acupuncture point. This one will go into your ear." God, I thought, what does she mean "try" a traditional acupuncture point? Have the other ones failed? Springy steel burrowed into gristly cartilage. The needle twirled, generating pain which ran all around the concavity of my ear. I opened my eyes, but saw only the brightness of chrome, and yellow glowing air. Then I slept.

A faraway radio announced, "We're going to sterilize you

now, Kenneth. This will be cold." Blobs of icy iodine solution spewed from the sponge that someone squeezed above me, stinging my belly and thighs and genitals. I shivered up and down my naked body. "Ten minutes," the voice said. "This will be a ten-minute scrub." Sponges rubbed hard against me and shook my body. My testicles were knocked together and hurt. "Ten minutes, Kenneth," I heard again.

A warm airy blanket floated down over me. They were putting on the drapes — the scrub at last was over! So thick and cozy and clean they felt. They were lavishly applied, layer after layer. For the first time, I think, I really understood that I was going to have an operation. "So this is what it's like to be under the drapes," I mumbled. After years of holding retractors above green-draped bodies I was myself the body under the drapes.

There was a sharp, sudden pain low in my belly. On a huge movie screen I saw a short curving knife blade rocking down through my left leg. I shook. It happened once or twice more. My God, I thought, they've begun surgery! They didn't even test me to see if the acupuncture is working. Do they think I'm asleep? Am I?

Dr. Moss's voice came from the loudspeaker: "I'm pinching the incision site with a hemostat, Ken. You don't seem to be getting much analgesia. We'll infiltrate with novocaine if it's OK with you." I was so thankful — somehow they knew I had felt pain. From the monitors, I figured. I saw sparkling plastic tubing and silver and gold wires attached all over my body, sloping down to ten different machines. They recorded my physiology.

There was an ellipse of wet, hooked pinpricks. Maybe novocaine works by acupuncture, I thought: the needle stick itself gives the analgesia, not the novocaine it injects.

"We'd better try more Innovar," I heard suddenly. Things apparently weren't going well in this operating room, the same one where Mr. McMaster's painful death was initiated. The Innovar must have made me sleep; I don't remember the skin incision.

In a dream I saw a shallow brown ditch of flesh. A surgical clamp scooped up a big lump of muscle from the ditch and twisted it over and over. There was pain, deep and spreading. I tried to say it hurt, but it was hard to speak. It was even hard to breathe because my neck was stretched back so taut. Dr. Weber's presence loomed dangerously above my extended throat.

I awoke from the dream, and separated my eyelids with all my might. Three blue heads bobbed in the bright air above my hernia, like Christmas tree ornaments on an invisible tree. The one on the right grew familiar: there was a pink freckled nose, and a pair of red eyebrows behind gold-rimmed glasses. Nancy! Of course my medical student would be at my operation. That's good, I thought. She'll finally be able to see my hernia.

There was more tugging and pain. I think I groaned. "OK, Kenneth, we'll give you more novocaine for your pain . . . OK, now."

Thank God, I thought, they know it hurts. But I never felt the novocaine go in, and the pain continued. They always seemed on the verge of giving me more novocaine, but then would get distracted and never give it. I shuddered — I was suddenly haunted by the memory of a spinal tap I'd done. "You should have plenty of novocaine, but you be sure and tell me if it hurts," I said to the patient, about to plunge a spinal needle into his back.

"It hurts, it hurts!" the frightened patient yelled as the needle burrowed in between the vertebral bodies.

"All right," I said; "OK." But I kept right on with the procedure, not doing anything more for the pain. "OK" I discovered, wasn't a very good analgesic. Maybe my surgery was patients' revenge.

There was more pain. I prepared for my woody-hollow body to lie on this hard operating table for eternity, traveling down an endless path with scoops and runs of pain for milestones. It would have been nice to have been a doctor, I thought. Only a year more and I would have made it. Twelve more months and I would have been Dr. Kenneth Klein, about to start my internship.

The loudspeaker came on again. It was Dr. Moss: "Well, Kenneth, we're almost finished now." Thank God, thank God, I thought. I can endure anything if the end is near. I slept.

I awoke a second or an hour later to more tugging and pain. "Well Kenneth, we're almost finished," I heard again. I realized that this phase of surgery could last forever too. Again my patient transgressions haunted me. It was my first sigmoidoscopy. I was trying to steer the foot-long steel tube up the rectum of the patient, looking for a tumor. "My God, doctor," the patient blurted out, "how much more? I can't take this much longer!"

"Almost done now. Just about finished," I lied.

"Here come the skin sutures. We're putting in the sutures now," I heard. There was a row of venomous mosquito stings. Then again I slept.

"Wake up, Ken. Wake up!" My nightmare was over. I smiled and opened my eyes with relief. But I wasn't in my bedroom and the voice wasn't Phyllis's. Someone was squeezing my arm. "Wake up, Ken," the recovery room nurse said again. "Move your legs. Your blood pressure is too low."

"That's *your* problem," I said. "Let me sleep." She packed a hard pillow into my tender belly, ignoring my request.

"Press against this and give me a nice deep cough," she ordered. I breathed three times and made a feeble rasp of a cough that tore into my groin. "No, no, that's not good enough. Do it again." Again I tried to imitate a cough to get the nurse off my back in this new arena of torture. It didn't occur to me to simply refuse to do what she asked.

I found myself back in my room on the eighth floor. A blood-pressure cuff encircled my arm like a giant gray leech. "Well, your pressure's finally back to normal," said Jane. "You were pretty hypotensive for a while down there in recovery." One of the other nurses asked me if I could crawl from the stretcher onto my bed.

"Sure," I said. I sat halfway up, and collapsed. The nurses carried me over on the drawsheet.

"Welcome home, Ken," Ronald said from his bed.

The next morning, as I lay in my postoperative bed, I reflected on my patienthood. What a profound experience it was to be a patient, even one who wasn't very sick! Other than being in prison or in the military, there must be few situations where a person has less control over his life. I was at the mercy of the hospital for food, for clothing, even for permission to sleep.

I reacted to my incarceration in two ways. On the one hand I wanted to succumb completely to this huge nurturing environment and let it care for my every need. In other words, regress to the hilt. At the same time, though, I wanted to take charge of the situation, by reading my chart, by participating in decisions, even by confounding the normal routine.

Each patient is different. Some, like Gloria Milner, do everything possible to maintain control. Others are only too happy to lie passively in bed and suck the hospital for all it's worth. But everyone, to some extent, feels the need to be both taken care of and in charge.

By the second post-op day I had had my fill of regression; I was raring to leave the hospital and run my own life once again. Dr. Moss relented, and let me go a day early.

9

The Home Stretch

Fourth Year

I CONVALESCED with Phyllis in Vermont. At first I was a total invalid — she did all the driving and lifting and cleaning and shopping. It was fun for about one day. But then being so dependent again gave me the willies. I must have been an awful patient for Phyllis.

After about two weeks my incision was finally painless. And I made an astounding discovery: my hernia was gone! I had almost forgotten that the point of all the trauma I'd suffered through was to get it fixed. It turned out to have been worth it. The dragging sensation was gone. No longer did I have to surreptitiously push the hernia back in. There was no more fear of strangulation. I celebrated my return to the world of the well — I ran up and down stairs, I drove a car, I carried books. Once again I felt whole.

Toward the end of vacation we returned to Boston and I went to see Dr. Moss for a checkup. I asked him if he had known I'd been in pain during surgery. "Yep," he said, "I sure did! Every time I cut, your leg went up in the air. Believe me, Kenneth, I was just as uncomfortable as you were!" He swore he'd never allow an acupuncture needle in his operating room again.

On examination he found that his unanesthetized stitches had held; I got a clean bill of health. So I was officially ready to return to the hospital, this time in a white coat instead of blue pajamas. The final year of medical school, the twentieth year of my education, was about to begin.

The fourth year was entirely electives. The idea was to give us the chance to pick courses that made the most educational sense for our futures. I chose a mixture of lecture courses and hospital rotations.

The lecture courses, which were each full-time for a month, were in nutrition, infectious diseases, and emergency medicine. Sitting in the big amphitheater again was surprisingly pleasant. I don't think it was just that the hours were regular and there was no night call; it was a return to the old and familiar. Every morning on the way to class I'd stop in at Vanderbilt Hall and get a Styrofoam cup of coffee. Then I'd walk across the street to Building C and settle down in a certain seat on the left side of the lecture hall, toward the rear. I'd put my feet up on the back of the chair in front of me, start sipping my coffee, and the class would begin. How comforting this old routine was in the face of the approaching end of medical school and the looming uncertainty of internship!

The year began with a pediatrics rotation at Children's Hospital. There was really no need for me to learn about babies since I was going into internal medicine. But how could I claim to be a doctor without knowing about the croup and mumps and chickenpox? As it turned out though, I never did learn about croup and mumps and chickenpox. But if I'd paid more attention I could have been an expert in the reticuloendothelioses, a group of diseases so rare that many pediatricians have never even seen a case. The reticuloendothelioses dominated my six weeks on pediatrics.

I had the bad luck to be taking pediatrics at the same time as John Defoe. John was an excellent student. He was bright, diligent, and aggressive — a real pain in the ass. He was going to be a pediatrician and wanted badly to do his internship at Children's. So he worked extremely hard, and made sure everyone *knew* he was working extremely hard. He carried an aura of unbearable enthusiasm. I've never heard diarrhea described with such rapture as when he presented a case on rounds. Sometimes I was certain that it was his constant smile, not gastroenteritis, that made some of our little patients vomit. Next to John I felt like a real sourpuss.

One of John's first patients was a five-month-old girl who had been sent in from another hospital. She wasn't growing well. She was jaundiced, and her liver and spleen were huge. At times she had fevers, and there were some funny blood tests. The doctors at the other hospital couldn't figure out what was wrong, so they transferred her to us for more tests.

The pediatricians at Children's pored over the case. Finally they decided she had an unusual type of reticuloendotheliosis, a class of diseases caused by the abnormal growth of a blood cell called the histiocyte. John was ecstatic. He rushed to the library and in two days had mastered the reticuloendotheliosis literature. He talked endlessly about eosinophilic granuloma of bone and Hand-Schüller-Christian syndrome and Letterer-Siwe disease. His eyes flashed with that same maniacal gleam I had seen in the eyes of Don Murphy, my first intern at the Beth Israel, that time he wildly lectured me about kidney stones at three in the morning.

Rounds became a reticuloendotheliosis hootenanny. John would sing on and on about this obscure group of diseases for which there is no cure, and everyone would clap and stomp their feet in time. All the while I sat quietly outside the circle of interns and residents and staff, bored and ignored. I couldn't care less about John and his diseases. And I wasn't especially happy for him that he was a shoo-in for the internship.

Day after day we talked about the miserable child. Did she have the Hand-Schüller-Christian variant, or was it Letterer-Siwe? Was her histiocytosis malignant or benign? Should we biopsy the liver or the bone marrow? Her infant body grew more and more pathetic under our watchful academic eyes. Through the window of her isolation room she looked like an exotic sea creature caged in a research aquarium: this rare specimen was yellow and bloated, with a big misshapen head. Its limbs were embedded with wires and tubes for close scientific monitoring. The creature was repulsive, and yet fascinating.

As they yapped on and on about their star patient, I found myself hoping she would die. I didn't want to see her suffer, I told myself. But I think the real reason I wanted her to die was to see *John* suffer.

I wasn't learning a thing. I blamed John and his patient for monopolizing all education at Children's Hospital. When the infant finally died, though, nothing changed, except that I felt guilty for having wished the death.

I was anxious to see measles and learn how to write IV orders. But measles wasn't admitted to the hospital much anymore, and my intern was bored going over fluids and electrolytes. It was easier for him to write the orders himself than to spend the time teaching me to do it.

Occasionally we did have formal teaching sessions. The topic of the month seemed to be epiglottitis. Epiglottitis is an infection of the tissues at the entrance to the windpipe. Sometimes there can be enough swelling to produce airway obstruction, which is of course a medical emergency. We had at least three separate talks on the treatment of epiglottitis. An otolaryngologist, an infectious disease specialist, and an emergency ward pediatrician each told us exactly when to intubate a child with this disease. Unfortunately, they all said something different. It didn't really matter though, because I couldn't remember what any of them said. Anyway, the only patient I'd ever intubated was dead Mr. Rosencrantz that night at the Beth Israel; this hardly qualified me to tackle a sick child, blue and gasping for breath. Luckily the whole thing was entirely moot, since I'd probably never see a case of epiglottitis in the first place. A lot of medical education seemed like that. We'd be taught different things by different people, little of which we'd remember, about diseases we'd probably never see.

In an effort to see some common pediatrics I convinced the head of the rotation to let me spend some time in the emergency ward. It was wonderful. I saw a constant crying parade of sniffles and fevers and tummyaches and rashes — it was hard-core pediatrics. After a few days I began to feel comfortable with the routine. I even made a few diagnoses. But one diagnosis, though correct, led to one of my most traumatic moments in medical school.

On a busy Wednesday night an eight-year-old boy named Ricky Gaines was brought in by his mother. His left testicle was swollen and painful. I cootchy-cooed the kid until he finally stopped crying. (At the time I didn't realize eight-year-olds are too old to be cootchy-cooed.) Then I carefully examined the delicate contents of his scrotum. The left testicle was indeed swollen and tender, especially toward the back. The posterior aspect of the testicle is where the epididymis runs, I recalled. That's the tube that channels sperm from the testicle to the penis. Of course, I thought, this child has an infection of the epididymis!

I went to look for Gabe Seltzer, the chief resident, to present my case of epididymitis. I found him doing a spinal tap on a fifteen-month-old girl, just brought in with seizures. After he was done I mentioned my patient; he said he'd see him when he could. But then several more emergencies came in and I knew there would be a long wait.

I went back to little Ricky and his mother and apologized for the delay. He was in a lot of pain, but trying desperately to be brave. I asked him if he wanted some juice.

"No thank you."

"Oh, come on, it'll make you feel better while you're waiting."

"OK."

In the refrigerator I found a can of apple juice and poured him a big cupful. Finally, I thought, I'm doing *something* for the poor kid. I gave him the juice and went on to other patients.

Half an hour later I ran into Gabe. "Listen, Ken," he said, "things are crazy. I'm not going to have time to see your kid.

The urologist is in the hospital now though. I asked him to take a look."

I went back to Ricky and his mother and again asked their patience. His mother prodded him as I started to leave. "Thank you for the apple juice, doctor," he said. "I forgot to say thank you."

"You're very welcome. Let me know if you want more."

After a few more sore throats and earaches I passed by the nurses' station. A tall blond doctor was standing by the desk, fuming to Joanne, the head nurse.

"What the hell's wrong with your nurses?" he thundered down at her. "Even a first-year nursing student knows you don't feed a patient who's just about to go to surgery!"

My God, I thought, how could anyone give a pre-op patient something to eat? When patients are being put under anesthesia they sometimes retch. If there's anything in the stomach they can vomit it up and aspirate it into the lungs. I pitied the poor nurse who did it; she'd really get roasted.

"I'm terribly sorry, doctor," Joanne said. "There's no excuse for that. You can be sure the responsible nurse will be found and appropriate action taken. I'll prep the boy's groin and take him to the O.R. for you personally."

My stomach sank. Could they be talking about *my* patient? The giant doctor had sat down at the desk and picked up the phone. As he started to dial, his nametag caught my eye. "T. Hubbard, M.D. Pediatric Urology," it said, confirming my fears.

"Doctor Hubbard?" I asked timidly, "are you by any chance talking about an eight-year-old boy named Ricky Gaines?"

"Yes. He's got a testicular torsion. We're taking him to surgery to untwist the testicle before it infarcts."

I cleared my throat and started to explain that the apple-juice villain was me, not an innocent nurse. But just then someone must have answered the telephone at the other end.

"Hey, Ray," Dr. Hubbard said into the receiver, "you're up for anesthesia? Good. Listen, I've got a probable torsion on an eight-year-old. It might be bad, I want to do him now. Only thing is some idiot nurse down here gave the kid a glass of orange juice or something. . . . Yes, I know they should know better. . . . I know. I've already talked to the head nurse. . . . OK, see you in the O.R. in twenty minutes." He hung up the phone, shook his head, and got up to go.

"Dr. Hubbard?" I squeaked.

"What is it? You want to scrub in and watch the surgery? Sure, fine. Be in room three in twenty minutes." He strode off down the hall. I didn't hold him back. I didn't tell him it was this idiot medical student, not a nurse, who had fed his pre-op patient. I felt terrible.

Half an hour later I was in O.R. number 3. It was my first trip to an operating room since I'd had my hernia fixed. This time I think I was even more frightened. What if little Ricky vomited and aspirated because of my stupidity? I'd assumed he had epididymitis. It hadn't occurred to me not to give him something to drink. I prayed that everything would go all right.

Dr. Hubbard and the anesthesiologist were already standing over their patient when I came in. Ricky had been lightly sedated and was lying on the operating table, covered with green drapes. The anesthesiologist snaked a nasogastric tube down the nose. He then squirted in a syringeful of air while he listened over the stomach. Even without a stethoscope I could hear the bubbling as the air percolated through my shameful apple juice. Next the anesthesiologist connected up the NG tube to suction. With a hiss and a gurgle, a column of pale golden liquid emerged from the nose and migrated down the tubing to the vacuum bottle on the wall. Ricky seemed to be doing fine.

"I wonder where they dig up the E.W. nurses from, these days," the anesthesiologist said. "I hope they crucify the one that gave the kid the juice, that is if she has enough balls to admit she did it."

Again I started to declare my guilt. But I just couldn't bring myself to say I did it; I was in it too deep. If I now confessed, Dr. Hubbard would know I hadn't spoken up in the E.W. when he had first discovered the crime, or even later when he hung up after talking to the anesthesiologist. And I'd already been in the O.R. with him for ten minutes and still hadn't said anything. It was too late. My initial crime was being overshadowed by a second one. A stupid medical judgment was now compounded by a big fat lie of silence. I felt terrible. Yet I didn't speak up.

I was learning what convenient scapegoats nurses were. Already I'd seen a nurse blamed for a medication error when it was the doctor who had ordered the mistaken dosage himself. And in the operating room I'd seen a surgeon scream at a scrub nurse when a stitch didn't hold, even though she had given him the suture he'd requested. I had already learned that you could avoid all nonmedical responsibilities by invoking the demands made by the profession. Now I discovered that it was possible to blame others for one's *medical* shortcomings too. I didn't like what I was learning. Yet I didn't speak.

There was a sound like the sucking on a straw at the end of a milkshake. The column of fluid in the tubing bubbled and broke up; the stomach was empty. Ricky lay peacefully on the table under his thick green drapes. The anesthesiologist seemed satisfied. He deepened the anesthesia, then gave Dr. Hubbard the go-ahead.

In the middle of the drapes that covered Ricky was a little hemmed hole, through which protruded his penis and his little fleshy walnut of a scrotum. Dr. Hubbard turned to me. "In torsion of the testicle," he said, "the testicle rotates on its long axis, twisting the tubular and vascular connections. Then swelling occurs. If it's not relieved the blood supply will be cut off, causing an infarction. When you suspect a torsion, you have to operate. And the sooner the better."

"Now," he continued with scalpel poised, "we'll cut along one of the oblique scrotal skin folds. Healing is better, and the scar won't show so much." He was relaxed and almost friendly, now that the apple juice was safely sequestered in the vacuum bottle and he had a scalpel in hand.

Basking in the congenial atmosphere I ventured a question: "Dr. Hubbard, I know very little about all this. But how can you be sure this boy has a torsion rather than just epididymitis?"

He gave me a technical answer which I didn't really

understand. The gist of it was that although there was a slim chance of epididymitis, the kid's age and the way the symptoms came on weighed in favor of torsion. "The only way to be sure is the knife," he said.

He plunged the scalpel into the scrotum. Then with what seemed like far greater delicacy he dissected the tissue that wrapped the twisted testicle. Surgery was careful and slow. The apple juice in the bottle on the wall kept catching my eye. It was a public display of my crime; it could have been labeled, "Exhibit A: The lethal apple juice."

"Well, son of a bitch!" Hubbard said as he parted the last layer between him and his prize. "It's epididymitis!" The testicle, it turned out, wasn't twisted at all. But on its posterior wall was a red swollen convoluted cord, the inflamed epididymis. He poked around a little, then sewed the scrotum shut.

The fact that I had bumbled onto the correct diagnosis did little to make me feel better. Dr. Hubbard was of course right that torsion had been more likely. Surgery was clearly indicated to be sure. But I hadn't even thought of torsion!

I left quickly so as to avoid Dr. Hubbard. Then I changed, drove home, and went to bed. I felt rotten. It didn't matter that my diagnosis was right. It didn't matter that there were no complications from the anesthesia. By not thinking straight I had exposed the patient to serious risk. And just as bad, I hadn't had the guts to admit my mistake; I let the blame fall on someone else. What kind of doctor was I learning to be?

I rejoiced when pediatrics was finally over. I was anxious

to leave this educational and moral disaster area for my next rotation, cardiology.

As the cardiologists say, their speciality is the heart of internal medicine. It was therefore important that I do well. So when I left pediatrics for the cardiology consult service I probably became another John Defoe, kissing cardiological ass to earn good internship recommendations. I chose to do my rotation at the cozy Mt. Auburn Hospital in Cambridge. It was the same hospital where I'd demonstrated my ignorance of gynecology in front of my brother and his girlfriend two years before.

Robert Siegel, the guy who argued that it was OK for patients to call their medical students "doctor," was now an intern at the Mt. Auburn. I heard his name paged hundreds of times a day, to the intensive care unit, to the wards, to emergency. And I ran into him so often I decided that for increased efficiency he must have cloned for his internship. Rob was always rushing. He always looked tired. How could I possibly do all that he's doing, I wondered. And even more to the point, how could I ever *want* to?

"Tell me, Rob," I asked during a frantic lunch break, "what's it really like?" He was the first person I'd known from medical school who had become an intern; he was my internship scouting party.

"It's no picnic, Ken," he said. "I was on call last night, didn't get any sleep. I've got eighteen patients on my service now, four sickies in the ICU. I can't stay awake. I can't think. I don't know what the fuck's going on with my patients."

"But you're surviving, right? You're not killing anyone and you do get to go home occasionally, right?"

"Yeah. I guess so."

"And the year is a quarter over already. *That's* got to be encouraging. Rob, tell me. It *is* worth it, isn't it?"

"No," he yawned, "probably not."

I tried to convince myself that Robert was having a rough day. Surely things were usually better. But every day seemed to be a rough day. I retreated to another defense — internship just lasted one year. Then came residency, which clearly was better than internship. And finally, you became a full-fledged doctor in practice. Certainly *that* must be better than being even a resident.

Or was it? What *was* being a doctor really like? It couldn't possibly be like being an intern, or there wouldn't be so many doctors. And hopefully it could be different than being like the booming cigared gynecologists at my parents' parties. But it was hard to know. I realized I had applied to medical school with almost no notion of what it meant to be a physician. And now, three years later, I still wasn't at all sure. It seemed foolish and dangerous to be investing such huge tracts of time in a future that remained almost totally unknown. Maybe, I thought, I should withdraw the letters I'd just mailed requesting internship applications.

My job at the Mt. Auburn was doing cardiology consults. I worked with a cardiology fellow and a staff cardiologist. We were called to help diagnose and treat patients with difficult heart problems. Many of our consults were on patients in the intensive care unit. I'd often see Robert there, carefully examining a patient's belly or calmly writing page after page of complex orders. Unlike the orders *I* wrote, his didn't need to be countersigned by a doctor — he *was* a doctor. Despite his disclaimers he looked so comfortable and competent in his white coat, surrounded by the intimidating illness and technology of the ICU. It was impossible to imagine myself in his shoes in less than a year.

But one time when he asked for a cardiology consult I wondered how competent he really was. The patient was a forty-four-year-old man named Charles Dugan. He had been admitted to the hospital after a fainting spell. There were recent bouts of chest pain, and shortness of breath too. Robert had heard a heart murmur and wanted some help.

I went to see Mr. Dugan in my new role as a heart specialist. I took a detailed history and did a careful examination. His heart murmur was classical for aortic stenosis, the narrowing of the aortic valve. His EKG and chest x-ray fitted with that diagnosis too. And aortic stenosis could entirely explain his recent symptoms. He needed a heart catheterization to measure just how severe the narrowing was — he'd probably have to have surgery to replace the valve.

It was all so clear. Yet Robert's admitting note was vague. He didn't really seem sure about the diagnosis. His interpretation of the EKG missed some important points, and he hadn't noticed the aortic valve calcifications on the chest x-ray. At first I was reassured. If I could discover things Robert had missed, maybe I wasn't out of his league after all. Maybe I could make it as an intern too. There was hope!

As I flipped through Mr. Dugan's chart, though, I realized what an easy time I had as a cardiology consult. In addition to his heart disease, the patient had a nodule on his prostate, a chronic skin rash, and a high uric acid level. I had no idea what should be done about these problems. But fortunately they weren't my concern. My job was simply to look after his aortic valve. Robert, on the other hand, had to worry about everything — not only on Mr. Dugan but on all his other patients as well. Hearts were just one organ competing for Rob's attention with brains and bones and livers and kidneys. If he were missing all those things about Mr. Dugan's heart, I thought, imagine what he was missing on other patients and in other organ systems. And Robert was smart, too, certainly smarter than I. Compared to him what a mess *I'd* make of things as an intern! How would I ever keep from making bad mistakes, maybe even killing patients?

"That's exactly what consultants are for, Ken," said Jim Campbell. Jim was the cardiology fellow. "Hell, the night Dugan came in Robert probably had four other admissions to worry about. He didn't have the time to go over the case in detail like you did. But he did the right thing. He knew the guy might have a serious heart problem, so he called you for some expert help. An intern doesn't need to be a walking textbook. He's doing a good job if he can recognize when a patient is sick and keep him alive until help comes. Don't worry Ken, you'll do fine. I survived internship; why shouldn't you?"

I presented the case to Jim and then we went to see Mr. Dugan. I was anxious to see if Jim agreed with my diagnosis. My presentation had been nice and snappy and Jim's pep talk had cheered me up. But my good mood didn't last long.

Jim heard a faint diastolic murmur I had missed. He agreed with my interpretation of the EKG but pointed out the left atrial enlargement I'd overlooked. He thought my diagnosis was correct but raised several other possibilities that hadn't even occurred to me. Once again I grew depressed. Sure I'd found a few things that Robert had overlooked, but I felt like a real amateur compared to Jim. I couldn't even claim to be competent in the little medical niche for which I was responsible. So at the Mt. Auburn as at the Boston City and the Beth Israel, I found myself on a seesaw. A little medical breeze would waft me up to feelings of accomplishment and exhilaration. Then its direction would change and I'd be blown down to frustration and discouragement. Up and down, Marjorie Daw.

I saw Mr. Dugan daily. Unlike Robert, I had time to sit and talk. "You know, doc," Mr. Dugan said to me one day, "I've never been so uptight. Before this I was never sick a day in my life and now you tell me I'll probably need open heart surgery. What if I can't go back to work? I couldn't stand being an invalid. And my family depends on me. I don't know what I'd do if things don't work out right." I listened, and gave what hope and comfort I could.

One day I found a second-year student in Mr. Dugan's room. She was seeing him as part of the Examination of the Patient course, a course I had taken what seemed like decades ago. As I came in she was just packing up her shiny new instruments. I introduced myself.

"Hello," she said. "I'm Ann Schroeder. I'm all done. You don't mind if I stay while you talk to Mr. Dugan, do you?" I didn't.

I sat down on the side of his bed and told him the results of the heart cath he'd had the day before. I'd gone over the data with Jim and Dr. Hughes, the staff cardiologist. Though the details didn't make much sense to me, the drift was clear — Mr. Dugan indeed needed surgery. "Just like I figured," he said, and shook his head.

Ann followed me out of the room. "Do you have a few minutes?" she asked.

"Sure."

"There are some things about aortic stenosis I don't really understand. Can I ask you a few questions?" I was ecstatic. Someone wanted to learn from *me!* We went over Mr. Dugan's EKG. We reviewed his chest x-ray. I drew her little pressure curves explaining the hemodynamic consequences of aortic stenosis that I'd barely understood myself two hours before.

Ann's questions seemed so naive. They made me realize how much I'd learned in the last two years. No, I wasn't a cardiologist, but I wasn't a second-year student either. For perhaps the first time in medical school I realized I was no longer at the bottom of the medical heap. I was making progress!

I invited Ann to come with me to Mr. Dugan's operation. Unfortunately she had a class then. But she said she'd come by later and see how things went.

"Hey, thanks a lot for going over that stuff with me," she said. "I think I finally understand aortic stenosis now."

"I think I finally do too."

I was in early Monday morning to see Mr. Dugan off to surgery. He was very jumpy. While we were talking, a nurse came in with his pre-op shots. I hoped he wasn't getting Innovar. The orderly soon appeared and I helped transfer

Mr. Dugan to the stretcher. "Well, good luck, Mr. Dugan," I said as the orderly cinched up the side rails.

"Hey, you won't change your mind about my needing this operation, will you, doc?"

"Nope, not a chance." It was easy to reassure him since I had had no part in the decision; if something went wrong it wouldn't be *my* fault. "Some very good cardiologists and heart surgeons have gone over your case. They all agree you need the operation. Without it you'd probably be dead in a year."

"Yeah, but with it I could be dead in an hour."

"Sure. Or live another thirty years. Good luck, now. I'll tell you all the gory details when you wake up."

He looked up at me and squeezed my hand tightly. "Good-bye," he whispered.

The O.R. was buzzing with surgeons, nurses, and technicians, all gathering to replace Mr. Dugan's aortic valve. It apparently took eight people to do the work of one heart.

The technicians calibrated the heart-lung machine while the nurses prepped Mr. Dugan's chest and arranged the instruments. Then, like a conductor tapping his baton, one of the surgeons asked for the scalpel. The room grew still. He hefted the knife once or twice, then pulled its blade down the middle of Mr. Dugan's chest. A blood trail appeared, separating right from left. The bleeders were quickly controlled. Next, with a carnivorous crunching the surgeons used instruments to split the breastbone. Then the rib cage was spread apart with a sort of surgical jack, revealing Mr. Dugan's huge ailing heart. Eight pairs of eyes watched its lurching attempts to force blood through the narrowed aortic valve. It was like a wounded animal, panting desperately for life in the glare of the operating room lights.

In open heart surgery the patient's body is possessed totally by machines. Machines monitor the temperature and blood pressure, machines do the breathing, machines pump and oxygenate the blood. It's probably as close as the body ever gets to complete rest, save death. I watched with awe as Mr. Dugan's circulatory system was progressively dismantled and given over to the machines. Now superfluous to life, the heart was made to stop. It shook and then lay still, cradled by the lungs. Its struggle against the tight aortic valve was at last over.

The green-gowned technicians swarmed over the heart-lung machine, constantly making the fine adjustments Mr. Dugan's unviolated body made quite automatically. They read a bank of monitors that told them how the dials should be set. These people thus became merely interpreters between one species of machine and another.

The surgeons meanwhile dissected the heart. It was carefully opened to reveal the cause of Mr. Dugan's shortness of breath and chest pains and fainting, the cause of his having to quit his job and the cause of the humiliation he felt in the eyes of his family. Where the supple, glistening aortic valve should have been was a crumbling skeleton of calcified tissue. This fossil of a valve was carefully excised. In its place was set an artificial valve, so precise and hard and cold. It lay like a sparkling jewel, embedded in the velvety red flesh of the heart.

The surgeons reconstructed and then warmed the heart. Then, to prod it into activity they stung it with a sharp electric current; it was ready to begin its new life with the capacious metal and plastic valve. But the musclebound heart was too tired to resume beating. The surgeons tried all their tricks, but each time the heart gave only a few feeble shudders, and was still.

They called Dr. Hughes to the operating room. "Surgery went extremely well," they insisted. "It's just that we can't get him off the pump." They shocked the heart again. "See?" they said. "It just won't start."

Dr. Hughes shook his head. "The patient had severe symptoms, and the cath data showed tight aortic stenosis. Surgery *had* to be done," he said, absolving himself of any blame for the death.

Dr. Hughes had properly recommended an operation and the surgeons had correctly done the surgery. So why was the patient's heart now lying lifelessly in his chest? "He had end-stage valvular heart disease," Dr. Hughes said. "When the left ventricle gets that big and dilated it's always hard to get them off the pump. I don't know what else we could have done." He shook his head again, and left. The surgeons felt better now that their colleague had endorsed the death.

"OK, turn it off," the chief surgeon said to the technicians. At the flip of a switch, Mr. Dugan was dead.

Ann came to the hospital in the late afternoon, exhausted from a day of lectures and labs. I was sitting at the nurses' station, reading a new consult's chart. "Hello, Ken," she said. "How'd surgery go?"

I told her what had happened. She didn't understand. How could anything have gone wrong? She had talked to him just the day before. He'd seemed so alive, joking about whether the artificial valve would keep him awake nights with its clicking. "Maybe I'll have to drink Pennzoil to keep myself lubed," he'd said. So how could Mr. Dugan now be dead? Ann sat down. She looked at the floor and began to cry.

Mr. Dugan was the first patient Ann had known who had died. Already I'd forgotten how hard it had been at first; I was startled to learn how quickly death becomes routine. I sat with Ann for a long time. I cried too, almost.

I told her she should come to Mr. Dugan's autopsy. Like intubating the Krantz the night he died, going to Mr. Dugan's autopsy was unpleasant yet important. "It won't be easy," I said, "but I think you should go. You knew his symptoms, you listened to his heart, you studied the chest x-ray and the EKG. Now you have the chance to consolidate it all by actually seeing the pathology."

The next day I met her in the morgue. Mr. Dugan's heart lay serenely in a white porcelain pan, surrounded by a pool of bloody water. The pristine artificial valve remained uselessly in place, rejected by the heart it was meant to help.

We sifted through the organs that together made up Mr. Dugan, all affected in one way or another by the narrowed aortic valve. The heart itself was gigantic. The walls of the left ventricle were grotesquely thickened. The left atrium was dilated and filled with blood clot, and the right ventricle was likewise enlarged. In another pan sat the lungs, violently red and filled with fluid. Even the liver wasn't spared. Its congested cut surface was dark and mottled, a result of the back pressure from the heart. I was moved to see how much disruption had been caused by the narrowed valve; I hadn't realized how sick Mr. Dugan had really been.

Ann and I talked afterward in the sweet and sour atmosphere of the morgue. She was shaken. She hadn't yet learned to pretend that seeing a dead person wasn't troubling. And not only was this her first autopsy, the body belonged to someone she had known, someone whose death it was now impossible to deny. Seeing the bloody mass of intestines and kidneys and lungs piled on the steel table was like having someone scream, "He's dead! Mr. Dugan is dead!"

So we talked and we learned from each other. From me Ann learned to push herself to get as much as possible from each medical experience. And from her I learned how much I'd changed since I'd been a second-year student.

Just as I began to get comfortable with cardiology, the six weeks were over. Once again it was time for the ritual move to the next rotation. This latest uprooting led back to the quadrangle for the emergency-medicine lecture course. Then it was on to the Mass. General for psychiatry.

On psychiatry it was finally OK to say you cared about patients without feeling like a softie. I loved it. I loved the chance to feel another person's emotions, to understand the things that made them feel sad and joyful and angry and satisfied. I loved the chance to talk, the chance to help. But something about psychiatry was disturbing. There were no blood tests or x-rays or monitors. There was nothing to hide behind; there was just me and the patient. I couldn't put off making a diagnosis or starting treatment by ordering another round of tests. Often I found myself put on the spot.

Much of my time on psychiatry was spent on the "acute

psychiatric service." Besides me there were two other students and a supervising staff psychiatrist. Our job was to evaluate new patients and arrange for treatment in an appropriate setting. Sometimes one of us would conduct a patient interview while the others watched. These sessions were videotaped. We sat around a big conference table, with the patient and the student-interviewer at the head. The others filled in the sides of the table, and at the foot was a camera with a big intimidating lens. I remembered how tense I'd been talking with the psychiatrist before my hernia surgery. But that cozy session seemed trivial next to this TV spectacular.

Our instructor was a psychoanalyst. The key to diagnosis and treatment, he said, was getting the patient to go back to childhood experiences. Under the bright lights of the TV camera I felt like the moderator of "This Is Your Life." After half an hour or so of trying to get the patient to talk about his parents and his siblings and his toilet training, the instructor would stop the session and ask the patient to leave the room. Then we'd discuss the case and play back especially juicy parts of the interview. Seeing myself on TV was excruciating. More than once I wanted to call the patient back and re-record the awkward moments. Videotaping was revealing, and in some ways fun, but learning somehow got lost in all the flashy technology.

The taping sessions were for patients who had appointments. We also saw emergencies, usually by ourselves. One of my first solo patients convinced me that he was going to kill himself and that his blood would be on my hands.

He was a very edgy man, in his mid-twenties. In the past

he had used tranquilizers heavily. He'd just gotten a new job, which made him even more nervous than usual. But he didn't want to talk about his job or his nervousness, or even about his mother. He just wanted Valium.

"I don't think it's in your best interest for me to simply prescribe a tranquilizer," I said. "You've already been addicted to Valium once. I'd like to refer you to our clinic for some therapy."

"I don't *want* therapy," he said. "I want Valium. I already know my problem. I'm nervous, I'm a neurotic. I need Valium to calm me down. I'll lose my job if I don't get Valium."

"Well, I'm not going to give it to you."

"All right then, I'll kill myself."

He got my attention. I asked him if he had ever thought about suicide before. He hadn't. Did he have a plan now?

"Oh I don't know, maybe I'll jump off the Longfellow Bridge, maybe the Pru. There are lots of places to jump from." I decided he wasn't serious.

"I'm sorry," I said; "I sympathize with you but I don't think Valium is the answer. I wouldn't be doing you a favor to prescribe it for you."

"OK, doctor, fine. I've given you your chance. If you don't mind now, please write down your name."

"Sure," I gulped. "Kenneth Klein," I wrote in small letters on a notepad. Then I added, "HMS IV," the abbreviation for Harvard Medical School, fourth year. "Kenneth Klein" alone seemed too naked, and I wasn't yet able to clothe my name with an M.D. My patient smiled, carefully folded the paper, and put it in his pocket. I asked him to wait while I talked to the senior psychiatrist.

"Why should I?" he said, and walked out.

I ran to my supervisor and told him the story. "So do you think he might actually kill himself?" I asked.

"No, of course not. Patients can really make you squirm, though, can't they?" We sat down and talked about how I might have handled the situation better.

Despite my supervisor's reassurance I combed through the newspaper every morning. In my mind I saw the headline a million times: "Rejected Psychiatric Patient Throws Self Under MTA; Doctor's Name Found on Blood-Soaked Note in Victim's Pocket." But apparently he decided not to kill himself. Or else I just missed the article.

After psychiatry I had only one more clinical rotation. Then I'd take six weeks off for an internship interview trip, and end the year with two lecture courses. This last clinical rotation before becoming a doctor was at the Harvard College Health Services. It was a rare chance to see medicine outside hospital walls.

I spent most of my time in the walk-in clinic. I saw four or five sniffles and sore throats a day — I got good at treating colds. A lot of patients came because they were about to travel abroad — I got good at ordering shots. And I became an expert at treating urinary tract infections and twisted ankles and headaches. Dr. Schaefer, an internist who was my supervisor, began signing prescriptions I'd written without even seeing the patients himself. My confidence grew. I swaggered around the clinic ready to take on anything that came through the door. Of course I can handle internship, I thought. At last I'm ready to be a doctor. But then a patient appeared who quickly demoted me back to medical school.

He was a custodian at the college who came in for a checkup. He had recently been hospitalized because of a rapid heartbeat. I quickly read the discharge summary he had brought with him. Then I did a detailed history and physical. After that was done I went to present the case to Dr. Schaefer. I was proud of my medical history; I had asked about every imaginable cardiac symptom. My exam was likewise thorough. I'd taken orthostatic blood pressures, felt for all the pulses, and listened to the heart with the patient in all sorts of positions. I was pleased at how much I'd remembered from my cardiology rotation. I was set to give Dr. Schaefer a brisk presentation.

"Mr. Banks is a fifty-six-year-old man without prior history of cardiovascular disease," I began, "who was admitted to Cambridge City Hospital two weeks ago for an episode of paroxysmal atrial fibrillation. At that time he . . ."

" — Wait," Dr. Schaefer cut in; "was it 'paroxysmal atrial fibrillation,' or do you really mean 'paroxysmal atrial *tachycardia*'?"

He stopped me dead in my tracks. "Uh, I can't remember for sure. It was 'fibrillation,' I think," I said, guessing. I had no idea which it was, or what the difference was between the two, or indeed if such a thing as paroxysmal atrial fibrillation even existed.

I went back to the examining room and sheepishly asked Mr. Banks for his discharge summary again. It was "tachycardia." I realized I didn't have the foggiest notion of what paroxysmal atrial tachycardia was, other than simply a fast heartbeat. But even Mr. Banks knew that — a racing pulse is what led him to go to the hospital in the first place.

I was headed down on the old medical seesaw once again. Here I was on the verge of doctorhood and I didn't even understand paroxysmal atrial tachycardia! I thought back to the first floundering week of medical school when Dr. Thatcher presented that woman with the pacemaker. In my own way I felt just as dumb about hearts now, four years and a cardiology rotation later. Only now there was no excuse for my ignorance — I was sure that at some point I'd been taught about PAT, and just forgot.

Dr. Schaefer went in with me and talked briefly with Mr. Banks. Then he listened to his heart and together we did an EKG. It was now normal. We left the examining room and Dr. Schaefer sat down and explained PAT, a fast heartbeat caused by the rapid discharge of muscle fibers in the right atrium. It usually lasted for only a few minutes or hours. As long as symptoms didn't recur, no special treatment was necessary.

I went back and explained all this to Mr. Banks. He was relieved; they hadn't told him in the hospital what was wrong. He gratefully shook my hand. "Thank you, Dr. Klein," he said. "I understand what was going on now. You make it seem so clear and simple." For not the first time in medical school I felt like a fraud.

As I wrote a note in Mr. Banks's chart I wondered how many other nuggets of medical knowledge had escaped through the sieve of my pre-intern brain. Each forgotten fact assured a missed diagnosis and a mismanaged patient. I recalled what my first-year tutor, Dr. Allen, had said to our little group more than three years ago: "Before you finish your medical training each of you will probably kill at least three patients. It's unfortunate, but there's no avoiding it." I had no doubt I'd meet my quota!

I went home and stewed about paroxysmal atrial tachycardia and morguesful of missed diagnoses as I prepared for my internship interview trip.

10

Filling an Intern's Shoes
Internship Interviews

A N ALARM BUZZED. I stretched in my sleeping bag, which lay on a foam pad on the floor, and opened my eyes. I was surrounded by boxes, books, and clothes. A heavy growth of medical journals, scattered and precariously stacked, held hostage the bed where I might have slept. I got up.

There was a note taped to the bathroom mirror: "Ken — Sorry I couldn't have breakfast with you. Decided to skip it so I could go over my patients before rounds. Plenty of food in the fridge. Make yourself at home — Harold."

Poor Harold. He had looked so tired when I'd arrived the night before. "Jesus, Ken, it's really been rough" was about all he said before he collapsed in his bed. Harold was just a year ahead of me in medical school. But now he seemed so much older.

I went into the living room and opened the drapes. From the twelfth-floor apartment I took in the grimy panorama of Rochester, New York, in winter. The view centered on Strong Memorial, Harold's hospital, only five blocks away. I wondered if I might end up there for my internship.

Rochester was the first stop on my search for the perfect internship. Over the next month and a half I would visit fourteen hospitals, have fourteen interviews, and get fourteen tours. How perverse, I thought, to apply willingly to do what Harold was going through now.

I ate Harold's breakfast for him. Then I shaved, got on my suit, and carefully brushed my hair. Suddenly I froze. All I had for shoes were the ratty old sneakers that I'd driven to Rochester in. What an idiot, I thought. How could I ever hope to be an intern if I couldn't even remember to pack my dress shoes! What a stunning impression I'd make at my interview in a three-piece suit and tennis shoes.

I frantically called the hospital and had Harold paged. After a long delay, he finally answered. "Harold," I said, "sorry to bother you, but what size shoes do you wear?"

"What? I'm in the middle of rounds. Are you going to knit me a pair of slippers or something?"

"Well, no. I forgot my dress shoes. I'm all set to go for my interview, but all I have to wear are my old sneakers."

"Jesus. I wear tens."

"My size is ten and a half. Do you have a pair I could squeeze into?"

"I don't know. You're welcome to use any shoes you can find. I think most of them are still in a Chiquita Banana box in the room where you slept."

"Harold, thanks a million. You've saved my life."

I found a pair of Wallabies that fitted pretty well if I curled my toes a little.

I made my way to the hospital and tiptoed into the interview. It went fairly well considering how foot-conscious I was.

Afterward I went on a tour with half a dozen other applicants. As we paraded through the intensive care unit I saw Harold, in hospital whites, listening to the lungs of a patient on a respirator. He seemed so professional — he was a doctor! I caught his eye as we started to leave. He looked down at his shoes on my feet, giggled, and waved.

I met Harold for a quick lunch in the doctors' dining room. He talked between mammoth bites of hamburger: "There's no time to eat, no time to sleep, no time to think. But I will say this, Ken, I'm learning a hell of a lot."

"But is it worth it?"

Just then he got a "stat" page to the intensive care unit, so I never did find out.

That afternoon I left Rochester and drove northeast toward Burlington, Vermont. There I'd stay with old friends, Fred and Esther. Fred was doing his internship at the Mary Fletcher Hospital, part of the University of Vermont. That's where I was going for my next interview. With luck Fred's feet will be size ten and a half, I thought.

After a few hours I left the interstate and picked up a small twisty road. The winter sun began to set, and I turned up the heat. The road entered a little town. In the gutters was the same hard greasy ice I'd seen that day almost three years ago when Phyllis and I drove to the Boston City to see our first autopsy. It seemed so long ago! It was hard to believe there was ever a time when I didn't know a heart from a thymus. It was hard to believe there was a time when I wasn't yet a medical student. Once, I thought, I was going to be a chemist. Then it was neurophysiology. All that was hundreds of years ago. It was all behind me; I was about to become a doctor.

I left the town and picked up speed. The air grew gray and heavy as the sun settled lower in the sky. Patches of ice and snow on the road became more frequent, but harder to see.

I thought ahead to the next six weeks. After Burlington I'd drive south to Goddard and visit Phyllis. It was her last semester. Then I'd go on to the Hitchcock Hospital at Dartmouth, for my next interview. Next it was back to Boston for a week, and then the big trip west. I'd fly to San Diego and work my way up the coast, visiting eight programs. Phyllis and I had decided to get married. We both wanted to live in the West, where we'd never been. It was time to leave New England, time for a change. The interviews I was doing now were to hedge my bets; I really wanted to go west.

I squinted ahead at the empty gray highway. Something was wrong. Thin black ropes were draped in the tree branches and curled down across the road. Then I noticed a telephone pole leaning 'way to the side — the black ropes were telephone wires. My car skidded as I gently pumped the brakes. A man in a red and black plaid jacket ran onto the road from around a bend, waving his arms. I coasted up to him and rolled down the window.

"Turn back, turn back!" he said. "Some power lines are down."

"What's going on?" I asked. "Has there been an accident?"

"Yeah, but that's OK. Everything's under control."

"Is anyone hurt?"

"Maybe, but we don't need no gawkers. Help is on the way."

"Listen, I'm a medical student. I can help."

"Well that's a little different. Follow me." I jumped out of my car and trotted beside the man. Unfortunately I didn't think to put on my coat.

The man said that he and his son had gotten there just a few minutes before me. The son had driven off to call the police.

As we rounded the bend I saw it. An old red pickup truck sat at right angles to the road, its front end crushed against a telephone pole. The pole was broken, lying almost horizontally across the remaining nubbin of a hood. It must have pulled over the pole that I had seen first, until the wires snapped. The mangled pickup's passenger door was bent open, hanging by only one hinge. Little triangles of sparkling glass were scattered over the icy road.

"He really must have been going fast," the man said. "Skidded on that patch of ice, I suppose. I think he's dead." I ran up to the truck, afraid of what I was going to find. I felt more like a voyeur than a physician.

In the driver's seat was a man wearing a blue windbreaker and a green baseball cap. He was slumped forward against the misplaced steering wheel. He was very still. From under the cap flowed thick gray hair, shiny in patches with matted blood. Deep lines shot out from the corners of his eyes; did he always look like that, or was he grimacing in pain? But how could he be in pain if he were dead? I quickly brushed some glass from the seat, knelt next to him, and put my fingers to the side of his neck. Yes, there was a pulse, fast and weak. The man opened his eyes slightly and groaned.

"He's alive!" I said. "He's *not* dead."

"I'll find a phone and make sure we get an ambulance quick as I can," the man in the plaid jacket said, and ran off down the road.

Suddenly I was alone with this man who seemed to be barely living. A seed of panic sprouted in my belly. I recognized that feeling well. It had been there on and off all through medical school. It was there that night in the emergency ward when Mr. Hastings had stopped breathing. It had grown stronger and stronger as I frantically wheeled him to the operating room. But at least I had been in the hospital. All the necessary equipment and help was at hand. Even so, Mr. Hastings had died.

"Oh God. My leg, my leg," moaned the man.

I put my hand on his shoulder. "Hello. My name is Ken Klein. I'm a medical student. You've been in a bad accident. Help is on the way."

"My leg, God, my leg!" he chanted. I found a flashlight in the misshapen glove compartment and shone it on his legs. The left one looked OK, but the right was badly broken — the foot was pinned beneath the brake pedal while the lower leg was twisted across the bent steering column. I dove down to the floor and tried to straighten things out. But he was wearing stiff icy boots; it was hard to maneuver. And when I finally began to make some progress, the man started to fall to the side. I stopped; moving him would take two people. So what should I do now, I thought. How could I help him? I lay back against the distorted seat to plan.

Then I smelled gasoline. After setting the man upright again I got out of the cab. Gas was steadily dripping from the ruptured tank. It ran into a little pool in the snow and made a rainbow with the last bit of daylight. I've got to get him out of the truck, I thought; the gas might explode. But even if I could free his leg and lift him out of the cab, where would I put him? The ground was packed with ice and snow. There was nothing to put under him and I didn't even have my jacket for a cover. But what if the gas exploded? Ambulance drivers knew the correct procedure in situations like this — why didn't they teach medical students what to do at the scene of an accident? The emergency-medicine course I'd recently taken assumed we were in a well-equipped E.W. The only lecture I remembered about coming on the scene of an accident was by a lawyer, telling us about our legal obligations as physicians. I had a sudden impulse to run back to my nice warm car and drive away. By leaving I could avoid the double dangers that faced me: the danger of the gasoline and the danger of responsibility for this injured man. Where was the ambulance? Where was the guy in the plaid jacket? He'd *already* run.

I decided to leave the man in the pickup. Maybe the gas would be less likely to explode since it was cold.

So I was stuck with this injured man in his time-bomb truck, waiting for the ambulance. What could I do for him in the meantime? Think, I said to myself, think! What would you do if he were just brought into the emergency ward? But the E.W. was such a different world. Here, I couldn't take his blood pressure, I couldn't start an IV, I couldn't even listen to his lungs. And I certainly couldn't give him any drugs or intubate him if he stopped breathing.

Again I thought of Mr. Hastings. There was blood caked onto this man's hair. What if *he* had a subdural? I took off his cap and surveyed his bloody head. The left ear was badly cut. It was slowly dripping blood—like the gas tank, I thought. I combed my fingers through his hair, feeling for fractures. But there weren't even any scalp lacerations; all the blood was from the ear. I pushed his eyelids apart and shone the flashlight into the pupils, first the right, then the left. They both constricted normally. "The pupils were initially round, equal, and reactive to light," I thought. That's what I'd tell the ambulance driver to tell the emergency ward doctor. Next I asked the man to move his hands and feet, but he just groaned. Then I tried to tap out his arm reflexes with my stiff fingertips, but his jacket and the steering wheel were in the way. I caught myself—what the hell are you doing? The guy is shocky and he's got a broken leg wrapped around the steering column and you're worried about his biceps jerks! You're not being graded on completeness anymore; this is for real. Do something to help him *now*!

His pulse was still weak, and even faster. I had to get him flat so more blood would go to his brain. Again I tried to free the leg, but it clearly couldn't be done without someone else to stabilize the upper part of his body. I decided to try to lean him back as far as possible with the leg where it was.

"Listen, sir," I said, "I'm going to lay you down a little so more blood will go to your head. It might make you feel better." With a bit of maneuvering I could get him lying to about 45 degrees. He lay against my chest; my arm supported him around the upper part of his back. It was nice to feel his body against mine; it made him feel more alive.

The carotid pulse was now stronger, and maybe a little slower. "Does that feel better?" I asked. He didn't answer. But he was breathing; I could feel him against my chest. I checked his eyes again. The pupils were still equal and reactive.

The smell of gasoline grew stronger. I began to think again about trying to get him out of the truck. Where's that damn ambulance, I wondered, why isn't it here yet? Ambulances certainly had no trouble finding their way to the Boston City emergency ward: a siren's shriek would announce an imminent emergency. We'd wait, coiled in anticipation, ready to spring one way for a cardiac arrest, another for a stab wound to the belly. It was always tense, but at least I was never alone. There was always an intern or a resident nearby to supervise.

A muffled wailing floated through the cold gray air. No, it wasn't another emergency arriving at the Boston City. It must be the ambulance coming to get this injured man next to me, my new patient. Never had I been so happy to hear a siren. But the sound disappeared. Maybe it had just been a howling dog.

Again I felt the pulse in the neck. It seemed weaker. I pressed closer to this man, to both give and receive warmth. There was little else I could do.

The wailing appeared again, and grew louder. Yes, it *was* the ambulance! Soon the spindly tree branches above us pulsed red and white and a bright yellow van shot around the corner, glowing with light and help.

It skidded to a stop and two men jumped out. "Boy," I said, "am I glad to see you guys!" They surged past me into the bent cab. One felt for the carotid pulse, the other shone a flashlight into the eyes. "The pulse is a little thready, but regular at about one hundred twenty," I said. "The pupils are equal and reactive. The only obvious head trauma is a badly lacerated ear, and he also has a compound fracture of the right leg. I don't know about internal injuries."

They stared at me. "What are you, a doctor or something?" one asked.

"Well, almost. I'm a medical student."

"Oh." The air vibrated with uncertainty. Who was in charge, a medical student or the ambulance crew?

I broke the silence: "Let me help you guys get him out of here." Once again I bent down to disentangle the twisted leg, but this time the other two supported the head and the torso. Even with the upper part of the body stabilized, though, how could I get the leg out without causing even more damage? I suddenly remembered reading long ago about what to do if you were first at the scene of an accident; was it in my boy scout manual? "If the victim is obviously hurt," it said, "especially if there are broken bones or a possible neck injury, *do not move him*. This could worsen the injuries, and even cause paralysis. Just make the victim as comfortable as possible and wait for expert help." The man groaned as I tried to free his shattered leg.

"Hey, maybe one of you guys could give me a hand down here," I said. "You must know all the tricks about stabilizing fractures."

"You're the expert, doc. Just do what you have to to get it out." I untangled the leg somehow, and we lifted the man out of the cab and laid him on the waiting stretcher. They covered him with a thick wool blanket and snugged a strap around his waist.

"Hey, can I follow you guys to the hospital?" I asked.

"Sure. It's about twenty miles from here. If you lose us, it's straight down the road, on the left." They lifted the stretcher into the ambulance and drove off.

I floated back to my car, free of the burden of responsibility for the injured man. As I followed the ambulance's flashing lights down the dark icy road I thought about what I'd do if I were the doctor in the emergency ward. I'd make sure he was breathing and had a heartbeat, of course, then get the blood pressure, start an IV, and draw blood for crossmatching. Then I'd stabilize the leg and do a neurological, chest, and abdominal exam. Next the patient would need a catheter in his bladder and x-rays of the chest and leg.

I soon lost sight of the ambulance and eased up on the gas pedal. How secure it was back in my cozy car, slowly gliding along the frozen black road. I was in no hurry.

After half an hour or so I saw a glowing red sign on the left that said "EMERGENCY." I parked in the little lot and walked into the warmth of the hospital. In the bright lights of the waiting room I noticed that my hands and shirt were smeared with blood. From his ear, I thought.

The room was empty so I walked through the swinging doors into the tiny emergency area. A balding middle-aged man with a handlebar moustache sat at a desk, writing. He wore blue jeans and an orange down vest, and there was a stethoscope around his neck.

"Hi, are you the emergency doctor?" I asked.

"Yep. You must be the medical student that took care of our patient at the scene of the accident."

"That's right. My name's Ken Klein."

"I'm Cal Peters, one of the GP's in this town. Those ambulance guys said you did a nice job out there, Ken. Good work."

"Where's the patient? Is he OK?"

"He's getting x-rays. His pressure was down so I started an IV, and we have some blood cooking. His leg seems pretty well smashed up, but I didn't find any serious head or internal injuries. Hey, it sure must have been scary out there without any equipment."

"It was. I was thinking that maybe I should keep an IV setup in the trunk from now on."

The doors to the x-ray room opened and the tech wheeled out the driver of the truck. His jacket and shirt had been taken off and a sheet covered his chest. The right boot had been removed too, and the pant leg was cut off above the knee. The man's leg was held in a plastic inflatable splint, and the ear was dressed with a bulky bandage that wound around his head.

Dr. Peters took the blood pressure while the x-ray tech went back to develop the films. "Pressure's down again," Peters said. "He needs blood." He called the nurse in from another room: "Karen, I need blood. Fast. Tell Nancy to forget about the crossmatch and just set up some O-negative. And call the E.W. at Mary Fletcher and tell them we're sending a patient. Also tell the ambulance crew we'll want transportation; I asked them to wait just in case. By the way, Karen, this is Dr. Klein, the one who found our patient at the scene."

"*Ken* Klein," I said.

She ran back to give the message to the blood bank

technician. Dr. Peters opened the valve to make the IV fluid run in faster. Then he turned to me. "Well, Ken, how far along in medical school are you?"

"This is my last year. Actually, I was on my way to an internship interview at Mary Fletcher."

"That's great. Well, the end is in sight, then; you've almost made it. Before you know it you'll be on your own. I think you'll like private practice. You have all the responsibility, you call the shots. It's a good life." The patient moaned.

Dr. Peters checked the blood pressure again, then rested his hand on the patient's thigh. He gently patted it with his fingers.

The x-ray tech came in with the films and handed them to Peters. We went over to the x-ray view box. The leg was badly broken, both the shinbone and the foot. Then Peters put up the chest film. "Well, doctor," he said to me, "what do you think?"

"Well, first of all I assume this is an upright shot."

"No. It would be dangerous to sit him up. I told Tom to take the x-ray with the patient supine. So what do you see? Any fractures? A pneumothorax?"

"There are no obvious rib fractures and the vertebral bodies seem normally aligned. The soft tissues, heart, and great vessels look OK. I don't see a pneumothorax, but there's a funny haziness in the left lung field."

"Don't worry about that. Remember, you're in the real world, not the Mass. General. Given our old equipment, I'd say that this x-ray is perfectly normal."

"I don't know, the left lung sure looks funny. I just wonder what an upright would show."

"The blood is running, doctor." The nurse was back.

"OK, Karen, good. Now I want you to ride in the ambulance, since we'll be giving uncrossmatched cells. Remember, if there's a transfusion reaction, stop the blood."

"Of course, doctor."

The ambulance crew came and took the patient back to the ambulance; the nurse followed, hand on the man's pulse.

A moment later the nurse came back. "The patient's family is here now, doctor. They'd like to talk with you."

"Certainly. I'll be with them in a jiff." He turned to me. "Well, quite a case, eh?"

"Sure is. So tell me, what do you think is going on with him, besides the broken leg?"

"I think that nasty fracture is the main problem. The belly's probably OK, and the head and chest seem fine too."

"So you'd say he's shocky just from the fractured tibia?"

"I don't know, could be he does have some internal bleeding somewhere. I suppose I should have put in a catheter to check for blood in the urinary tract. But they'll do that at Mary Fletcher. A patient as sick as he is is better off at a bigger hospital."

I said I thought I'd follow the patient; I was headed there anyway. This was a rare chance to follow a case through right from the beginning. I went to the men's room to wash the blood from my hands.

On my way out to the parking lot I passed three people talking softly together—a woman in her sixties, a younger woman, and a man. The younger woman was crying. The man looked up at me as I passed by; I think he spotted the blood on my shirt. "Excuse me," he said, "are you the doctor who found the gentleman out on the highway?"

"Yes. My name is Ken Klein, I'm a medical student."

"I'm David Shelton, his son. Dr. Peters said that you helped a lot out there. We want to thank you, doctor."

"Well I did what I could. Unfortunately, I didn't have much to offer without any equipment."

"Doc said Dad's hurt pretty bad, that there might be some internal injuries. What do you think; will he make it?"

"Well, it's too early to know just what's wrong. They'll have to do some more tests at the other hospital to sort things out. They're very good there; I'm sure they'll do everything possible. I'm headed that way for an interview; I'll look in on him. If I see you I'll let you know how things are going."

"Thank you sir, thank you very much." The patient's family got into their car and drove off. I followed them down the dark country roads. Soon I lost sight of their taillights, though; they were driving fast.

It was nice to be back in my warm car once more. It was nice to be free of this dangerously injured man. I tried to tune in a radio station, but there was too much static.

My thoughts again turned to what I should have done when I first arrived at the scene. After almost four years of medical school, fear of doing something wrong was almost automatic. I fretted endlessly over mistaken diagnoses. I replayed cardiac arrests over and over in my mind, deciding what might have been done differently. I still thought about Mr. Hastings. I knew I would always carry the fear that I'd killed him by not bagging him properly. But in this case I couldn't think of anything I'd done that seemed grossly wrong. Not that I had many options out there on the highway. I'd have to ask someone about the danger of a gas explosion, though. I might have made a mistake by not trying to get him out of the truck.

Then I began thinking about Dr. Peters in the emergency ward of that little hospital. There were no surprises there; I think I could have handled it as well as he did. I think I'd have even done a few things he didn't do. But who knows; he was on the firing line, not me.

I kept wondering about the patient's fast pulse and low blood pressure. Could he really be going into shock simply from a broken leg? Dr. Peters didn't give a very reassuring answer. I didn't know either, of course, but I was just a medical student. Then I realized I wouldn't be able to use that excuse much longer. In just a few months I'd be a doctor. No longer could I hide behind my studenthood when I didn't know something, or when I was being introduced to a nurse or to a patient's family. Just as Dr. Meyer had told that fourth-year student on my first day of ob-gyn, soon I'd be "playing for keeps."

Ahead I saw city lights, and soon I was in Burlington. Signs led me to the hospital; I parked and walked quickly into the emergency ward. It was busy like the Boston City, but everything was newer. I closed my jacket over the bloody shirt and asked the clerk if the transfer from the little community hospital had arrived.

"Yes, they're working on him now," she said; "can I help you?" After I explained my connection with the patient, she led me back around the desk, through the double doors.

Lying on a table in the middle of the big trauma room was the driver of the red pickup, surrounded by doctors and nurses. All his clothes were off. There was only a small towel across his groin, symbolically preserving his dignity.

Mr. Shelton had sprouted tubes since arriving at Mary Fletcher. A second IV had been started; both were running in blood. There was a catheter in the bladder. And, coming out of the left side of his chest, was a plastic tube attached to a series of bottles on the floor. Thick magenta blood oozed out from the chest and crawled down the tube to the waiting bottles.

I inched my way up to the doctor who seemed to be running things, introduced myself, and explained what I was doing there.

"Hey, that's great that you're following up on this case," he said. "I'm Jim Fagan, surgery chief resident. Let me tell you, this is one sick dude."

"What do you think is going on? Why's he so shocky?"

"He's bleeding; into his belly and into his left lung. And we made the diagnosis sooner, thanks to you."

"To *me?*"

"Yep. Your friend Dr. Peters called while the patient was on the way. He told me a medical student found the guy on the road and had come with him to the hospital. He said you wondered if the supine chest x-ray might be obscuring some pathology. He thought about it and decided you might be right. He suggested we ignore the x-ray he'd sent with the patient and take an upright. We would have done it eventually, of course, but it might have taken a while to figure out that his x-ray was supine. See that chest tube? Well, look at the x-ray." He nodded to the view boxes on the wall. I recognized the x-ray taken at the other hospital, with the hazy left lung field. Next to it was a new film. The lower portion of the left lung was obscured by an abnormal shadow.

"See that fluid level?" said Fagan. "That's blood. This guy has a big hemothorax. Peters missed it because he took the film with the patient supine. The blood layered out behind the lung and just made things look a little hazy. The patient is looking better since the chest tube went in."

"Wow! You say he's bleeding into the belly too?"

"Yep. His abdomen was tense and there were no bowel sounds; Peters should have picked that up, too. We tapped the belly and got back blood. He's probably got a ruptured spleen. At least Peters had enough sense to send the patient here; I'll say that much for him. He might not have known exactly what was going on, but he knew the guy was sick."

"OK, Jim," said one of the nurses, "the O.R. is ready."

"Great. Call the other guys and send the patient right up."

"Dr. Fagan," I said, "would you mind if I watched?"

"Not at all. That would be great."

My friends Fred and Esther were expecting me, and I was already late, but I just couldn't pass this up.

Mr. Shelton's body was a three-ring circus. Surgical drapes strung up by metal rods divided him into three fields, each controlled by a different team. At the head was a plastic surgeon, repairing the mangled ear. The center ring was run by Dr. Fagan, who, with the assistance of a junior resident, worked on the abdomen. Below them were the orthopedists, piecing together the puzzle of a leg.

I watched over Fagan's shoulder as he opened the peritoneum. Would this ringmaster be able to deliver on his lavish promises of what would be seen? Yes! There *was* blood in the belly. And its source was indeed the spleen, a red meaty fist with a crack down the middle. As Fagan and the junior resident began the process of removing it, I flipped back through my mental card catalogue of splenectomies. I was surprised to find there was only one other entry. It was the time I'd removed the spleen of the black and white mongrel in dog surgery lab. I hoped Mr. Shelton would do as well as my patient had.

The three surgical huddles worked quickly and with few words. The chest tube's water seal gurgled contentedly, and the heart monitor beeped out Mr. Shelton's heartbeats with proud regularity. All was well. How nice it was to be here in this smoothly running operating room rather than by myself out on the highway, or even back at that little hospital, alone with Dr. Peters. How secure to be a medical student, in league with these competent physicians that surrounded me. What a luxurious, safe life! It was hard to make a serious mistake as a medical student — there was always an intern or a resident around to supervise. If I had ordered a supine x-ray on Mr. Shelton for example, my intern would have been right there to correct me. Yes, being a medical student really wasn't so bad.

"So what time is your internship interview, Ken?" It was Dr. Fagan, disrupting my idyll. The spleen was out, and they were sewing things back together again.

"It's at seven-thirty," I answered. As I did so I saw a huge clock, ticking away the last moments of medical school.

The simultaneous surgeries all went well. Each team closed up the anatomy under its jurisdiction and Mr. Shelton was wheeled off to the intensive care unit. I finally called Fred and Esther from the surgeons' locker room and promised an exciting explanation for my tardiness.

On my way out I passed by the ICU and found the Shelton family in the tiny waiting room. All three stood as they saw me. The lines of hope and worry I had seen in the dimly lit parking lot already seemed more deeply set into their faces. In the last few hours these people had acquired a new identity — they were now relatives of a critically ill patient. Until he either got well or died their lives would center on the double doors to the intensive care unit.

"Surgery went well," I said. "He's in good hands." Mrs. Shelton cried and hugged me, bloody shirt and all.

I arrived at Fred and Esther's house at about eleven, tired but euphoric. "You guys won't believe this," I began, and told them the whole adventure. After I had finished no one was ready for sleep, so we attacked some leftovers. I'd forgotten how long it had been since I'd eaten.

"Well, Fred," I said over the cold chicken, "your turn. Give me the lowdown; what's internship really like?" Fred told stories even more amazing than mine. He had an incredible amount of responsibility. The number of very sick patients under his care was astounding. His days were long and he was getting hardly any sleep. Yet, he was surviving. In fact, he said he basically enjoyed the work. "I have a lot to learn," he said, "but boy, have I grown this year. I can handle common things all by myself, and I feel comfortable managing just about anything until help comes."

Fred seemed so competent. Like Harold, he seemed much more mature than I, and obviously knew so much more. And like Harold, he was only twelve months ahead of me in his training. How could I ever hope to catch up to him?

Finally Esther yawned and we all acknowledged that it was time for bed. After brushing my teeth I suddenly remembered my shoeless state. I sheepishly told my final story of the evening and begged a pair of Fred's shoes.

"Sure Ken, no problem," he said. "What color is your suit?"

"Tan." He went into his bedroom and brought out a pair of brown wingtips.

"Jesus," I said, "they look enormous. What size do you wear?"

"Eleven and a half."

"Boy, Fred, I don't think I could ever fill your shoes."

Despite my lack of sleep, the interview the next morning went well. The subject of my adventure on the highway came up, and I got to tell the story again. The interviewer complimented me for what I'd done. "I think the patient would have fared better if you'd been manning the E.W. yourself, instead of our friend Dr. Peters," he said. I floated out of his office and went to join the tour.

For the second of what would be fourteen times on my internship crusade I was shown the medical wards and the blood bank and the coronary care unit and the cafeteria. All hospitals were the same. There were the same overworked nurses, the same feeble gray patients, the same harried interns. I cornered these interns, hospital heros, and asked them how they liked their program. But I already knew what they'd say: they didn't get any sleep last night, and there was never time to go to the teaching conferences. They had no sex life anymore, and it didn't matter what city you did your internship in because you never had time to see it anyway. But beneath the tiredness and the cynicism there was a spark of excitement and pride — they were somehow managing to do their work, and they were slowly but surely evolving into competent physicians.

The tour passed by the intensive care unit. Among the anonymous row of the critically ill I saw a familiar face. I ducked out of the tour and went to his side. I stared at the quilted-together ear that had bled on my shirt, at the thick chalky cast which held the leg I'd untangled from between the pedals of the truck, and at the chest tube which still sucked the blood that wasn't there on Dr. Peters's x-ray. Mr. Shelton was still intubated from surgery, lying passively as the respirator took his breaths. A nurse came by to adjust his IV. I asked her how the patient was doing and she got the chart for me to read; I guess she assumed I was a doctor. After fiddling with the IV, she started to reposition him in bed. I put down the chart and slipped a hand under his back and his thigh, to help her. "Be gentle," I said; "he's someone special." Suddenly I understood how it was possible to be sustained through an internship.

As I left through the double doors I passed the I.C.U. waiting room. It was filled with small groups of people, huddled extensions of the suffering going on nearby. Again the Sheltons looked up and recognized me. "Doctor, hello," said the daughter. I didn't flinch. "How's Dad?"

It was too early to say how he would do. But he clearly was very sick. I walked the uncertain line between discouragement and unrealistic optimism. Again I told them that he was in good hands.

They thanked me again. It didn't matter that I'd really done little to help the patient. And it didn't matter that I was only a medical student. For them I was a doctor, like it or not. They were grateful for my interest and for the comfort I was able to give. I couldn't avoid the responsibility that went with their gratitude and trust; I accepted that.

I went back to Fred and Esther's house. After lunch I exchanged Fred's wingtips for my sneakers, packed, and drove off to Goddard to see Phyllis.

This day was much warmer than the day before; the sun was shining. Yesterday's ice was melting into shimmering little pools on the shoulders; the road was almost completely clear. I rolled down the window and sang into the beautiful afternoon.

I was gathering strength. If I could have a good interview on only a few hours' sleep, if I knew how to care for the victim of a serious accident, and if I was able to give comfort to a distressed family, surely I could get through a dozen more interviews. And more important, I could survive my internship. I was ready to become a doctor.

Epilogue

I CALLED Fred from San Diego to see how Mr. Shelton was doing. "I just saw him yesterday," Fred said. "He looks great." He had apparently had a few setbacks, but left the I.C.U. a week before my call. Then a few days later he walked for the first time, with the help of crutches, an intern, and a nurse. "He's still a little shaky," Fred said, "but he's going to make it."

I asked Fred how work was going. "Just fine. Ken, do you realize that internship is more than half over? *I'm* going to make it!"

"Of course you will. I could have told you that a year ago."

"Well tell yourself the same thing now," he said, "because that's true too." I thanked him for the good news and the encouragement, and said good-bye.

"By the way," Fred said, "before you hang up, did you remember to bring your shoes this time?"

"I sure did. I even brought along an extra pair."

"Well in that case, you're *definitely* ready to be an intern!"

I interviewed my way up the West Coast, then returned to Boston for the last few months of medical school. I sat

impatiently through my remaining lecture courses, antici-
pating the momentous events to come. Soon I'd find out
where I was going to do my internship. Then Phyllis and I
would get married. Finally we'd both graduate, and move to
wherever my internship would be.

On the day of internship notifications my whole class was
buzzing. It felt like Vanderbilt Hall the night before our first
biochemistry exam. We'd all find out about internships at
the same time because of a computerized matching system.
Internship applicants listed the programs to which they had
applied in order of preference, and the programs ranked
applicants likewise. Then the lists were fed into a computer,
which determined who would go where.

We gathered in a fancy faculty room in one of the
buildings on the quadrangle to receive the results of the
match. It was the same room where we'd come to register on
the first day of medical school, almost four years ago. After
filling out endless forms that long-ago day we all trooped off
to the auditorium at the Peter Bent Brigham Hospital. There
we had our first clinic, the one with Dr. Thatcher and
Evelyn, the pacemaker lady.

They began handing out the envelopes. At last, I thought,
my student days are over. At last I'll receive a salary instead
of paying tuition. Finally my orders won't have to be
countersigned. I was ready!

My turn came. Just as I had with that fateful special
delivery letter four years before, I took a deep breath and
tore open the envelope. Yes! I had matched with my first
choice, the program in Portland, Oregon. I ran to the phone
to call Phyllis. We were going west, to begin our new lives.

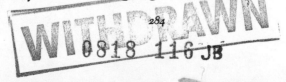